BITING THE BIG APPLE

A memoir of life, love
(*okay, and sex*)
in New York City

BELLA VENDRAMINI

HACHETTE AUSTRALIA

All characters and events in this book are true (except winning the Town Hall drinking competition), though I've changed some names to protect the innocent, and to save my own ass. Also, to Rosie and Danny, none of the sex, heavy drinking or profanity ever happened. And to anybody that isn't Rosie or Danny, it did.

HACHETTE AUSTRALIA

Published in Australia and New Zealand in 2008
by Hachette Australia
(an imprint of Hachette Livre Australia Pty Limited)
Level 17, 207 Kent Street, Sydney NSW 2000
www.hachette.com.au

National Library of Australia
Cataloguing-in-Publication data:

Vendramini, Bella.

Biting the Big Apple / Bella Vendramini.

978 0 7336 2184 0 (pbk.)

Vendramini, Bella. Actors – Australia – Biography. Australian students – New York (State) – New York. New York (N.Y.) – Social life and customs. New York (N.Y.) – Description and travel.

792.028092

Cover and text design by Sandy Cull
Cover photographs of the author by Peter Lueders
Typeset by Post Pre-press Group in Adobe Garamond 12.5/17 pt
Printed in Australia by Griffin Press

Hachette Livre Australia's policy is to use papers that are natural, renewable and recyclable products and made from wood grown in sustainable forests. The logging and manufacturing processes are expected to conform to the environmental regulations of the country of origin.

To my parents
Rosie Scott and Danny Vendramini . . .
for everything

1

Don't they know who my mother thinks I am?

I DON'T KNOW WHY, but I felt suspicious of this new LA opportunity. I feared I wouldn't be good enough, that I wouldn't be strong enough or talented enough – Heath Ledger said the same thing about filming *Brokeback*, that he secretly thought he had tricked everybody into believing that he could act when he couldn't. Though it's true that doing the harder things in life are the most rewarding. Like those times when you don't plan to go out and a friend makes you, then you end up meeting the love of your life or something. Or at least getting laid.

But let me start at the beginning. I'd gotten the acting bug early in life when I was a whippersnapper in sunny Brisbane, where I'd lived with my parents and sister since flying in from the green shores of Kiwiland aged twelve. I toured in a children's theatre troupe and even played Juliet to a chorus of shuffling parents. I wasn't exactly a Shirley Temple, I was a kind of, well, a female version of Danny DeVito, as one helpful audience member pointed out. At seventeen, when at last I discovered boys, I figured the whole DeVito thing had to go, so I moved to Sydney where my parents had a house, and did stretching exercises to try to make myself taller. By that stage I'd been surrounded by so many of those intimidating, tall actor types who sighed a lot and spent their time emoting and looking unnecessarily troubled that it put me off the whole acting thing, and I spent most of my time watching DVDs. Not that I was depressed or anything.

I lied on applications for jobs as a dental assistant, a circus performer, a secretary, a journalist and a film coordinator. I got the coordinator job. I looked on the internet to see what a coordinator actually did, then travelled down to Melbourne to be a production coordinator on a low-budget feature film called *The Merchant of Fairness*. I had me some fun. I got to break up fist fights between crew members and learned the craft of film production. And although I did meet lots of producers who sighed a lot and looked unnecessarily troubled, the pay was good and I got to carry a clipboard, so I happily stuck at it.

But back in Sydney, after getting a few more jobs in production and even producing a couple of films myself, I could tell something still wasn't quite right. I tried going to university to study business, but there were only so many statistic and quantitative methods a girl could handle. The reality was, I'd begun to secretly and wistfully watch actors and fantasise that one day I would join their ranks again. But this time, not as a four-foot fat guy.

When I finally found the guts to change my title from Paid Producer to Unpaid Actress, it wasn't exactly what I'd hoped for. I didn't suddenly become glamorous or skinny, and, strangely, there was no limousine waiting for me after work. Instead I got acting jobs in films with fellow nerds, and played mostly girlfriend roles and died gruesomely a lot. I played far, far too many 'chick that gets killed by cool alien' characters. But I liked my new friends, and I even snaffled a best actress award for a short film at the TAP Gallery Awards. It felt good to be part of a group of people who were all in the same boat together, learning our craft while playing wingmen to try to get one of us laid.

At the beginning of the year, my acting agent had sold us, like the cattle we were, to another agent, who looked like Tom Selleck. I had even graduated from alien films and was earning a bit of money as I had hooked up with a talented filmmaker named Robbie Baldwin. But when I heard Robbie yell 'It's a wrap', my knees sank into my shoes and I did what any self-respecting actor would do: I plugged my thumb into my mouth and sucked it. Then I went off to buy chocolate and brood.

On my way back from buying dinner (three packets of Tim Tams and a sushi roll), I was eyed by a stranger on the street.

'You're that actress!' grinned a teenage boy with greasy curls and a few pubescent hairs on his chin.

Ha ha, see! Brooding did work.

I cleared my throat and swept back my hair like I'd seen it done in the movies. 'Yep, that's me.'

'Yeah. Like, you were pretty rad,' he mumbled as he lazily scratched his arm.

There was an awkward pause.

Should I autograph his school bag or something?

'Soooo,' (cough) 'which film did you see me in?'

'I can't remember what it was called. But you had like a bad disease or something, and, like, your boyfriend didn't understand you, and, like, you threw that bottle at him, and, like, smashed it everywhere,' he said, as he flicked his hair at me and I wiped a splotch of grease from my eyeball.

Like, great, my fan base was really extending. A while ago,

I'd won a well-paying job for a Department of Health educational film about a girl dealing with Hepatitis C. A generation of Aussie kids were therefore growing up knowing me as Bella Vendramini: the Face of Hep C.

Lovely.

'I don't have it, you know,' I said.

'Cool. Whatever.' He winked.

'Er . . . really,' I said.

'I don't care if you have it or not,' he replied significantly eyeing my breasts.

I turned back to the shop to buy more chocolate to fill the newly created void.

ıılıılıılı

Sometime later I got a call that I'd won the role as the Flying Fairy in a production of Gilbert and Sullivan's *Iolanthe* at the Sydney Opera House. Woo hoo! No more depression or diseased-people roles; time to be glamorous! They dressed me in a glittery garish tutu with blue stockings and a big blonde wig that kept falling into my eyes, making me feel very Farrah Fawcett-ish. Yep, Hep C had nothing on this. Under my costume I wore a tight harness (or 'the nappy') that got connected to two steel cables that were rigged to the top of the Opera House ceiling. Each night I was supposed to fly out over the stage, flap my wings and land gracefully in the centre of a group of excited fairies. Some nights it wasn't so graceful. The technicians, who were nice, salt-of-the-earth kind of guys who wore 'I Love Beer' T-shirts, had sometimes had a little too much Victoria Bitter in their cereal, and when they would pull their ropes to make me fly I would look more like an out-of-control racing car than a swan-diving fairy. My plastered-on smile would tremble as I was yanked violently left and right then suddenly plunged down to the floor, *à la Mission Impossible*. One night I got stuck up there and there was nothing for it but to keep on flapping and flapping until the entire first act was over and they got a crane lift to bring me down. I couldn't masturbate for a whole week after that one. (Mum, if you're reading this, that was a lie.)

After *Iolanthe*, I auditioned for the lead role in an independent feature film and, lo and behold, a few weeks later I found out I had won the coveted part.

The character I was to play was a challenging one. Mardi was a deeply depressed girl who lived in a kind of haze of self-inflicted sadness. Then, to add salt to her already fragile self, her father gets diagnosed with cancer, her dead brother haunts her in her dreams, her friends abandon her, then her boyfriend cheats on her with her best friend. And there wasn't a single hammy death scene or alien in sight. I had my work cut out for me.

Acting put the fizzle in my lemonade. I loved the complex game of truth and mistruth, of exploration and creativity, and damn in hell it was fun. I was over the moon to sink my teeth into such a serious and three-dimensional role that didn't come with a character description of 'Hot Chick Who's Really from the Planet Zion'. I think I went a tad overboard in preparing for it, though: I quit my day job, cut my hair and spent months creating her character and her physicality.

The shoot was a success, but perhaps I had been a little too, um, rigorous in my preparation of Mardi. I had spent so many months morphing into her grief-stricken shoes that I'd eventually taken on her depression as my own. And when the film shoot was finally over I couldn't shake off the damn depression. At least they can't say I'm not a committed actor, I thought, as I sucked harder on my thumb and licked the Tim Tam crumbs off my ILB T-shirt.

I didn't know the acting techniques for shaking off a character and leaving it at the set door, so, trying to be romantic about the whole thing, I thought of Martin Sheen's breakdown in *Apocalypse Now*. But the damn depression obscured my attempt to glamorise it. I felt like the insides of Sid Vicious' liver.

The strange thing about depression is that if you leave it unchecked it develops into a force of its own. You almost forget the reason you got depressed in the first place. You end up just existing in a kind of continual fog. I mooched around the house, making my housemates' lives hell until the threat of eviction had me applying for temp jobs.

ıılıtılılıı

I walked into my new position as a medical secretary at a hospital cancer ward and introduced myself to my new boss. She looked mean as hell, with severe black hair, pale vampire-ish skin and hard-looking features. I gulped and covered my neck.

'Hi, Petra, I'm Bella, I'm supposed to be starting here today.' I smiled, scanning for the exit signs.

She glared at me. 'Call me Ms Reeves,' she said, as her false nails made snail trails through her white make-up as she slowly scratched her face.

'Yes, Ms Reeves.'

'We don't have breaks here. You can eat lunch at your desk. A maximum of ten minutes per day to stretch your legs. You will enter cancer patients histories into the computer.' She eyed me from under her heavily pencilled brows. 'Any questions?'

Perhaps this wasn't exactly the best job to get me back into the land of the cheerful people. But what were my options? My landlord's scornful face billowed in front of me like my second-grade teacher's had done when I had eaten her pencils. I resolved to bite the bullet.

'Nope, no questions.'

I swear she clicked her heels together. 'Get to work then.'

I spent my days hooked up to a pair of earphones listening to a monotonous oncology doctor's voice detailing cancerous metastases of the heart valve or adenoma of the thyroid, and which patient was going to die in what time period. The women in the other cubicles would ignore me and sometimes fart. My only solace was a kind-faced office girl from the Outpatients section who would bring fat, left-over coconut and cream cakes, which I wolfed down as a kind of anaesthetic. I also became slightly paranoid, as if an army of judgemental women were tsking at me whenever I'd step out of line. Although, in retrospect, I don't think it was my imagination. At night, I would dream of cancer until the wee hours of the morning.

One Wednesday afternoon, a month into the job, I took my ten-minute break to slump onto a bench in the grounds and feel sorry for myself as my depression deepened. One of the patients, Beatrice Rose, was out walking. She perched her frail frame down on the bench and turned to face me.

'You don't look well, dear. What medication are you on?' she asked, concerned.

'I'm not a patient, Beatrice, remember? I work here.'

'Oh yes, of course,' she replied, flustered. She stared off into space for a few beats then turned to regard me again.

'Dr Powers is the best cancer doctor here. I can get him to see you too, if you like?' she suggested as her gnarled old hands twisted the fabric of her slip.

'I really don't have cancer, Beatrice, truly.'

'Yes, dear, of course, dear,' she replied, looking entirely unconvinced.

Okay, if I was being mistaken for a cancer patient, it was time to do something drastic. I had to get out of this death-riddled hell I was in. A flurry of excitement was building in my stomach at the thought of what I was about to do. Feeling hopeful and terrified, I marched into Ms Reeves' office and told her in one breath that I was giving my notice.

Her severe face looked up at me. 'Why?' she demanded. 'What about your promotion?'

I took in her vampy black clothes, her hair pulled back into a painful-looking bun, her unhappy eyes.

'Um. (Cough) Family commitments.'

She stifled a laugh and her voice was amused. 'That's what they all say.'

I studied her again. Her eyes were twinkling and her make-up cracked as her face seemed to soften.

'You've done well. I didn't think you'd last this long. Good luck to you.'

Who was this woman? In all the time I had been here, I hadn't seen anybody smile, let alone the wicked witch of the cancer ward. That small offering filled me with an inordinate amount of pleasure, and with her smiling face imprinted in my head and a skip in my walk, I ate the last of my coconut and cream cake and made my way home.

ıılıllıllılı

The next morning, my enthusiasm was nowhere to be found. What had I done? I'd quit a job where they wanted to make me a manager, to give me a pay rise, and for what? Sitting in my room, in a state of panic? My alarm clock rang and I instinctively felt a nasty plunge in my stomach. Then it clicked. I didn't have to get up and go to Cancer Town. I could do whatever I wanted. I threw the clock at the wall for that added dramatic touch.

For a few days I was on a high, and I woke to the sun pouring through my windows and my cat stretching beside me, her extended paw neatly inserted into my nose. I wore a pair of bunny slippers and some old flannel pyjamas and padded around the empty house, had eggs and bacon with fresh orange juice, and randomly watered plants while dancing to golden oldies. I felt at peace, I was alive in the moment, and my optimism was growing stronger with every hot cup of marshmallow-laden chocolate that I gulped down.

Then the phone calls started coming.

'So, what are you going to do now?' stormed my manager at the temp agency.

'How will you pay your rent?' asked my concerned parents.

'Don't leave meeee!' wailed my coconut-cream-cake contact from work.

I still had enough confidence to ward off the blows and keep them happy with my excuses. But I knew it wouldn't last long.

A friend of mine, Clarice, a recent law school grad with long legs and a tough smile, came around to see me.

'Bella, I understand what you are doing, but . . .' she started.

Ah, here came the but.

She looked at me. 'You're not a child any more, Bella. You have responsibilities. To yourself, to your family, your friends, your career, your future. You really are being just a selfish child,' she remonstrated.

I didn't think that was fair so I stomped my foot. 'But I am trying to grow up and take responsibility for my life, that's what I'm trying to do.'

'By leaving your job!' she said incredulously.

'I know what I'm doing, Clarry.'

We looked at each other.

'Okay, I don't know what I'm doing,' I confessed. 'But I have to follow my instincts. My head is calling for an insanity plea, but I just gotta do this.'

Clarry left with well-wishes and warnings, and I was left with a growing seed of uncertainty. Then, just in time, the cavalry arrived. I opened the door to my friend Rene, and her amused left eyebrow sky-rocketed to the ceiling as she smiled her impish smile.

I love Rene's eyebrow arch: filled with warmth and wickedness, it makes me feel that everything will be all right, she understands. Rene is a talented woman, beautiful, witty and intelligent. If she wasn't my friend I would hate her thoroughly. We went to high school together, partied like faded sixties rock stars and talked about our ambitions. We lost contact for a few years, but she was back in my life with a vengeance, which was great.

We sat together in the sun on my patio, drank hot chocolate and talked about the bigger picture. She scolded me for taking my time quitting and reminded me of all the things we used to plan and dream about. That evening, filled with Rene's reminders, I experienced a burst of panic.

Despite my showdown at Cancer Town, I still felt like I was in a Kurt Cobain song – and I needed to do something drastic to get out of it. I wanted to find a happy place – and fast. I logged onto the internet and up popped a website of exciting travel destinations. I always travelled when I was in denial or unhappy, as it was sure to give me fresh perspectives and a skip in my step. Feeling like a naughty schoolgirl and with my heart in my mouth, I entered my credit-card details and pressed 'confirm'.

2

Goodbye Celine: surf's up

I SPENT A MONTH capering around Hong Kong and China, in the middle of one of the coldest winters on record. I climbed the Great Wall and paced around the frozen Forbidden City. I ate a lot of dumplings and was robbed more times than I can remember. I didn't find my happy place. My confidence still felt like it had had an all-over body wax. Towards the end, I caught a dangerous and virulent Asian flu that had me in my hotel room literally wringing out my sweaty sheets. I had a cough that felt like a potato peeler was loose in my throat, and I was gradually resembling an advertisement for anti-smoking. I arrived home with too many fake Asian antiques, and on doctor's orders, had to be quarantined in my house for two weeks until I improved. Not the most successful of trips.

I still didn't have the confidence to audition for any acting roles, and rent had to be paid, so I got a job. Bored solicitors leered at me over a faux mahogany receptionist's desk in an office in Circular Quay as I intoned, 'Good morning, Hilton and Rodgers Law Firm, Bella speaking, how can I help you?' Syrup dripped off my tongue as I pointed my index finger at my temple and thought 'click'. I felt like crap. Like a crap sandwich. I had turned into one of those people who reminisce fondly about high school.

After four gruelling months at Hilton and Rodgers, I actually found myself at a hairdresser's waiting for a perm when sanity came snapping back. I really needed to get out of that office. I had to be an adult and think things through. My choices loomed in front of me: running away? Setting the place on fire? Tough one. I checked my bank balance on my newly purchased I-want-to-fit-in diamante-encrusted phone with Celine Dion ringtone (*I know, I know!*), and found that I had a whopping fifteen dollars. So I settled on chocolate and cigarettes instead.

I had to reassess my life. Technically, I had done everything by the book. Nine-to-five job, good income, nice Saab (okay, my dad bought it for me); I'd said 'please' and 'thank you' (occasionally), laughed at bad jokes (sometimes) and hadn't come too loudly. But I still felt like shit. Even dunking dumplings in Doijiang didn't disrupt my damned depression. And if my new perm was anything to go by, I was in danger of seriously losing it. Celine didn't even make me happy any more.

The next afternoon, Saturday, I found myself still in bed at 4pm, feeling like road kill. I thought about my future and my heart felt like my fingers did when I plunged them into the snow.

I drove to my parents' house in Glebe. My mother opened the door to me in her eternal floral dress and smiled her beautiful smile. The floodgates opened. I stood there, like an idiot, feeling the tears sliding down my face.

My mother, Rosie, has always been my rock. The author of

nine books and a successful person to boot, she has soft intelligent eyes sparked with cheekiness and a beautiful oval face with metal-rimmed glasses. She seems to know more words than the *Oxford* and her unpretentious compassion, good humour and gift of perception affect everyone who meets her. The thing about Rosie is that she looks tiny and fragile, yet inside that delicate shell is such an extraordinary, almost shockingly huge world of ideas and passion, strength, searing intelligence and immense love, it often takes my breath away. She and my father are the first I want to tell good news to and the first I go to when the bottom falls out.

I looked into her comforting eyes and cried like a baby. I hadn't cried like that since Tom Gruber bit the head off my Cabbage Patch Kid in primary school.

'I'm aaaa looooser,' I wailed. 'I didn't know how' – hic – 'to stop being Mardi' – hiccup – 'and I wanted to do a good job' – hic – 'and now, I'm, I'm, I'm just a loosssaaaa.'

A fresh flood of tears was released as I saw my fuzzy perm reflecting in the window.

Mum sat me down, force-fed me some vitamins and gave me a loving cuddle.

'Bella, you haven't been your happy self since the feature film finished,' she said, smoothing my hair. 'You did a good job, but it took over a bit, didn't it?'

I nodded, drying my eyes. 'But even before that –'

'I know, baby, and now you're at the accounting firm and it isn't exactly finding your G-spot, is it?'

A laugh broke through my tears.

She smiled. 'Don't be so hard on yourself, honey. You've learned, and next time you'll know how to do it differently.

'Know yourself. And trust yourself,' she continued. 'You're a talented actor, my girl, you just need to be confident about that.'

I couldn't really believe the nice things she said, as my confidence was still at the bottom of my tennis shoes, plus I was filled with fear. In my heart of hearts, I knew what I wanted, but, as Rosie guessed, I was just plain scared to go out and do it. What if I returned to acting and got depressed again? . . . And what if I sucked? . . . What if I didn't book any jobs? . . . What if I ended up old and alone, collecting Coke cans and reciting Ophelia monologues to a multitude of stray cats? I needed to think.

I drove out to Bondi and sat on the cliff top like a monk, overlooking the thrashing waters below. The burning sky lit up the clouds around me, making the tips of the waves light up like a child's crayon drawing. I thought about my friends and family and all the suggestions and advice they'd given me in the past few months, from swallowing my dissension and keeping the job, to quitting and becoming an actor. (Oh yeah, and setting off the fire alarm at Hilton and Rodgers and running away to Bolivia to sell cocaine, thanks for that gem, Tozza.) I was more confused than ever. Everyone was so helpful, but I had come to realise that their well-meaning advice was coming from their own experiences, which, really, is the only place any advice *can* come from. I realised my decision had to be made through my own experiences, through my knowledge of myself, through my dreams and, damn it, from a place of honesty.

It was hard to reconcile the different parts of my personality. Sometimes I felt as strong as an ox and as sexually savvy as Sharon Stone. Other times I felt Mary Poppins-ish and naive, like a kid. Often I dreamed of pure luxury in my life – to marry Prince Charming, wear beautiful clothes and have enough money to light cigarettes with. Other times I wanted nothing of the sort and found the notion soulless, stupid and alienating. Sometimes I was the life of the party and would joke with vitality. Other times I entered a room and was socially uncouth and timid, analysing every gesture and word until it paralysed me next to the food table.

I sat on my rock, feeling the pebble imprint on my bottom.

Yeah, yeah . . . Sharon Stone, Prince Charming . . . blah blah. But what did I want?

I felt a crisp wind blow up from the ocean and turned to face it.

I wanted to be a pirate. I wanted to stifle the lady in me. I wanted to be full of courage, and notorious. *A pirate, huh. Okay, that's not very helpful.* I knew I didn't want to be in an office, no matter how much chocolate it would buy me. *But what did I want? Be specific.* I wanted to be making films that I was proud of, embodying characters that fascinated me and learning the craft of acting. *And?* I wanted to travel, and . . . *And what?* To love hard and see new places and be happy in my own skin . . . I wanted to feel alive again. I had nothing to lose!

And that definitely included my diamante-encrusted mobile phone. I took the offending phone out of my faux alligator handbag and felt a dirty chuckle rise from my belly. I looked at the vastness of the ocean in front of me and I flung it with all my might into the crashing waters below.

'Take that, Celine Dion!' I shouted into the wind. 'Woo hooo!'

And it was as easy as that. All the doubts and turmoil over the past few months gave way to a great ball of joy that rose in me. I was going to be an actor. I wasn't going to be as false as a no-frills chocolate bar any more. All along, I had been 'acting' the good worker, the (er . . . sometime) dutiful adult. When, really, all I wanted to do was to *act*. I knew with every buzzing cell in my body that I was finally back on the right path.

Now, with my goal firmly in place, I could look ahead, plan and choose my battles more strategically. Steer myself in the right direction, towards acting and away from the coconut cream cakes, so to speak. I brushed my knuckles on my lapel and blew the dust off them. I'd been waiting passively for my dreams to materialise, but now I was damned well ready to fight for them.

That night, I slept like the dead. I dreamed I was surfing on a giant computer-generated wave as it swept through a stunning futuristic city of skyscrapers. I arched my back and pressed into the pixelated wave and steered myself through the streets of the city with a newfound happiness.

The next day I woke early to an explosion of noise.

Half-asleep, I picked up the phone.

'Surf's up . . .' I stammered.

'Bella? Bella, it's Bianca.'

My cousin Bianca is a stunning model-turned-actress with giant soft brown eyes and scarily high cheekbones. Being a successful model for years, winning the Ford Supermodel of the Year competition, she'd moved to Los Angeles to change careers and make it as an actor.

'Bella, we've just got funding for a full-length Hollywood feature film. You've produced films before, will you come over and help me produce it?'

My jaw dropped to the floor and I was suddenly wide awake, looking around the room in shock. A Hollywood feature film? It felt like a grand universal joke. All I had to do was have faith in my goal, trust a little in myself and in life, and then this happens. Just like that? I liked this goal thing.

I only had a week to swot up on American-style producing, quit my job (without setting off the fire alarm), pack my bags and say my goodbyes. When I boarded the plane for Los Angeles, I didn't know what to expect, and even though it wouldn't exactly be me up there on the silver screen, I could damned well smell it from there.

3

Cracking it up in La La Land with Like People and Leto

O N THE PLANE TRIP over, I read up on Los Angeles. I discovered that forty per cent of women had hurled their footwear at their husbands, that it was prohibited to drive more than two thousand sheep down Hollywood Boulevard at any time, and that it was unlawful to beat your wife with a strap more than two inches wide without her consent. I also discovered that zoot suits were illegal, as were crying on the witness stand and hunting for moths under a street lamp. I wasn't exactly sure what a zoot suit was, but I had stopped moth-hunting years ago, so I figured I would be okay.

After shaking off the effects of the free vodka, I took in my new surroundings. The first thing that hit me was the absence of anything that could be a zoot suit; the second thing was the heat. It got caught in my bones and was trying to escape out through my skin in rivulets of sweat. A tissue jammed under my armpit did the trick. Licking the wrappers of my stock of melted duty-free chocolate, I excitedly caught a bright blue bus to the address in West Hollywood that Bianca had given me.

It was an extraordinary house, once owned by Marilyn Monroe, set just below Sunset Boulevard on a graceful sloping hill. The giant white mansion was split into apartments, each with its own intricately carved balcony, and surrounded by tall, rubbery palm trees. I climbed the meandering white steps (through the throngs of my imaginary paparazzi) that led me to the top of the slope and the house itself. At the top of the grand stairway, I took a sharp left and found myself at the door of Bianca's studio apartment, my new home for the next couple of weeks.

'Welcome bitch!' came Bianca's enthusiastic greeting. 'You made it!' We gave each other a hug and settled down to catch up on our lives over white wine and chocolate. I was loving it already.

We had a few days before we started pre-production on our film *Japan* – enough time to get over my atrocious jet-lag and to orientate myself with the City of Angels. I wanted to explore Los Angeles, go to Hollywood and let my ringlets down before the work started. Oooh yeah!

It was as if I were awake in a dreaming world. The sun was out and blond people were everywhere – I'd arrived in Barbieland. It was just like being in the middle of a movie set, with the sun providing the lighting and all the trees and cars and houses merely props for this giant Hollywood game. I was like a stunned-mullet movie-extra catching glimpses of the bold and the beautiful as they tossed their golden curls at one another.

People didn't walk, they either glided or strutted. On the street they talked in loud stage whispers and glanced over their shoulders self-consciously at an imaginary audience. The cab drivers affected De Niro-esque grimaces as you got in, and the valets swaggered and winked at you *à la* George Clooney. Everybody wore designer sunglasses and nobody was without the ubiquitous

Hollywood prop, the take-out Starbucks Grande coffee cup. When I watched them from my vantage point on Rodeo Drive, I realised they weren't being *like* people in the movies – they *were* the people movies were made about. It made me uncertain about what was real and what wasn't. I ordered another martini to think more on it.

On a jaunt to the local grocery store for supplies of ice-cream and seaweed (don't ask), I overheard a conversation behind me in the checkout line, which later I discovered was a stock-standard piece of LA dialogue.

'What about [Sandra] Bullock?' said one woman.

'She's totally MIA. Old news, not hot,' replied the other.

'Left field: Madonna.'

'Are you kidding?'

'Sure, she can't act her way into bed – or her marriage from what I hear – but she'll bring the hype.'

The other woman didn't even bother to respond.

'So, has Tom's agent gotten back?'

'Nope . . . the cunt.'

By that stage I had reached the checkout and had to repeat myself over and over again because the checkout chick couldn't decipher my accent. The two behind me stopped talking to, er, rudely eavesdrop.

I also noticed the plastic-faced wives creaking about the place, shopping and driving, their bejewelled old hands gripping the steering wheels of their Mercedes and BMWs. Their faces were a tight and painful-looking stretch across bone, and their collagen lips burst out like cooked German sausages. I always fantasised that women like that were somehow both glamorous and tragic. I imagined them staring drunkenly out the windows of their prison-mansions, suffering their cheating husbands and inept housekeepers.

I felt an uneasiness around those women, and it wasn't just the atrocious bright gold designer sunglasses: it was because I couldn't read them. Over a lifetime we develop lines on our faces that are a map of our personalities. I figured that a person with lots of lines stemming from their upper lip has got into the habit of pursing their lips from feeling disapproving or from keeping quiet. People with smile lines around their eyes and mouth have obviously smiled a lot, so are probably easy and open. With these face-lifted women, I was unable to read their faces and see who they were or what they were thinking, and that made me uneasy. Or perhaps it was just the nuclear explosion of perfume that followed them everywhere.

I was introduced to one of these society wives who was connected with our film. She was in her fifties and had an air of sadness; she was talkative, incessantly moving her hands and head. She sighed a lot. She offered us water and apologised profusely that it was local bottled water. She held herself upright, her brown-lipsticked smile unwavering, but when she excused herself to get something from another room, I could see her through the door, and her straight posture and smile dropped instantly as she rummaged through her papers. As if putting on a well-practised mask, she emerged from the room upright and smiling again. It was as though she was always on show. I imagined how exhausting it must be, and the little sighs that kept escaping her seemed to confirm it.

The effort I had put into choosing my wardrobe back in Sydney was completely in vain. I looked like a downright country-bumpkin, yodelling hick compared to LA women. I began to feel even more daggy when Bianca swanned me around to meet her sexy, skinny and beautiful friends. My rubbing thighs and a belly protruding over the top of my jeans didn't do much for my confidence. Everybody was so beautifully . . . well, beautiful. And, unlike me, they weren't wearing jandals they'd purchased in high school. When I met people, they would flick me over with their eyes and find me wanting. Their gaze would settle a little too long on my frayed hair, chipped nails and daggy clothes; then they would dismiss me with a glance and a toss of hair.

Determined to experience LA life to the full, and not to embarrass my cousin, I tried to make an effort with my appearance. I stopped wolfing down hamburgers and started squeezing into Bianca's trendy clothes when we went out to party. The transformation was instant. With a bit of make-up and my stomach rolls hidden from view, I was suddenly visible and accepted. I was asked out to parties, asked who my designer was (St Vincent de Paul) and who my stylist was (my mum). And, just like in the movies, men approached me asking if I would like to 'go out on a date' with them. Heh, heh, now this was the Hollywood I'd heard about.

One day, Bianca's friend Cary picked us up in his convertible Mercedes and drove us through the heat to his Hollywood Hills home. We arrived at a stunning mansion of elegance, comfort and finery with a view of the burnt-looking hills all around us. I was happily fantasising about owning such a place when I got a text message from my bank threatening to close my credit card if I didn't make a payment. My response was immediate: I sent out for more booze. While we waited, our host pointed out a beautiful old building below us that was used as Rydell High in *Grease*, which prompted me to do my Travolta impersonation, which prompted him to stop my alcohol supply. But even sobriety didn't dampen my spirits. I relaxed into the luxury and the host's witty banter. He regaled us with amazing Hollywood stories about celebrities and decadent parties. He told us about the time he met Robert De Niro, who had held a small hand-held camera throughout their dinner party, interviewed everybody with it, then proceeded, to everyone's surprise, to eat nonchalantly off other people's dinner plates. My host and Bianca laughed delightedly, while I put back the chicken wing I'd swiped from her plate.

In LA there was one degree of separation, not six. Everybody but everybody was somehow connected to the film industry. In fact, the whole time I was there I don't think I met one person who wasn't somehow connected with the Hollywood moving-making machine. It was so stimulating being around many of these people, but there were also some bottom-feeders too: small-time entrepreneurs with shiny suits and ponytails, with backgrounds in the 'adult entertainment industry'. Talking with them felt like getting the hard sell at a used-car lot. And no, I wasn't interested in acting in *Sperms of Endearment*.

ıılıtıllılılı

We wove our way through the Friday-night crowds and the warm LA air to Sunset Strip. There were so many diverse groups of people out and about, from plump, boobed-up girls with shiny shoes and Gucci handbags to crews of cool-looking black men in jeans around their ankles and gleaming gold chains. Men in hotted-up cars with pounding rap music filed by shouting incoherent things about our asses and mothers. Mexican delivery boys darted between the crowds, carrying their parcels.

Bianca got us into the Château Marmont, the notorious celebrity castle where John Belushi died from an overdose, where Robert De Niro lived, and where a stoned Jim Morrison got hurt when he dangled from a drainpipe, attempting to swing from the roof into the window. Yep, just my cup of vodka.

Inside the château was a dark and glamorous world. Exciting and debauched at the same time. The tuxedoed wait staff were from a romantic era, yet the young celebutantes with their designer casual clothes added that touch of modern Los Angeles. I tried to copy the pouts of the passing actresses but then caught my reflection in a mirror and stopped.

'So it's, like, Bella, isn't it?' asked a beautiful woman, as thin as a snake. She didn't wait for an answer. 'Nice dress, it's gorrrgeous,' she purred. 'So. You are Bianca's cousin, yes?'

'Ye –'

'That's, like, just great,' she interrupted. 'So,' – brief pause – 'who else do you know?' She asked the question as if it were a test.

'Well, I'm new to –'

'Oh. I see. Well,' she said with another brief pause, 'nice meeting you.' And with a thin smile and a nod she abruptly turned on her heel and left.

I think my mouth did the goldfish thing as another woman nearby shook her head and laughed lightly. 'Don't worry about it,' she reassured. 'It's just Hollywood,' she said, as she laughed again and shook her fingers like they were covered in glitter.

I felt at a bit of a loss, as if I had entered another world entirely and didn't know the rules. The last time I had felt like that was when I crashed a snow-boarders' convention on Bondi Beach. I figured high-fiving people and saying 'Radical, dude' wouldn't work here either. I slunk into a corner to watch the beautiful people and throw back a cocktail.

'You don't look very happy,' mused a handsome man wearing what appeared to be a safari suit.

If he told me my dress looked gorrrgeous I was going to smack him.

'Annalise over there is the worst thing possible, she's a real-estate broker,' he said, motioning towards a stunning model-esque woman laughing in a sexy, throaty way. 'Dan over there is a waiter,' he added. 'It's all smoke. This place can make a star out of anyone.'

I smiled back at him. Then he asked me what I did for a living as he leaned a little closer.

I wondered if I should say I was Danny DeVito's love child.

'I'm a real-estate broker.'

His face dropped like my knickers on laundry day. Then he abruptly broke into laughter. He was even more handsome when he laughed.

'I like you.' He smiled. 'Let me buy you a drink.'

Gabriel was a lawyer for an entertainment firm and had moved to LA five years before from somewhere in Nebraska. He told me LA was made of 'smoke, sun and dreams', and after we'd had a few drinks he asked me out on a date.

Cool, I would get to use the line, 'Sorry, I don't date lawyers', like in the movies. But before I could answer him, he suddenly dropped his hands under the table and started making these weird little convulsing movements with a look of fierce concentration on his face. I wondered if he could be masturbating. I took a peek and caught him trying to manically twist off his golden wedding ring. I stood up abruptly.

'Sorry,' I said, 'I don't date assholes.' Then I sauntered off to find Bianca.

'Nice strut,' she said when I walked up to her. 'You learn quickly.'

'It was supposed to be a saunter.' I replied into my drink.

ılılılılılı

LA was a city of disparate groups. So many different types of ethnicities, cultures and socio-economic backgrounds. But it seemed that they lived in their own fortified worlds, occasionally merging like that night on Sunset. I saw this same merging-of-tribes phenomena again when a friend of Bianca's invited us to Jared Leto's birthday party.

Jared Leto, the sexy blue-eyed actor from *Requiem for a Dream* and *Fight Club*, had a low single-storey house nestled in the Hollywood Hills. Inside was a life-sized plaster-of-Paris sculpture of two people having sex doggy style, and outside was a large pool with a sunny terracotta patio. I went out to the bar, where a chlorine-drenched Jared passed me a drink and a smile. He was slight, had a sexy way of moving and very saucy bedroom eyes. I liked him. Otherwise, there were three groups of people near the pool: a bunch of Like Girls (you know, like, girls who say 'like' all the time), who laughed with confidence and examined each other's jewellery; Jared's old high-school buddies, boisterous and loud, posturing in their well-tanned skins; and in the corner, a bunch of CGTCs (country girls turned city), with faux designer handbags and surreptitious faces. The three groups eyed each other as though they were from different planets, which didn't seem that far off the mark.

Then the Olsen twins arrived, and their appearance just seemed to highlight the disparity of the groups. As the twins' thin frames, swathed in flowing hippie material, sat near the pool, their robes sticking to the cement as they shifted positions in the sun, the Like Girls reacted by huddling even closer together, examining and re-examining their accessories. The Boisterous Buddies began flexing and shadow-boxing each other, while the CGTCs stared at each other with limp jaws and closely clutched drinks. It was like tribes of schoolyard kids eyeballing each other. But it wasn't just the twins' celebrity that caused it because when a group of preppy guys arrived, the groups did the same thing: huddling even closer together, occasionally glancing over at the strangers with slightly bemused expressions. It seemed to go beyond social anxieties with strangers; it was as if their very existence, or place in the world, was precarious, and only their stringent unity and exclusion of others would keep them safe from harm.

Then Jared climbed onto his roof and, screaming like a banshee, flung himself into the pool, splashing everybody in the process. The soaked groups grinned, then laughed. Water sports: the great uniter.

⷟⵿⷟⵿⷟⵿

Before we started pre-production on *Japan*, I went to see my childhood friend Zoë, who lived in Venice Beach.

Zoë and I had grown up together on Waiheke, a small island nestled in the Pacific Ocean, off the coast of New Zealand, and had spent most of our time getting into and out of scrapes. We'd go on adventures together, egging each other on to climb tall trees, shimmy along precarious cliff tops and swim out past the breakers. We'd come home with skinned knees, our grinning, exhausted faces caked with salt and dirt.

In her twenties, Zoë's penchant for getting into scrapes led her to excel in both martial arts and gymnastics. She landed a job as Lucy Lawless' stunt double on the TV series *Xena: Warrior Princess*. When the show eventually finished, she flew to Los Angeles to kick ass in the movies. And that she did, literally. She doubled for Uma Thurman and her gutsy performance as The Bride in *Kill Bill* earned her an award for Best Overall Stunt at the Taurus World Stunt Awards.

Not having seen her for years, I was unsure what to expect. But from her slightly ramshackle beach house, infectious laugh and the offer of a beer, I could see she was still the same down-to-earth, funny chick that I remembered from childhood.

We spent the day at the beach, drinking cold beers and belly-laughing. It was just what the doc ordered.

The following afternoon, Zoë had rehearsals for a film, so a friend of hers, Daniella, took me out on the town. We started at a beach bar then made our way up Venice Beach to a summer festival that was just kicking off. We met a very LA-looking bleached and boobed-up actress called Sally who invited us to share her picnic, which we hungrily accepted. Sally told horrific and fascinating stories about her casting-couch experiences and said she'd 'screwed more directors than light bulbs'. Daniella was tired and had to work the next day, but I was having fun, so Sally suggested we kick on to a CD launch party.

At the launch, Sally and I swanned around a glass-walled venue filled with rappers and faux-gangsters with thousand-dollar haircuts and bling. With the aquarium-like walls and the bright gold bling everywhere, it felt like swimming in a giant fish bowl through gleaming, posturing goldfish. As the bright glare began to dissolve my corneas, Sally offered to give me a lift back to Venice Beach. On the way home, she piped up, 'I need a pick-me-up.' A light bulb flashed above her blonde head. 'Let's get some crack.'

'Whaat?' I drunkenly slurred.

'Crack. I need a little pick-me-up,' she repeated through glossed lips.

'And I suppose a shandy wouldn't do the trick, huh?'

Other than jumping out of her car in the middle of LA with no money and no clue as to where I was, my options were limited. I tried to talk her out of it, but she was bloody persistent. We drove through an innocuous-looking suburb with neat rows of houses and tree-lined streets and stopped near an intersection.

'What now?' I asked fearfully.

'We wait,' she said, as she fixed her hair in the mirror.

After a while, I could make out a shadowy figure loitering near the corner.

'Bingo!' she said as she turned the car around.

A baby-faced black guy limped up to the car as Sally rolled down her window. She passed him fifteen dollars and he handed her a small package, all without a word spoken between them.

It was completely surreal, sitting next to this woman I'd just met, with her fake boobs profiling her model-esque frame and her Valley Girl accent, as she bought crack from some random stranger with a weeping eye.

As he merged back into the shadows, Sally put the car into gear and roared away, elated and laughing. I began to feel more and more uncomfortable as she kept fingering the small bag on her lap. Eventually she stopped the car, avoiding the bright street lamp nearby, and took out a pipe.

'You're not going to do it here, are you?'

She laughed and told me not to be so green.

'Go ahead then!' I blurted out. Then I climbed out of the car not knowing what else to do.

'Get back in here, people will get suspicious!' she roared.

'No fucking way. I'm not breathing that crap into my lungs.'

'Fine,' she said, as she packed the small crystals into the pipe and lit it up with a plastic lighter.

As I watched through the window, her face contorted and it looked like she was going to be sick. I came around to her side of the car and opened the door so she could vomit if she needed to. But then her expression changed into a strange energised mask. Her features had stopped moving, but I could see the sensation pass through her closed eyelids like an electrical storm.

She opened her eyes and laughed.

'Wooo hooo!' she yelled, and hammered at the dashboard. 'Climb on in,' she laughed.

With no alternative, I gingerly got back into the car and she drove me home at a blood-curdling speed.

Ah, the City of Angels. There were so many contradictions there. Bianca drove me through the 'bad area' of LA once, and it seemed like an apocalyptic vision. Fires burned freely as figures huddled, and mad, bare-chested men yelled abuse as we sped past. At Sally's record launch a musician had told me he'd spent seven thousand dollars on his shoes. The sub-cultures were so clearly defined, meeting through common spaces and the sharp splinter of the Hollywood dream. That was the real commonality: the lure of the Hollywood dream. Scratching the surface of its gleam was the insistence for love; the need for nourishment, acceptance, attention, affection. The city divided into those who had it, those who never thought they would, and those like Sally, who'd smoke their mothers to get it. Love and Hollywood, together forever.

4

Swimming in fire with eyelash flutterers and wonky birds as Aretha provides the soundtrack and I wait for the Big O

*J*APAN WAS THE BRAINCHILD of Bianca and her producing partner, Fabien. The drama was set in a hotel and revolved around the unlikely friendship between a hitman, code-named 'Japan', and a baseball-capped dad-like character. We'd received permission from the Screen Actors Guild to make it under the 'low budget agreement' so the pay-rate and budget were fairly low, which was going to make it that much harder to crew and shoot. But the passion was there.

Pre-production was a real shambles. Back home, I would have had an army of contacts to call upon for help. In LA, I didn't know a soul. We hired some dilapidated offices in Burbank and had less than ten days to cast and crew an entire feature film, organise catering, locations, equipment and transport, and draw up schedules. All of us in production became pretty overloaded and our stress levels began climbing Everest. I began to feel like the Energizer Bunny's shoddy counterpart. As the fifteen-hour days passed I could feel my synapses fraying and snapping like carrot sticks as my mind ran a thousand conversations at once.

I sat in my office on the Sunday and watched the ketchup roll out of my hamburger and make pretty patterns on my shirt as my left eye twitched. I sucked in a great lungful of air then breathed out. My nervous breakdown would have to be put on hold for the time being: we were off to location in Arizona.

For the set, Bianca had cleverly obtained a defunct forty-million-dollar resort called the Montelucia, near the beautiful Camelback mountain range near Phoenix, Arizona. Apparently, in the fifties it was the place to be. Movie stars floated in the extensive maze of swimming pools dotted with grottos and palm trees. The interior was wonderfully garish with gold fittings and huge ballrooms that could seat hundreds. The owners thought it would be cheaper to tear the whole thing down and start again than to renovate it, and, as luck would have it, our film was shooting right before the scheduled demolition so we had the entire place to ourselves.

Bianca managed, through sheer Aussie doggedness (and a few eyelash flutters), to secure Peter Fonda (of *Easy Rider* fame), Michael Buscemi (Steve's brother) and Shane Brolly (the sexy star of *Underworld*), as well as Kiera Chaplin (granddaughter of Charlie) and Aimee Graham (Heather's sister). The first night Peter Fonda arrived in his bright yellow Ferrari was one of the best nights we had there. We sucked back margaritas and sat out by the swimming pool drinking and talking well into the morning. I liked Peter, he had a razor-sharp memory and a wicked wit. He was very tall and as thin as a pole, with a lined face, small eyes and a wide expressive mouth. He sat listening to the conversations around him, his body and face as still as a statue, then he would single out one of them and his distinctive voice would rise above the fray and his body and face would become lively and animated. He told us extraordinary stories about life in Hollywood, about playing in Bob Marley's band and the eighty-plus movies he'd made. He sat on the edge of the dried-up fountain like a king. His white baseball cap, the peak twisted to the back, read 'Easy Rider' in embossed letters. He liked talking about his past, about the pot, the parties, the movies, but he also liked talking philosophy. He had very definite ideas on religion and society. We got into a heated debate about the battle of the sexes and decided to settle it by seeing who could drink more. I unfortunately proved we were the lesser sex.

A month in the middle of the Arizona desert in a huge, empty resort – think *The Shining* on acid – with a bunch of crazy actors and a crew that wore T-shirts reading 'Who do I have to screw to get off this film?' was, needless to say, both heaven and hell. My life went from trying to find happiness at the bottom of a bowl of shark fin soup to a manic state of coordinating fifty or so horny actors and irate crew members through the trials of a full-length, underpaid feature film. And the heat was extraordinary. I was used to Queensland heat and even the heat of Africa, where I'd travelled a few years earlier, but this was something else entirely. It was like swimming through fire, with temperatures up to 46 degrees Celsius. I imagined the faces of the Hollywood plastic wives melting like ice-cream.

I worked well into the heat of the night on schedules and paperwork as shooting continued. The actors would come into my office to invite me for beers, and sometimes I would join them, but most nights I stole glimpses of them through my window, playing in the pool, and having a good time. I would look down at the figures I was working on and remember why I'd quit producing in the first place. Acting was so much easier. *Splash in a pool? I could do that*, I thought as I gritted my teeth.

I would sometimes call my father for advice. Danny was a

successful film director before he became a writer and was always on hand with practical help. I swear he could craft a camera out of a wine bottle and a couple of screws, but it was his faith in me that was my real weapon. His love is as warm as an oven, completely, deeply unconditional and as strong as the ocean. It is something I think of, like a treasure, whenever I feel hopeless or lost. But even with my father's good advice and support, there were times when each of us cracked like a crack ho. My limit arrived about three-quarters of the way into the shoot. I was trying to finish mountains of paperwork, my day's to-do list was seventeen pages long, we'd lost two overworked key members of the crew the day before and I was frantically trying to find replacements to allow shooting to continue. I hadn't slept in what felt like days, I was trying to negotiate a cease-fire between a number of irate crew members, the caterer had suddenly pulled out (wanting more money), one of our actors had heatstroke and finally the cinematographer came to me with a broken camera that needed urgent attention.

One afternoon I became overwhelmed. My heart began booming like a demented cannon in my chest and a flood of tears gushed from my eyes. I stretched out a smile, managed an 'excuse me', went into an empty room and let loose. I felt hopeless and stressed and pissed off that I was being such a cry-baby, but the exhausted tears wouldn't stop. My mind fondly flicked back to stealing Post-it notes from Hilton and Rodgers. So I did what any normal person would do: I called my mum.

'Bells,' she said. 'The situation is not going to change, so you have to. You have to be aware that stress is the demon here, take initiatives to de-stress so that you can work more effectively. Take a break before you break,' she said, sounding just like Dr Phil.

On Mum's orders I looked for a chance to leave the set for

the afternoon. Someone had to take a meeting with an out-of-town art designer we wanted to snaffle for the movie so I oh so kindly consented to take on the arduous task. I lit a cigarette, turned the AC and the car radio on full blast, then head-banged along the dusty and deserted highway shouting the lyrics to 'Bad to the Bone'. I liked this whole de-stressing thing. The scenery was magnificent. Moonscape-like craters and rocks lined the desert road. I kept expecting to see a posse of cowboys in hot pursuit emerge from the dust that my speeding car created in its wake.

Oblivious to anything other than my fantasies of cowboys and Indians, I snapped back to reality as a sinking feeling in my chest (and the complete absence of any other cars) told me I was hopelessly lost. I swerved to the side of the road to phone the designer for directions and, yep, Murphy's Law, the production phone battery was dead. The sinking feeling went to my belly. I turned the ignition on and the car spluttered then fell silent. I checked the gas dial – I had run out of gas. The sinking feeling went to my feet.

As it was 44 degrees and I was in the middle of the desert sitting in a tin can, my mind flicked to the Aussie survival manual I had been given in primary school. I dramatically thought of peeing in a palm frond and drinking the evaporation, but settled on the large bottle of Evian in my handbag. With nothing in sight, I got out of the car, hitched up my jeans and strode into the heat with a strut I imagined was John Wayne-like.

The heat was unbearable. The burning yellow road looked like water, with the heat emanating from it in thick golden waves. My head was burning, my lungs hurt and I could feel my eyelashes start to frizzle. All around me was desert and rocks as far as the eye could see, huge hot rocks and heatstroked birds that were zig-zagging wonkily. Images of me as a romantic, adventuring fifties movie star gave way to images of me dead in a ditch with a wonky bird pecking at my innards.

After days (okay, an hour) of walking in the middle of nowhere, exhaustion setting in, I rounded a hill and discovered a highway exit. Turning the corner I spied a bustling metropolis with a neon Kmart sign glowing next to the golden arches. Talk about surreal. Who the hell lives out here? Suddenly there were people everywhere. Shopping, going about their business, unaware of my dramatic escape from the clutches of certain death.

I found a service station, bought a small petrol can and began filling up. A guy with a square jaw and sunglasses was watching me from his pick-up truck. He got out, ambled over and asked if I would like a lift back to my car. Dreading the wonky birds and the walk back, I accepted gratefully. As we waited together for the can to fill, we got to chatting. The thing about the man was that I couldn't read him. Unlike the plastic-surgery women, it wasn't the lack of smile lines or wrinkles, it was something in his eyes. They were somehow blank, cold. Cold and curious at the same time. I wasn't exactly afraid of him, but I knew something wasn't right. Exhausted, I brushed away my paranoid thoughts and went to line up at the cash register. Inside, a crazy-looking woman with missing front teeth and badly bleached hair stared at me intensely.

'Do you know that man?' she asked between chewing at her nails.

'Um, no, he's giving me a lift to my car.'

'I know, I heard yer talking. I don't think yer should go with him.'

'Huh?'

'There's somethin' not right about him.'

My head was clearing with the help of the air-conditioning. I knew the woman was right: even if he was as harmless as a hamster, I shouldn't be taking the risk. I nodded at her and resigned myself to death by wonky birds.

'I'll give ya a lift,' she said, with an unnatural smile.

The theme song from *Deliverance* crashed through my head. I sized her up to see if I could take her: she was about a hundred years old, so I thought I could just about manage it.

'Thanks, that would be great.'

'Yer don't mind if I take a few detours on the way, do yer?' she asked.

Uh oh.

'Ah, no . . . um, sure, thanks,' I stammered.

'Juz tell the man I'm a friend of yer mom's,' she added with a conspiratorial look. She paid for her gas and went out to her pick-up truck. I could see her talking to the hillbilly guy behind the petrol pumps. Their body language was unusual, they both looked tense and, unlike country people, they were standing very close to each other. Then they parted without formalities. I wondered what they had been talking about.

I paid for my fuel and went up to the would-be psycho or possibly harmless nice guy who saves women, and told him my mum's friend would be giving me a lift, but thanks anyway. He didn't say a word, gave me a blood-curdling smile then got into his truck. In a fume of burnt rubber, Elvis left the building.

I climbed into the old woman's pick-up truck. The passenger side and the back of the truck were packed with all sorts of rubbish, bits of material, shoes, empty cans and tools. I hitched my legs up against my chest and turned to look at her. She turned the ignition on, raised her eyebrows at me and let out a dirty chuckle. I buckled my belt as I tried not to think of tomorrow's newspaper headlines – 'Sydney Girl Murdered by Mother and Son Team'.

Down the road, we stopped at a pet store to pick up her giant bulldog, which had been getting washed. Psychos didn't wash their dogs, did they? The next stop was at a low and grimy brick building with an American flag festooned on the door. She was gone for a few minutes and came out with a black bag of something horrible smelling.

'Fer Chuck here,' she said, motioning to the brutish dog salivating down my back.

We drove slowly on for a while, and I was getting more and more nervous at the behaviour of this strange woman next to me. She was animated and lively one second, then strange and secretive the next. Not good with directions at the best of times, I was also getting suspicious about where we were going.

'Are we lost?' I asked, trying to keep the shake out of my voice.

She looked at me shrewdly and laughed.

'What? Yer thunk I'll murder yer, do yer, girl?'

What? How does she . . . ? I decided to do what any sane person would do in this situation. I laughed hollowly.

She turned to look at me.

'Ah crap, girl, don't be scared, I'll be lookin' after yer . . . Are yer afraid that guy will come back?'

'Ah . . . yeah, that's it,' I answered.

Her face bunched with anger. 'Don't you worry about him, I gave him a good telling off,' she said emphatically. 'Darn it, men shouldn't be picking up wee girls like that!' Her calloused old hand reached across and patted me sympathetically on the leg.

'I got his number plate!' she said, smiling cheekily. 'I also gave it to Cary at the butcher's just in case,' she added, narrowing her eyes.

Relief flooded my body. What a sweetheart! Here I was thinking she was going to knock me off and feed me to her dog, or her son. Finally able to relax, we spent the rest of the journey chatting fondly like old hens. I told her why I was in Arizona and about my acting plans; she told me about missing her daughter who worked on an oil rig in Texas. When we arrived at my car, I invited her back to the resort for dinner to thank her.

She laughed. 'Not an old bird like me. What would all the movie stars think? No, no, not me, love.'

I really wanted to somehow repay her and kept asking until finally she relented.

'Well there is something I wouldn't mind havin'.'

'What? Anything for you, Carol,' I said.

'Well, I think yer gonna be a big movie star, I can tell that about people. Give us yer autograph.'

Embarrassed, I scribbled a thank you and my name onto the back of a receipt and gave it to her.

She looked at it appraisingly. 'This might be worth something in the future. Thanks,' she said, smiling.

᠁᠁᠁

We had a couple more nights of shooting on location and then *Japan* wrapped. I could almost feel the pressure dripping off my shoulders and gathering in a puddle at my feet. But I had been so busy with the dramas of the film, I had forgotten to dislike myself. My depression, I realised with a shock, was well and truly on the mend. Every day, the secret gleeful knowledge that I was healing and following my own path was growing stronger, and it was putting a fine old jitterbug in my step.

Back in LA I went to see Aretha Franklin in concert. Hers was the first album I ever bought and my feelings for her vacillated between thinking she was the most incredibly talented woman on earth, and thinking she was the most incredibly talented woman in the universe. Yep, I was a fan. And it was extraordinary. Her talent was so breathtaking, you couldn't help but be floored. When she shuffled on stage, though, I was pretty taken aback by her size. She was sewed into a huge bright red, blindingly sequinned gown, which I unkindly thought made her look like a giant disco ball. She belted out some of her new stuff then began in with 'Respect'. I got shivers as her powerful lungs pumped for all they were worth, but as she neared the end of the song, she seemed a little unsteady on her feet. By the last lyric she looked in distinctly bad shape. I mentally plotted out my path to the stage, ready for CPR and a personal thank you from the great songstress herself for saving her life. Then, with a slow-ness matching a stoned sloth, she ambled off stage while the big band continued to play. After ten minutes lost from view, I saw her in the wings making her way back to the microphone. The crowd let out an almighty roar as she valiantly walked back on. And she was a different woman. She moved easily and quickly. She was upbeat and had a huge smile on her chops. Her hands didn't stop moving or rubbing at the sides of her dress, and I wondered if she liked to chase the tail of the dragon. Regardless of whether she needed a little pick-me-up, I was so aghast at her talent, nothing seemed to matter. It was a real highlight, I had truly been in the presence of royalty.

ılıltılılı

I left Bianca's lovely house on Sunset Strip to catch up and crash at Zoë's house on Venice Beach, where we spent long sunny days with no pressure. It was so soothing after the last two months that I relished every second of it. One evening Zoë got a phone call from Darryl Hannah who she'd gotten to know from her *Kill Bill* days. She invited us to her house for dinner and drinks. I was going to Splash's house! We dressed up as elegantly as we could and got into Zoë's old pick-up truck and hightailed it to Beverly Hills.

The caterer was serving strange smelling vegan food, which Darryl prompted me to try. She was very tall and slim, seemed rather shy in her movements and her voice was small like a child's, all softness and squeaks, which made me warm to her immediately. I took a bite of something lentil-y and nodded approvingly as my eyes bulged and my throat refused to swallow. She laughed softly and offered me a drink.

I'd met a lot of celebrities in Los Angeles and I was struck time and time again by the fact that they were human. A bizarre thing to think, perhaps, but I still had that childish image of celebrities being somehow untouchable, silver-ish, with larger-than-life values and beauty, gracing the silver screen like lovely gods and goddesses. Watching Darryl extract a piece of spinach from her teeth as she ate set me straight.

The next day, with a hangover and lentil breath, I woke to find that reality had annoyingly started to crash into my world. The film was over and I couldn't sleep on Zoë's sofa forever. With a steadily growing hole in my pocket, I was forced to figure out what to do. I thought about being responsible and returning to Sydney, my house and job. The option made me shudder all the way up from my toes.

Then, like a fresh breeze, a vision of New York swept into my sights.

I'd always had a secret love affair with New York and its history of artists, immigrants, boot leggers and poets. It was like lusting after a boy who didn't know you existed – the thought of it was tantalising and also a little scary. I didn't know that much about the place – just rumours I'd heard, scenes from novels I'd read and the occasional bullet-ridden news special on TV. But somehow I had it in my head that it was a special place where artists, thinkers, outside-of-the-boxers and crazy people were accepted and encouraged.

In a strange way, I had been saving New York. I'd been all round Europe and Africa, Asia and bits of America, but never to New York. Not that I didn't want to go. I did, desperately. But my instinct was to wait until the time was somehow right to take on that city. It was like saving a special present at Christmas or waiting for the Big O. Now I found myself in the United States with no plans and the perfect opportunity to visit New York. I wondered if, finally, the time had come.

Zoë and I sat outside on her balcony with martinis. We talked about Mardi, my depression, jobs, fears, family, the trip and *Japan*. As I reflected on all the things I'd been through to arrive at that point, they began to lose their threatening undertones and became genial, as though I was supposed to have gone through them all, to become a better person, a better actor even. I felt supported by life: it was my mercurial teacher, and the opportunity to go to New York was life giving me a surprise present. The small niggling joy I had been carrying at the thought of going to New York burst out of my chest and splashed onto my face in a huge grin. I jumped up on the chair with my fist in the air and commenced my recently practised Travolta dance.

'So I take it you've decided,' said Zoë as she giggled drunkenly and attempted to high-five me.

'Yep,' I answered, grinning like a maniac. 'I don't know what I'll do when I get there, I don't even know how I'll get there. But I'm going.'

We beamed at each other like idiots, then burst into a drunken rendition of 'New York New York' – *'If you can make it thereeeee, you can make it anywhereeeee. It's up to you! Neew York, Neeew Yooork . . . Neeeew Yooooooork! Chi-chaaa!'*

5

I Love New York and adventures with serial killers, Flipper and farting clam shells

I GOT SEARCHED THREE TIMES by airport security. Perhaps they thought the 'ILB – I Love Beer' T-shirt I was wearing was a clever terrorist disguise. Finally, after officially declaring that 'No, I did not have any affiliations with known terrorist groups' I made it through to my destination: New York, New York.

I was excited as hell to be there but also sleep deprived and somewhat terrified. Images of American serial-killer TV shows flashed through my half-awake mind. I was worried I looked like a tourist and an easy mark, so I made myself walk calmly and nonchalantly across the wide terminal. A tall thin man in a hooded top watched me as I studied an information map. Definitely a serial killer. He shoved his hands into his pockets and started to head towards me. *I knew it!* Was I about to get robbed and cut up into little pieces? I could see the occasional glint of his cold-looking eyes as he studied me under his hood. I hurriedly jammed my bags under my arms, then dove through the glass doors to get outside, where two massive black women sat cackling and smoking on a bench under the darkening sky. I needed to get me some protection. The big chicks looked like they could take the hooded man at a pinch. I felt tougher. Serial my ass! I strolled up to the women and asked one of them for a light, affecting an 'I'm with them' glance around me. The bigger of the two stared me down as though she were deciding whether to eat me or not. I responded by gulping. Then, with a *Pulp Fiction* coolness, she struck a match from a book with only one hand and held it out to me, as if it were a dare. I slowly leaned over and tried to suck in the flame through the end of my cigarette, but I couldn't get the damn thing to light. My faux cool was dissolving rapidly. I tried again with a sheepish smile. Suddenly the two women burst out into machine-gun cackles, bending over, their huge frames vibrating madly with their crazy belly laughs. I looked around. What fresh hell was this? Every time they managed to stop laughing, more peals would break out as they regarded my befuddled expression. Was this some weird New York thing? Finally it clicked. I had lit the wrong end of the cigarette. I was super cooool. New York, I had arrived. After they'd dried their tears, they invited me to share their bench and asked me about kangaroos and the Crocodile Hunter. I asked them about serial killers, but they looked at me strangely so I changed the subject to *Pulp Fiction* instead.

The bus chugged through the night towards Manhattan. The lights were amazing. The blinding yellow of car headlamps, the white of the huge buses, taxi lights flashing on and off as people entered and exited like a stream of ants. Traffic signals popping away, shops brilliantly lit to sell their wares. An invigorating cacophony of multicoloured lights that reminded me of a mad acid flashback, I – er, a friend – once had.

We drove past streets that looked so familiar. Giant racks

of fire escapes bolted to the outsides of buildings, hundreds of steely yellow cabs hurtling down the streets, honking at each other: and pedestrians, hundreds of them, walking, milling and darting about. People were smiling animatedly in restaurants and bars as I caught brief glimpses. The excitement was so profound. I felt a fresh rush of adrenaline, of being in the sexiest city on earth, not a single person here who knew who I was or where I was going. I didn't have a boss telling me what to do, no commitments, just the start of a heady new adventure, and I was scared shitless.

ıılııılıılıı

The next morning I took to the streets. The first thing that hit me was the buzz. It was tangible. Real. Almost violent in its excitement. What everyone had said about New York was true. The energy was astounding, it was everywhere and it made my skin goose-bump and a smile split my chops. The second thing that hit me was the reek, and it smacked me in the gob. Piles of overflowing, wilting garbage bags, like fat black ticks embedded into the pavement, were everywhere. As the day wore on, the stench got worse. The heat expanded the bags and released noxious gases into the air. I found out it was a regular, run-of-the-mill garbage day in New York City.

I came upon a poets' park, where sunlight cast shapes on the top of buskers' heads as they sang and talked amongst themselves. There was a small enraptured group gathered beneath a stone statue listening to a poet with a black cape and a hypnotic singsong voice. I listened to the Count for a while but the poetry was undeniably Vogon, so I slipped away and left them to their chanting. Cobblestones gave way to roadworks, where three guys in hard hats rested on their shovels and had a smoke. Ah, some things were universal. I saw the yuppies buying coffee and taking miniature dogs for walks. I saw a giant man kissing a gnarled old woman dressed in furs. I saw a fat doughnut-eating policeman watching the world through lazy eyes. And I saw the men. Oh my, did I see the men.

My gods. So many handsome men. Tall, well-dressed, smiling and winking as I walked past. I was stopped by a man in a corduroy jacket who asked me out on a date. My ego went spinning out of control but I declined on the grounds that he might be a serial killer. The other thing I noticed was the politeness. I had been given a taste of it in LA, but New York was another matter entirely. People stopped what they were doing to help you with your bags, open doors, tip their hats and offer a good morning. It was like a replay of the ceremoniousness of the past. This contrasted with the very vocal abuse from cab drivers to their patrons, or customers to their shopkeepers. It seemed the rules allowed you to slap a cab on its rump as it cut you off, shout 'mother fucker' at regular intervals then tip your hat and offer a 'good day'. Cool. I saw a cab driver honk his horn at a little old lady with a thin mouth, who yelled after him, 'Stop your damn honking, you stupid ass.' You go, girl.

I was staying in a hotel near East 17th Street. It was a small, hundred-dollar-a-night, boutique number with gold-leafed pink wallpaper and a tiny yet ultra-modern pink bathroom. It looked like a Barbie Dream Home, but pinker.

On my second evening in the city I spent hours on my laptop surfing the fabulous Craigslist – the 'Bible of New York' – where you can buy a sofa, get a house, swap a kitten, get laid, or all the above at the same time. It is a veritable goldmine of entertainment and information. A smorgasbord of everything that New York has to offer. The singles' pages were the most horribly enthralling. People wanting to meet up for foot fetishes, group bangings, true love, a casual hook-up or a 'man to dominate me thoroughly and make me come like a train'. There were ads for jobs too, thousands of them. I saw some ads for film production interns and vaguely thought of applying for them. Then I stumbled across the actors' auditions page and my heart did a little leap frog. There were hundreds of opportunities, even excluding the 'sexy actress wanted for sexy shoots' ads. My eyes lit up like firecrackers.

But Craigslist could wait. I had more pressing concerns: what to do that night. I sat down on my hotel bed, looked around me and twiddled my thumbs. I got up and looked out the window into the apartment that was three feet away from my room, but my neighbours' sex acts weren't very interesting, so I sat down on the bed again. I turned on the TV and flicked through the hundreds of channels but there was nothing to watch . . . I thought about the exciting city just metres from my hotel door. But it was eleven at night, and I *was* in New York City, where a girl had to be careful, right? I ummed and ahhed and weighed up the odds. I could stay in the comfort of my room and watch reruns of *Miami Vice,* or I could go exploring and potentially end up in a gutter, one hand clasping an unfinished hot dog bought from a street vendor, the other clasping the bullet hole in my chest. I scratched my head, which prompted a spark of sudden realisation. In all my life, the best things have happened to me because I took a chance. When I stopped thinking about right and wrong in societal terms, and threw caution to the wind, then good things happened. It was time to take a chance. I got dressed in jeans and a jacket, picked up my room key and some cash and left the building.

I walked out onto East 17th Street and turned left. The adrenaline was pumping through my body so much I hardly noticed the activity around me. I bought a map from a street vendor and sat on a park bench to get my bearings and ground myself.

The city was seething with action. It was a Tuesday night, nearing midnight, though the bustle was more like a Saturday night on Mardi Gras weekend in Sydney. People were everywhere, shopping and out on dates. The bars and restaurants were groaning with people. A fifty-something man in a dark business suit, wielding an old leather briefcase and a paunch, sat down next to me to eat the biggest sandwich I have ever seen. I just couldn't take my eyes off that sandwich. He sensed my ogling and stopped mid-bite to raise his eyebrows at me. Embarrassed, I turned away.

His nasally voice rose above the din of the traffic. 'Want some?' he asked, with what I would come to know as a New York smile.

I turned to check him out. He seemed normal enough, and I was hungry as hell. But I knew I wasn't supposed to accept candy from strangers, so I figured a sandwich was also a no-no.

'No, I'm good, thanks, mate, just never seen anything so big.'

'That's what all the girls say,' he answered with a grin.

I laughed a bit too hard. He frowned. Then eventually laughed too. Once I had affirmed that yes, wombats could take your arm off, he told me about all the things I should do in New York City while I was here.

He looked me up and down and nodded. 'Yep, you look cool enough,' he said, 'you'll like Bleecker Street.'

A New York person said I was cool! Okay cool *enough*, and from Willy Loman, but it was a start.

I took a bite from his sandwich, wiped the mustard from my cheeks and said goodbye. I was off to try and look cool on Bleecker Street.

I followed my map like a third grader learning their ABC, until I spied what looked like a shortcut to Bleecker. I turned down a long, empty street and watched the moon eerily reflect off the old stone walk-up buildings above me. The noise of the traffic became a distant roar and the sound of my feet hitting the pavement sounded like atom bombs going off, giving me the creeps. Loud, regular, a little crunching of small rocks, a small slide as I descended the pavement. The scene felt straight out of a B-grade horror flick – secretary with green eyes and laboured breathing takes shortcut – close-up on stranger's eyes watching her from behind. Damn, my imagination was starting to kick in.

Dramatically, I turned around to check if I was being followed. I did a double-take. There was a figure behind me who ducked out of view as I looked. Holy shit. I was as good as dead. I slowly turned and started to walk again, but I heard the footsteps behind me break into rhythm. I sped up a little, but with a cold flash of fear I realised the footsteps were speeding up as well – matching my pace. *Be cool, be cool.* I plunged my hands into my pocket, fished out my hotel keys and spaced them between my fingers to improvise a weapon, as a mad aunt had once taught me. The footsteps continued to speed up; they were coming faster and faster behind me. A hot flush broke out onto my skin and a cold fear flashed through my head making my thoughts clear and sharp. What would I do? I spied a busy intersection ahead but I calculated the footsteps would reach me before I got there. There was nothing left for it. I turned around to face the stranger. In the black shadows only a few metres from me was a shadowy jerky figure coming at me full steam. I lowered my stance and grasped my keys tighter. As I got ready to shout and wave my arms like a crazy person (another excellent tip from the mad aunt), the figure emerged like a deathly demon into the light.

Wha –?

Where had the demon gone? There was just a tiny old woman

wrapped tightly in a tweed suit, clutching a small white handbag to her chest like a frightened child. She took in my dropped jaw and confused expression.

'I'm sorry,' she panted, 'I was getting scared and I wanted to keep up with you in case there were robbers.'

My lungs exhaled a rush of air.

'Don't worry, really. There's nothing to be frightened of,' I reassured her, as my eyes shifted from side to side.

We walked arm in arm to the brightly lit intersection and said our goodbyes.

I walked on until I finally found Bleecker Street, and it was everything Sandwich Man had said it would be. Cool people were everywhere. There were cute little shops packed with treasures, ultra-modern bars next to old-style Irish pubs and tiny cafés nestled side by side. I had heard that New Yorkers didn't make eye contact and rushed everywhere, but I didn't see any evidence of that, it seemed just the opposite. People smiled and tossed out unthreatening compliments as I walked past their perches. I felt ecstatic and on an unnatural high just to be walking the streets of the bustling metropolis: I was a cool person in Manhattan.

I walked on, as if in a dream, until a detonation of amazingly soulful music stopped me in my tracks. It was deep and down home dirty blues of Lindt chocolate quality. I stood there, as still as a statue, letting the throb wash over me and pound my senses as New York whirled in the foreground. It was coming from an upstairs venue; the sign on the rickety door read Terra Blues.

The beauty about being in a foreign country is that you do things you normally wouldn't. Back home, there is no way on earth I'd walk into a bar alone, even if that tasty music was luring me with all its might. But here, in New York, the rules had changed. I felt stronger and somehow braver, probably stupider. I had nothing to lose.

With a tickling of excitement in my belly, I climbed the stairs and made my way into a dark room with small white-clothed tables and walls strung with artworks and framed photographs of musicians. I could make out only about four other customers. I quietly slid into a chair at one of the tables to listen. The lead singer was a massive black man who sat on a stool looking just like a giant bullfrog regarding his kingdom before him. He croaked out song after song that made the hairs on the back of my neck stand up. If this band was in Australia, the queues would be a mile long, but here in New York City, crazily, this was evidently the norm. As my body moved to the music and my smile started to hurt my cheeks, Frog Man turned his huge eyes to face me.

'Stop, stop, stop!' he ordered the other musicians.

In perfect unison they halted, fingers poised over their instruments.

'It's a crime! A crime I say!' he sang, as the cool-cat band members nodded and 'ah haa-ed' and 'right on-ed' back at him in perfect harmony.

He pointed his huge sausage-like finger at me and his voice rose with rhythm. 'All alonnne! What for? It's a crime, I tell ya! A crime!'

I winced/smiled back at him and sank into my chair.

The band started up again as his rich voice rose with the chorus: 'It's a crimmmme, a crime, I tell ya!'

Then he began to improvise a serenade in his earthy song voice.

'What's your name?' he sang at me.

'Huh!' accented the chorus behind him.

'Bella,' I yelled back to the stage.

'Bella! Huuh! Sheee don't want nobody,' he sang. 'Sheee just wanna dance. She don't need nobody, she just wanna dance, yeah, wanna dance . . .'

When the song finished I wanted to hug the old frog, but didn't in case he thought I was mental. I moved up to the bar to order another drink and settled in excitedly for the second half.

At the bar, I noticed a man nearby watching me. He had tanned skin and was handsome in a Clive Owen kind of way, with a high and serious brow and a dimpled American-style chin. He had neat dark hair flecked with salt, which he patted as he regarded me. He reminded me of a storybook aristocratic prince, but what struck me most were his eyes. They were startlingly blue. Glittering like Christmas tinsel, they were one set of fantastic peepers. I found myself staring into them and getting kinda lost. I think my jaw hit the floor and I drooled a little as well. Blue Eyes took pity on me and smiled slowly, then asked if he could buy me a drink.

'Th-th-thanks,' I replied, wiping away my drool, which put lipstick all over my fingers, which I wiped on my shirt front, then tried to take the mark off with a wet tissue, putting white dots all over my left breast. I was doing well.

He watched me like a naturalist would an exotic bug. Eventually, he spoke.

'I'm James.'

Oh yes you are.

'I'm . . .' I stuttered. 'Um . . .'

He gave me the naturalist look again.

'. . . Bella,' I remembered.

'Bella. I like that. Nice to meet you, Bella,' he replied, his eyes twinkling.

We got to talking and he told me how he was born and raised in Monaco, went to Yale University, lived for a year or so in New York, then moved to Chicago to start an advertising firm there. He said he'd missed New York, so was back in town to open a branch of his company, which would enable him to move here permanently. Two hours ago, he said, he had been sitting on the plane, fantasising about the first thing he would do when he landed in New York. An air-hostess had tapped him on the shoulder and asked if he would like a snack.

'Peanuts or chips, sir?' she'd asked.

For some inexplicable reason he'd felt that the decision was somehow important. At length, he'd decided on the chips.

She had smiled and handed him a packet of Terra Blues Chips. He'd remembered the very bar we were sitting in was also called Terra Blues, and decided then that visiting Terra Blues would be the first thing he did on arrival. Thus, here he was.

I told him about Australia and why I'd come to America, and about my indecision that night sitting on my hotel bed wondering if I should go out or not. The conversation took a detour to my hotel neighbours' sex acts, and then, when I finished my tale, we paused and looked at each other. It was as though there was something gleaming in the air between us, as though we were in on a shared secret. As though fate was somehow involved.

As the good red wine started to flow and his conversation was by turns hilarious and interesting and shocking and inviting, I got to thinking. He was charming as all hell, and his witty *Rosencrantz and Guildenstern Are Dead* style banter was rapidly dissolving my fear that he was a serial killer. I was in New York, for god's sake. I had to do the cliché and date a handsome millionaire while I was there, didn't I? Who was I kidding? I'd watched *Sex and the City*.

As sunlight began to slip through the doors, and my tact and motor functions were drowned in liquor, he turned to me.

'Can I take you out again?'

'Ash long as thoshe eyes come with yoo . . . cowboy,' I slurred, confusing myself with Greta Garbo.

A tiny sober part of my mind winced.

'Done, Greta,' he replied.

'Huh? How dud yoo . . . ? Okay, thatch it, you're reading my mind, we're destined. Letsh have babies . . .' I said, then grinned drunkenly.

'Let's go on a date first,' he answered with a wry smile.

I gave him my number with a caution. Something about 'babiesh shouldn't be had as they eat too much'. Then I uprooted myself from the barstool and made my way back to the hotel with a lopsided skip in my step. James' blue eyes swam in my head as it echoed with 'she just wanna dance, yeah! She just wanna dance . . .' I tried to dance, got confused, then gave up and crashed on the bed as the ceiling whirled me to sleep. My first day in New York was finished and I was as happy as a drunk could be.

The next day I woke, pulled myself into the foetal position and kept time with my throbbing brain as it threw itself against the wall of my skull. I'd met a guy, hadn't I? What was it I'd said to him? Fuck, it all started coming back. The dancing (badly), thinking I was Greta Garbo and asking him to have babies – cringe. I vowed never to drink again, dragged myself up like a dying dog and got dressed in a crisp white dress that I was convinced made me somehow purer. (Every little bit helps.)

My stomach was reeling and my skin was covered in a light film of sweat as I strolled through the streets. I sat under a tree in Union Square Park and ate a ham sandwich. The park was a surprising oasis surrounded by four lanes of heavy traffic on all sides. People sat on the grass in groups and ate. Some danced; others painted on canvases or read in the sun. Dogs barked from the nearby pet run, breaking the strangely soothing hum of traffic all around. I watched an angelically beautiful black man with porcelain features and a kind smile, play with a soccer ball. He bandied the ball around his legs like Beckham, cuffed it with his chest and balanced it on his head like a pro. An ancient homeless guy with blackened clothes, a yellow beard and missing front teeth watched him. Without a word spoken, the young angel kicked the ball to Yellow Beard and they began to play together, passing the ball between them in silent harmony. Eventually, a Serbian tourist in his twenties with bleached blond ends and a blue-and-white soccer jumper was welcomed into the game by Yellow Beard. And then there were three.

All of them had soft and keen smiles, their eyes catching kind, quick glimpses at each other as they dribbled back and forth. People dotted around the park watched smiling at the strange group, at their absorbed game.

A tall Mexican stood nearby eyeing them off. The Serbian raised his eyebrows and offered him the position of fourth man. The guy shyly shook his head and said he just wanted to watch.

A large gay woman with cargo pants and holding a diary asked me if she could share my tree. We chatted amiably about the smells of clean fresh earth and the countryside.

When I looked up again, The Shy Mexican had overcome his timidity and had joined in.

They were starting to sweat, but their passes were still gentle and encouraging. Yellow Beard had a smile that nearly split his chops, The Angel was dancing with the ball like a conjurer, The Serbian was shooting admiring glances at The Angel and The Shy Mexican was sweetly chuckling to himself. NYC is like that. Seemingly disparate strangers sharing unspoken intimacies every day.

I glanced across at The Lesbian and she had written in her diary:

I am here!
I am here!!
Oh my god, I am here!!!!!!

A black guy in a park uniform, with cornrows whipped back from his temple into a mullet asked in a southern drawl if the players could please stop.

'I sure do appreciate it folks, but it's just the rules,' he added.

All four men came together into the middle of their small playing field. Smiling, they shook sweaty hands. The Angel walked away, humming to himself, The Shy Guy went to buy a hot dog and Yellow Beard and The Serbian settled into the grass together to share a cigarette.

It was a beautiful absorbing example of what New York seemed to have to offer. People had a generosity of spirit and a kindness that I hadn't expected to find here.

I threw myself into New York with an exhilaration matching a broke ho on Sailor Night. I went shopping, saw Central Park and got lost in the Metropolitan Museum of Art. I ate delicious stale hot dogs from the street vendors and spent fascinated hours people-watching. I felt the pulse of New York as soon as I hit the pavement. But it wasn't just the twenty-four-hour restaurants and cafés, bars and hotels, and it wasn't just the thousands of fashion houses, shops and art galleries that created the buzz. It was the people. From their sparking minds came ideas and businesses and artworks and designs. The 'buzz' seemed literally to be the white noise from millions of these seething, animated minds, combined in creativity and freedom to create the gem in the crown of America: New York. It truly was amazing. I knew after those few heady days that I badly wanted to get a visa to stay in this extraordinary city. Well, at least until I got laid, or saw a celebrity or something.

6

Meeting Mr Big and so long Sour Receptionist Chick and thanks for all the killer bees (and policeman's balls) and shaving rash

M Y KNIGHT IN SHINING ARMOUR, Craigslist, helped me secure a twenty-dollar-a-night room in the Garment District of Manhattan, home of New York's fashion industry. It was an old theatre the owners were renting out to travellers on the sly. Just my kind of place. From the ceiling they strung rolls of black cloth which hung down to create small sleeping compartments. The 'rooms' fitted a tiny single blow-up bed, a small lamp, a blanket and a marshmallow-sized pillow. I slept crammed up against my suitcases listening to a couple having sex with less than a millimetre of fabric between us. But if it meant being able to afford a few extra weeks in NY, I was all for it. Plus, on the bright side, my neighbours' regular grunting marathons were helping to rock me to sleep each night.

One night I lay tossing and turning on my inflatable bed, unable to sleep: I wasn't getting my usual lullaby as the nymphos had selfishly gone out for the evening. Plus, I'd seen so many things that day that my head was reeling from the stimuli. I thought of the elegant lady climbing gracefully out of her limousine on Park Avenue, of the group of students rallying in Bleecker Street over rent increases, of the old couple walking hand in hand through Central Park. I imagined myself as each character I'd seen. I imagined going home to an elegant apartment and smoothing out the wrinkles of my silk sheets before I slid into them. I imagined being one of the students, lying awake at night, thinking of global warming in a share house. I thought of sleeping next to my husband of forty years and waking early to stroll with him in the park. But I didn't see *me* in any of them: I saw parts of me, desires or attitudes, but there was nothing that jumped out and screamed 'Yes, that's what I want for my life'. I suddenly felt empty, and frightened. How did I fit into all this? Into this city? How would I end up?

I climbed out of bed and opened the front door to perch on the stone steps and smoke a cigarette. I thought about the kind of person I would be. Do people choose that? Or are we predestined to be a certain way? Like a hammer banging through glass, a sudden and primal thought broke through. *It didn't matter, as long as I had acting. It didn't matter, as long as I loved what I did.* (Cue wind machine in hair.) But that thought really was like a train smashing through my senses. It was absolutely true. I looked down at the cracked stone I was sitting on, then out at the stairwell before me, and I felt a giant sense of relief flood through me.

Then my mind exploded with all sorts of options. I could get an acting job here! Why not? I could even do an acting course – great for the résumé! I felt such a fire of optimism in my belly that I shouted myself another cigarette and happily thought through all my options until my neighbours came home and grunted me into peaceful oblivion.

I woke and felt that same fresh wind blowing, like a longed-for day arriving, or a wink from a stranger on a bad-hair day. It's funny, you learn lessons in life, often many times, often the same lesson more than once. But even when you have learned a lesson, it has to be fuelled regularly, affirmed, kept alive. The night before I had refuelled my commitment to acting. I had stuck the mother of all logs on my fire and I was dancing around it naked. Those stone steps were imprinted in my mind like my first kiss, or sitting on the cliff top back in Sydney. I felt thoroughly excited to be alive, straining at the leash to dive head first into this glorious city and become an actor.

With my heart in my mouth and a skip in my newly purchased Manolo Blahniks, I put my plan into action and plonked down a deposit to move into a room in a two-bedroom apartment in Chinatown. It was cheap by New York standards – eight hundred dollars a month, utilities included – and was positioned on the east side of downtown Manhattan. It was probably so cheap because you risked a heart attack every time you walked up the seven gruelling flights of stairs to reach it. Plus the 'bedroom' was the size of a doll's teacup. My new flatmate was an affable shaven-headed ex-punk rocker named Ricco who got laid from Craigslist on a regular basis, which was helpful for me given my newly developed sleeping technique. It wasn't exactly the Taj Mahal but it was home.

As I took to the streets, the myth of man-less NY was shattered again. NY men were thriving like the beautiful rats they were. On any given day you can get stopped by a leather-elbow-patched poet, a waiter at a café, a well-suited stockbroker or a Midwesterner in the big smoke. Unlike in Sydney it is acceptable for men to approach you on the street and ask for a date. I thought it kept happening because I was bombastically cool looking, but realised, with the help of Juan the waiter, that it was because I looked like a tourist and thus an easy pick-up mark. (I thanked Juan for his insight then gave him a lousy tip.)

ılıılıılılıı

Soon after the move to Chinatown, James phoned to ask me out on a date. A date with a handsome New York socialite, I could do that. I didn't have any glam clothes, so improvised with a pantsuit and a scarf, and tried to flatten my hair with a book then gave up. I looked like a construction worker. I nearly called to cancel, but I was here for new adventures so I did the best I could, hushed the niggling feeling in my belly and waited for him to arrive.

He picked me up in a chauffeur-driven car and regarded me as I got in.

'You look awful,' he said, deadpan.

Huh?

He broke into a boyish grin. 'I'm just kidding. You rival Charlize Theron.'

Oh, you think that was funny, huh? Okay, game on, Mr Big.

'And you look like a wanker. Just kidding.'

'A wanker? What's that?'

One point to me.

I tried to brazen it out. 'It's when you, er, um . . .' I coughed.

Damn, this was not going well.

'Get intimidated around beautiful women?' he suggested.

Hmmm. An auspicious start. 'Yeah, that's it. Shall we start again?'

'Okay.' He paused and regarded me. 'Seriously, you look lovely.'

'Thank you, James,' I said, fluttering my eyelashes. 'And do you have unwholesome feelings towards Charlize Theron?'

'Completely.'

'That's okay, she's the only one I'd jump the fence for. Well, her or Angelina Jolie.'

'Ah, at last we agree on something,' he twinkled.

He took my hand in his, brought it up to his face then breathed it in. 'I like your smell,' he said.

I looked at him and popped up my left eyebrow.

He had the grace to blush.

I retaliated with a brighter blush.

Then I think I actually giggled.

With him blushing like a clown and me giggling like a school-girl we looked like a couple of idiots, and I'm pretty sure I heard the chauffeur snigger. But the fact that there even was a chauffeur had me at 'hello'. Superficial, who me?

James whisked me off to a gleaming restaurant high up in a skyscraper and made me feel like a princess for the whole evening. Disarmingly clever, he kept me on my toes, and I loved that. He was seven years older than me and had a kind of sexy world-weariness about him, but also an underbelly of boyish excitement that would bubble up when he talked about travel or his work. He told me how he'd built his advertising company up from scratch and how it was now one of the fastest growing in America. That it took 'perseverance, good risk management – and a lot of balls'. I felt inspired by him, so told him about my acting plans, and his blue eyes gleamed as he nodded.

Then he asked if he could be my manager.

'My what?'

'Manager.'

'Um, what for?'

'Acting. I meet a lot of people, and I think you're very special. I could help you,' he said.

It felt like the beginning of a hard sell. Was he about to make me buy into a pyramid scheme?

'You're going to make it,' he continued. 'And I want to be there at the beginning, so you can thank me at Oscar time. Purely selfish reasons,' he said.

'Sooo, *this* is a New York pick-up line, huh? Not bad.'

He smiled. 'Okay, kill me. Though I was serious about the Oscar thing. So what would be my first duty as your manager?'

'I want you to set up a meeting with the Coen brothers, book me a space flight to the moons of Jupiter, have flowers delivered daily and, oh, I only drink vodka in the mornings,' I said, as I flicked my hair and ruffled my imaginary pearls.

'Your wish is my command,' he replied with a spark of amusement playing in his ridiculously blue eyes.

ıılıılıılıı

I liked James a lot and felt inspired by him and his go-get-'em attitude, so the next day I did a massive résumé send-out and, as luck would have it, got a response straight away.

A New York University grad student named Lauren emailed me the script for a lovely short film about a woman who was a commitment-phobe, liked 'the sound of ice crashing into water' and 'eating chocolate as the sun goes down'. Typecasting, I liked it.

I fumbled my way through the subway system to West 40th Street and turned up at the audition unnaturally nervous. It was for an unpaid role in a student film, yet my knees were shaking like a boat sail in high winds. I rallied myself by thinking of the twenty-plus alien films I'd done in Australia, playing Juliet at La Boite Theatre, the best actress award I'd received. Who gave a shit? This was different, this was New York. I gave myself a quick slap on my face to settle my nerves.

I walked in.

'What happened to your face?' asked a concerned Lauren.

'Shaving rash.'

She laughed. Then paused, then took a closer look at me.

Mental note: Find another way to settle nerves.

'Okay, Bella, you are home alone and the phone rings. It's your boyfriend; he tells you he has cheated on you. Start now, please.'

Easy enough. I was still embarrassed about the red handprint on my face, and when I get embarrassed I get pissed off at myself, okay, and often at innocent bystanders too. I could just use my natural pissed-off-ness for the boyfriend's call and be out in time to ogle the Polish Parade on Fifth.

After breaking up with my 'boyfriend' with the warmth of a glacier, I hung up my imaginary phone, allowed a few beats for the calm before the storm, then let rip on an innocent chair. The room became my dominion and I was the avenger for all the girls who had been cheated on before.

'Wow,' came Lauren's reply as she moved the chair out of my reach. 'Thank you, Bella, we'll be in touch.'

I closed the door behind me then bent down to tie my shoelace and eavesdrop.

I heard Lauren's muffled voice talking to the producer. 'She's . . . wow, she's incredible.'

I grinned. I loved her! 'Incredible' he-he. New York, here I am! Just call me Ms Incredible! The Incredible She-hulk! Your Incredibly She-hulk-ness. Hulky for short. I couldn't think up any more, so I jumped into the clanking elevator and graciously accepted my Oscar from Meryl Streep all the way down. Wait . . . Incredibly good, or incredibly bad? Fuck.

Whatever. My first New York audition was over, and other than the director thinking I had a facial hair problem, nothing at all could dampen my mood.

ıılılılılılı

A few nights later, I wanted to go to Union Square and sit in the park. But as is usual for me, when it came to directions, my feminine wiles went toes up and my masculine side came out with a vengeance: that is, I got very lost. I sat down on a stoop and lit a cigarette. A homeless man ambled up to me. He was smothered in grey rags with a shiny rat-ish tooth sticking out of his mouth like a broken door.

'Can you spare some change, ma'am?'

'Yeah, sure,' I said, as I fished out a crumpled note from my pocket.

He looked at me. 'That was your last, wasn't it?' he pronounced like a soothsayer.

I did a squirm/nod combo.

'Well now, if I were a gentleman I would return it to you,' he said. 'But I'm not,' he added with a chuckle.

I looked in the other direction.

'I'll give you some hard-won advice for free, though. One: love as hard as you possibly can – because great things will happen. Two: stay away from the cops, they'll eat you . . . And three: watch out for the killer bees,' he said mysteriously.

I knew I shouldn't ask, but I couldn't resist. 'The . . . what?'

'The killer bees,' he repeated, grinning. 'You can see one go by now.' He pointed his bent finger at a speeding yellow taxi.

I chuckled, and he joined in.

'Yep, they'll run you over faster than a cop'll eat you,' he said with a light chortle.

I got up to go and promised I'd look out for them, then eyed my bill in his clenched fist.

'Remember, there are no gentlemen in this town, it's all smoke,' he said, swiping his hand across his face like a closing door.

Back at the hotel, I hungrily logged on to my email but there were no more responses to my frantic résumé send-off. I had to think like a New Yorker. How had De Niro or Pacino made it in this town? I needed to get me some inspiration. Well, they had both been trained by teacher extraordinaire Lee Strasberg. An Academy Award nominee himself, Strasberg had taught Marlon Brando, Al Pacino, Robert De Niro, Marilyn Monroe and Kim Stanley, amongst others. He was the American godfather of the Method and an expert scholar of Konstantin Stanislavsky, the Russian director who initially devised the famous acting technique. He'd been artistic director of The Actors Studio for years, and in 1969 established The Lee Strasberg Theatre and Film Institute in Manhattan. He died in 1982, but his teachings and school live on through alumni including Angelina Jolie (drool), Matt Dillon, Steve Buscemi, Sissy Spacek, Adam Sandler, Alec Baldwin, Rosario Dawson, Clare Danes, Scarlett Johansson, Uma Thurman, Sienna Miller, Harvey Keitel, Val Kilmer, Dennis Hopper, Sally Field and Christopher Walken. Not a shabby bunch of people by any means. I figured I would go and find the school and visit it for inspiration – and perhaps even sit in the bum prints of Marilyn Monroe herself.

Reverentially I opened the famous little red door of the Lee Strasberg Institute on East 15th Street and entered. But it wasn't what I'd expected. It was slightly ramshackle with a small reception desk and a narrow hallway. Framed photographs of Marlon Brando, Marilyn Monroe and Al Pacino bustled for space near a huge painted portrait of Strasberg himself. Excitement rose into my throat, then my nerves clenched as it sank in – I was standing in the Strasberg Institute.

I stood in the entrance, staring around me like a tropicana-shirted tourist ogling everything, breathing in the same air as De Niro. A tap on my shoulder broke my reverie.

'Excuse me, can we get past?' smiled a handsome boy.

'Oh shit, sorry!' I said, as I slithered back against the wall. I watched the crème de la crème of New York actors file past me and I was shocked. They looked normal! I didn't know what I'd been expecting, but shouldn't they have been wearing furs, or have had horns or something?

I was swept along in the line of people entering and found myself sitting inside in a hallway, on a long wooden bench near a giant blackboard listing all the classes for that day. There was movement and vocal production, great playwrights and theatre history, method training, character work and script analysis. I licked my lips as I imagined going to such wondrous classes.

A woman with blonde hair loomed into my imaginings.

'What are you doing in here?' she asked rather sternly. 'Can I help you?'

Oh shit, busted.

'Um. Yeah,' I blustered. 'I came to find out about taking some classes,' I lied.

'Okay then, you can wait in the reception area. We can talk there,' she said.

I sheepishly left the inner sanctum and stood near the receptionist who was to guard me. I looked at her. She was a large woman without much humour.

'Sooo . . .' I began.

She looked at me, eyebrows disapprovingly waggling.

'Ahem. Nice weather, isn't it?'

She looked at me like I was mad. The rain was pelting down outside.

'Sooo . . . how do you get into a school like this?' I asked, trying to change the subject.

She looked me up and down with a snooty expression. 'Don't even try, it's impossible . . . dear.'

Why, you little . . .

When the blonde woman appeared again I reaffirmed my

desire to go to classes. I knew I wouldn't get in but I figured Sour Receptionist Chick needed to be taught a lesson. Blonde lady gave me an application form and a run-down of the school and I thanked her and left. Ha! Take that, Sour Receptionist Chick.

I left feeling inspired. A year before in Sydney, I'd taken a brief Method class taught by Tim Robbins and it had done good things for my work. But the little glimpses of the classrooms I saw at the institute, the gluttony of fantastic lessons on the board, the young dynamic-looking students, the handsome boy, even the troll at reception filled me with delight and a hunger for more. That evening, with my heart in my mouth, I decided to throw caution to the wind and apply for the institute.

I'd been seeing James almost every day over the past week and his belief set me afire to work on the Strasberg application like a possessed demon. I wrote and rewrote my application essay into the wee hours; I emailed directors I'd worked with for references, and updated my résumé. Then, a week or so later, we blew a kiss onto the bulky envelope and posted it off.

ılıltıllıllıı

James was wining and dining me, taking me to elegant restaurants and private clubs with tuxedo-suited wait staff, stiff drinks and even stiffer price tags. They were amazing evenings of skyscraper views, crystal goblets, private entrances and thick red ropes ushering us in to exclusive places. He needed to re-establish himself in New York, so we were both thoroughly enjoying painting the town red 'for work purposes'. He was so charming. Funny and fresh and wry and intelligent and supportive and appreciative. He (gulp) seemed like the perfect man. He made me laugh from my belly and snort things from my nose. A man who can do that and drink me under the table had got me.

One of the places we began to go to fairly regularly was the fantastic Friars Club of Manhattan. It felt like going to a secret men's club. Entering the 1909 building with pool rooms and gleaming bars and wood panelling was like entering another era. Pictures of past members adorned the walls: Sinatra and his rat pack, comics like Billy Crystal, famous actors, entertainers and politicians. You can only get a membership to the Friars Club if you are either very famous or very influential, and whoever happens to be the hot property at the time is king at the club. *The Sopranos* were the 'it' thing while we were there, and the cast members were dotted around the place looking like something straight out of a *Godfather* film. They'd sit on their cushioned sofas drinking tumblers of golden whisky, with jewelled pinky rings and expensive suits, talking in animated whispers.

One night I watched transfixed as a relatively slight man with greying hair and an incredibly powerful presence walked into the room and took his seat amongst them. As he sat, the men at the table rose simultaneously and bowed their heads in submission. He was evidently a man with large knackers. As he sat drinking with his entourage, young, good-looking, well-dressed Italians filed past him and gave their respects. He didn't talk to any of them, perhaps an occasional nod of his head or a slight raising of his glass. He simply sat there, dripping with power. I really couldn't take my eyes off him. I was so absorbed in the tension at the table and his amazingly considered movements, I forgot to be inconspicuous, and when he looked up from his drink he caught me staring straight at him. A smile plastered itself onto my face and I hurriedly looked away. But when I looked back, he was still staring at me intensely. His gaze mesmerised me, sucking me in like a piece of spaghetti. We kept eye contact for what seemed like a year, then he raised his tumbler to me along with his eyebrow in a 'Care to have a drink with me?' way. But it wasn't a question, it was a command. I froze. Then inexpertly dropped to the floor. Why in hell I did that, I had no idea, perhaps a primal I-don't-want-to-sleep-with-the-fishes instinct. As I pressed down into the carpet, I knew my fumble had seemed totally fake. Where the hell were my acting skills now? Between the legs of the chair, I counted to five then peeked up over the rim of the table. He was still looking, god damn it. And this time a smirk played out on his features. My face went beetroot red and I grasped at a fork and held it up in the air with a little flourish. He smiled as if I were a Chianti he wanted to gulp down. Not what I was going for. Just then, James came back from the bathroom and I was able to hightail it out of there.

'Before I end up like Michelle Pfeiffer in *Scarface*,' I told James conspiratorially.

ıılıılıılıılı

From mobsters to cops, the next week, James invited me to go with him to the NYC Policeman's Ball Benefit. We drank wine in the Heroes' Hall with high-ranking officials, socialites and the sporadic beat cop who was in line for promotion. It was somehow eerie, and most of the time I felt vaguely paranoid and somewhat naughty.

Then we were ushered into the ballroom, where the elegant tables were festooned with white tea roses and crystal glasses for red and white wine – and tequila shots. Probably a cop thing. Everywhere you looked were handsomely suited men with their equally glamorous wives. I refastened the safety pin holding my dress together.

At our table were seven society people and their spouses. I singled out the least ferocious-looking person to talk to, which was Amit, a twenty-something Jewish guy, and his favourite subject was New York.

'Okay then, if France was a forty-year-old woman in a red

dress holding a cigarette,' I said, 'and Italy was a crinkled old man wearing a fedora, New York would be a . . . ?'

'Street dog,' he answered. 'Ingenious, brazen and unkempt.'

Amit told me he was 'addicted' to New York. He said he travelled a lot for work, but got anxious if he stayed away too long and didn't get his fix of the Mad Hatter's tea-party.

A seven-chinned man with a jet-black toupee and a pug nose quipped, 'New York is a place for the *best,*' as his chins wobbled ferociously. 'The *best* of everything,' he continued, as he significantly patted at his wife's arm.

'One word to describe New York?' said James to the table at large.

'Unabashed,' answered Amit.

'Stuff adjectives,' said an emaciated woman with red nails. 'Agglutination,' she uttered from the bottom of her throat.

Intakes of breath and murmurings of appreciation were heard all around the table.

'Heroic,' said Jet Head enunciating every syllable and looking extremely pleased with himself as he patted his chins.

'Fashionable,' said Jet Head's wife as she curved her fingers around her bangs.

James turned to me and smiled. 'Bella?'

They were all so . . . *New York.* Well, except for Jet Head. I tried frantically to think of something – anything – clever to say. What the fuck was an adjective anyway? Okay, calm down, think clearly. Fuck. Can't. Too much pressure. Say anything – quick. Oh, I know!

'Myopic!' I blurted out.

The table went deathly silent, then, almost immediately, a collective inhalation sounded. I wasn't sure exactly what faux pas I'd made, but I gathered it was on the same level as Hiroshima. Jet Head almost burst his buttons as he busied himself scoffing and making eye contact with whoever would have him. His fashionable wife pushed out her incredulous smile from her mouth like she was trying to give birth. Even Amit was joining in on the slippery coughs and half-born smiles. *Why were they being so mean?*

'Myopic, you know: all-encompassing, inclusive and broad-ranging . . .'

A marshmallow-haired woman with a bad face-lift burst out laughing and then made a great show of trying to stop herself. 'Broad-ranging,' she tittered to her neighbour.

I was at a loss – and I couldn't work out whether I felt more humiliated or pissed off. I wished my PMT would kick in so that I could at least yell at one of them.

Then, the penny dropped.

'I meant *panoptic*.'

'She meant panoptic,' repeated the face-lift woman, nearly splitting herself with laughter.

Okay, I was a dickhead; okay, I used the wrong word; but hell, it wasn't like I'd flashed my punani at them. I quickly looked down to check my knees weren't splayed.

I looked over at James but his face was unreadable. Was he about to pitch in on the smirk-fest too? Then I saw James pull back his chair and rise to his feet, his wine glass raised. 'To myopic New York,' he said, looking down at each one of them significantly. I could have had sex with him right there and then. Then it got even better: I saw his eyebrow raise ever so slightly as he continued to regard them. Immediately they scraped back their chairs and joined the toast. 'To myopic New York!' they agreed, as they licked their lips and looked uncertain.

It was my turn to keep from laughing. James turned to me and his eyes were burning bright blue. He held out his hand and I took it, and he led me away onto the dance floor.

'The worst I can do is cut off their funding, although I'd prefer quick deaths all round.' He looked wrathful.

'Forget them,' I said, '*you* were fantastic. The way you made them toast themselves like that – damn, you have balls of steel, James. And, to see them actually do it!'

'They didn't have much of a choice. I make more money than all of them. The pecking order triumphs.' He paused and looked off into space then abruptly turned back to me. 'I go to these functions and I spend money to get more clients, which in turn makes me more money, which I then give away to get more. The order never changes, the process, the rules, always the same. And the slivers of time in between are filled with moments like that. They used to amuse me. Now they just make me feel sick. Sick and guilty.'

'Well, we've got to find more appropriate uses for your "slivers of time" then, haven't we?' I said, as I thumped my eyebrows up and down suggestively.

He shook his head and laughed. 'Forget what I said, your suggestion is infinitely more interesting.'

We both looked over at the table and could see the group still collectively huddling over their drinks and watching us as their animated faces alternated between sycophancy, confusion and sullenness.

'I think those are their sex faces,' James quipped.

ılıllıllılı

The next night we went to the annual Friars Club Roast benefit. The Friars Club has an annual comedy event, where they would 'roast' a celebrity. The Friar members would gather famous people in a giant hall and spend the evening taking the piss out of the Roastee. The tradition has been going since 1950 and past Roastees have included Chevy Chase, Bruce Willis, Hugh

Hefner and Whoopi Goldberg. It sounded fabulous – despite the fact that the price of dinner could have housed a hundred Afghani orphans. That night they were roasting the infamous boxing promoter Don King, with Donald Trump as MC.

We entered the Hilton ballroom and were ushered to our table, which was piled high with alcohol and delicacies. I quickly summed up our fellow diners and breathed out when I didn't notice any red nails or jet-black toupees.

The stage was lined with tables and chairs for the panel, an amazing mix of people from the world heavyweight champion to well-known comics and celebrities. Because it wasn't televised, the panel could do and say anything they wanted, and they did. Donald Trump, to my surprise, was utterly hilarious. He opened with a classic.

'Don, you are a fucking murderer and a fucking thief – and a downright asshole. I suppose that's why so many people compare you to me.'

And it got worse. As the panel took turns in crucifying King, they joked about his two murders, his hair, his women. Nothing was safe. The crowd were choking up their food and doubling over in laughter, and some of it was so obscene and so downright fucked up, some people actually walked out. James and I kept wiping the corners of our eyes and back-slapping each other.

At the end of this hugely enjoyable tirade, Don got a chance to rebut his tormentors. He got up slowly and walked towards the podium. People were braying already, but the laughter dried up quickly as he began to talk. He was either on drugs or old age had tapped him a little. He didn't crack a single joke, but spewed out a biblical rant about sinners not believing in Jesus. Donald Trump retorted with: 'You're a fucking nutcase.'

As the event was finishing and I was drying my eyes, Carol-Lee, a friend of James', turned to me.

'I'm going to fuck him tonight,' she said, waving her arm towards the stage.

'Who?' I asked incredulously. 'Don King?'

'No! Him,' she said, indicating a handsome young actor from *The Sopranos* signing autographs.

'Don't let me stand in the way of the kill. Off you go then.'

With that she got up and made her way up onto the stage, elbowing celebrities out of the way as she did.

Two days later she turned up at my apartment with a large smile and a pair of his boxer shorts.

ıılııllılıı

I'd be out at one of these glamorous events, chatting with dignitaries and people who owned countries, then the next day I'd find myself at a shop trying to barter down the price of chewing gum. I didn't have much money, and even though James was generous to a fault, I still wanted to pay my own way. Sometimes, though, I got embarrassed about my poorhouse status and made excuses as to why I couldn't do something – headache, saving orphans, syphilis – but soon I realised it was pointless being embarrassed about it, so I tried to accept the situation for what it was. It made things a lot easier. James started calling me his 'poor church mouse'. Or 'Churchy' for short. I called him my 'Zealous Rockefeller', or 'Rocky' for short, or occasionally 'capitalist pig'.

'Rocky' and I were spending a lot of time together and, though I'd only known him for a bit over a month, I couldn't seem to remember a time without him. I'd never, in all my life, met anyone like James. In terms of my checklist, he had it all. We seemed so easily and familiarly to slot into each other's lives, into our dreams. I mean, we were different, sure, but those differences made it all that much more exciting. There was always a kind of silky pleasure dangling between our words for each other. It felt good. Right.

He really was an extraordinary man, a man in hyperbole: he did nothing half-heartedly. He threw himself into his blossoming company, into his social engagements and into me. He was the kind of person who made you feel as though nobody else existed to him. He excited me: his sharp intelligence, his easy acceptance of new ideas, our ferocious verbal battles over politics, his generosity of spirit, his abilities and strengths, even his softness as he lay hungover in my arms. There was not a single boring thing about James. I liked how he loved the unexpected: he would think up new and diabolical plans for us and instigate them at a moment's notice. His was a reckless nature, but it suited mine and we would invariably egg each other on, into more dramatic and crazy situations and places. And, magically, he believed in me with all he had.

7

Accessing the Lee Strasberg Institute and commitment issues

O NE SUNNY AFTERNOON I was in the Lower East Side doing
my laundry. As I whiffed the clean, warm smells and watched
the dryers turn, I took stock of everything that had happened in the
month since I'd arrived. It felt somehow unreal. Almost as though
it were happening to somebody else, and I was watching the adventure unfold from the sidelines, invisible and enthralled. I tried to
work out how I felt. Simply, I was happy. Really happy. But it was
tinged with sadness when it dawned on me that my New York
fairytale would have to end soon. Out of the blue, my phone chir-
ruped. It was the blonde woman from the Lee Strasberg Institute.

'I wasn't in the inner sanctum . . .' I began hurriedly.

'What?' she asked, confused.

'Er, nothing.'

'I am pleased to tell you, you have been accepted into the
institute for the year-long course commencing in January. Congratulations, Bella.'

'. . .!'

I mumbled something unintelligible back to her, but I was so much in shock I didn't make one iota of sense. It couldn't be true, could it? I hadn't really expected to get accepted. A year in New York at the Strasberg Institute? Perhaps it was Rene playing a prank on me? Why, the little . . . But no, it *was* real. I looked around the laundromat and caught the eye of the woman next to me, who had been eavesdropping. She grinned, then said 'Congratulations, girl.' I felt the hairs on the back of my neck stand up and salute. Holy hell! This was the biggest thing that had ever happened to me. Everything I'd been through had culminated in this one moment. It was my break.

I excitedly called James to tell him the news.

'Where are you?' he yelled down the phone.

'Bubbles Laundromat.'

'Where else?' he said dryly. 'Stay where you are, I'll send a car for you.'

When the car arrived, it whisked me off to meet him and we sunk bottles of champagne and toasted the world as the sun slid down behind the skyscrapers.

'Bella, I hate to say it, but I told you so,' said James.

I grinned like a maniac.

'I believed in you. Your talent, your face, your freckles, your bad politics. Absorb this and start to believe in yourself.'

I felt on top of the world. Like bubbles were bursting in my chest and a fresh new wind was blowing on me in all the right places. I was going to stay in New York and I was going to Strasberg. And I had James by my side. There was nothing else for it: I did the Travolta dance.

But as the evening played out and the champagne bubbles flattened, the realisation dawned on me: apart from a few coins amongst the tobacco at the bottom of my faux Prada handbag,

I was broke. Very broke. There was no way I could afford the tuition, or even the living expenses for a whole year. What the hell had I been thinking?

Disappointment flung itself at me like a mad thing and I felt hot tears pricking at my eyes as my stomach did a nasty plunge. I lowered my champagne glass. Strangely, I realised I felt only a little suicidal about it, because I was so chuffed that I'd had the guts to try and had been accepted (even though a huge part was due to Sour Receptionist Chick – credit where credit is due). I turned to James.

'I can't go.'

His glass was poised in midair and a look of bafflement came over his face. 'Why?'

'Because I'm not ready to turn to prostitution,' I answered. 'I can't afford it.'

James let out a sigh. 'Is that all?'

'Like the sympathy there, James,' I retorted. 'Let's get obliterated!' I added as I poured out more champagne and reverted to my 'Who the hell cares about anything? Let's go to the Bahamas' mode.

We raised our glasses again and I met James' blue eyes. I saw sparks in his eyes and a deep well of amusement.

'What's so funny?' I asked.

'You are, Bella.'

'Granted. But why?'

'You're quite pathetic at "brave face".'

I grunted.

'I'll pay for the first year,' he said simply.

A sudden prickle of fear rocketed up my spine, and before I could stop myself I blurted out an emphatic 'No!'.

'Bella, your tuition fee is a good night out on the town for me. I have more money than you've had hot breakfasts.'

Alarm bells were ringing. No way. It was cliché enough to date him, but having him pay for my schooling turned it into a farce. 'No.'

'Bella. I believe in you. I want to help you. I am being self-serving, allow me my amusement.'

I was too independent. Boyfriends in the past used to get shitty about it, but I hated feeling as though I was in somebody's debt. 'Thank you, James, really, but no.'

He turned away as though I'd hurt his feelings.

'James, really, I mean it. Thank you so much. It's so kind of you to offer, it's amazing, but I can't.'

'Just promise you'll think about it, okay?' he said, looking more cheered up. 'Let's have another drink.'

We drank well into the morning until the bars closed at four. Neither of us had an off switch so we hightailed it to the only bar open in Manhattan at that time, a strip club in Midtown called Bejingles. As an exotic Hungarian named Pamela gyrated on my lap, I thought about what James had offered and a million questions buzzed at me: Was I being an idiot to refuse? Here was this amazing man, ready and willing to enable my dream, so why was I refusing him? I didn't want to be owned. Would I be, if I accepted him? Was Pamela wearing underwear? And how did I feel about James? The Sunrise drink hit me and a gurgle of clarity broke through: it was that I wasn't sure what was expected of me in return. James maintained that he expected nothing but the satisfaction of seeing me succeed. He liked to be 'godlike', he half-laughed. But there is always something for something. I couldn't be bought by him or anyone else, I knew that. Don't get me wrong, I could probably be bought for a chocolate bar at a pinch, but this was very different. Would my independence, which I protected so fiercely, be challenged by accepting his offer? Would it change things in our relationship?

Would it mean I would have to be an exemplary girlfriend and not let one go in bed, for example? When James went to the bar again, Pamela spoke up.

'He's a regular in here, you know.'

'Really?' I asked, a little shocked as I lifted her off my lap.

'Yeah, he brings his big advertising clients here to get some.'

'To get some what?'

'Some backroom.' She laughed in a wonderfully fiendish manner.

That was a turn-up for the books. Evidently he was not the untarnished godlike character he depicted.

ıılıılılılı

The next day I shrieked down the phone to my parents about being accepted at the institute. They were overjoyed at the news and cheered. They said not to worry about money, they would mortgage the house if need be, but that it was such an extraordinary opportunity I couldn't let it go.

'Honey,' said Rosie, 'I've never heard you so happy. This is your path, Bells, you've found it. And we are going to help you come hell or high water.'

I felt sunk in a deep, rich pool of love. Encased in it, as though it were flowing through me and filling every crevice inside me. Tears sprang out of me like Bambi on acid.

I thought back to my depression in Sydney and how that small decision to 'act', to 'do', had led to this, this feeling of unadulterated happiness. I was making my parents proud, I was falling in love, and I had just been accepted into one of the best acting schools in the world. Telstra commercials had nothing on this.

When I got home, I logged on to my email and found that James had sent me twelve messages, each with a single word:

Bella,

don't

be

an

asshole,

accept

the

offer

from

the

nice

gentleman.

Over the next few days, I battled with my pride, ambition, independence (and my shoelaces), then decided to accept the gift from James: he would pay for my tuition. And my parents would pay for rent and living expenses while I studied. With the help of the people that cared about me, I was going to do it.

A few nights after accepting James' offer, we sat together at Tavern on the Green in Central Park and swapped our fears and dreams and toasted to the future. The restaurant was lush. The beautiful nineteenth-century baroque building was filled to the brim with lavish flower arrangements that tumbled dramatically from the overflowing tables. The floor-to-ceiling mirrors sent romantic candlelight ricocheting across the rooms onto the rich tapestries and pyramids of chandeliers. I looked around in wonder. Then down at the wine prices and had a small seizure.

'What a place,' I said, gawking around like a schoolgirl.

'Let's buy it then,' James joked.

We worked out where we would put the jacuzzi, the cocaine room and the pinball machines, then he leaned over to me.

'Bella, will you marry me?'

Whaa? I did the deer-in-the-headlights thing.

'Well, what do you say?' he prompted.

I looked at his beautiful blue eyes glistening with champagne.

'Ask me when you're sober,' I joked, smiling uncomfortably as I skolled the rest of my billion-dollar glass of wine.

So, that was the catch.

ılılıllılı

We had been partying like Kate Moss' alter ego and my life had steadily become a swirl of Seabreezes, cocktail dresses and fried fugu fish. We liked to party, that was certain, but it seemed as if that was all we ever managed to do. It was as though we existed in a kind of fantasy bubble world of chauffeur-driven cars, bars, games, alcohol and more alcohol. I was enjoying myself, but I also felt that something was missing, something that was just out of reach of my understanding, obscured, I guess, by the fog of alcohol I was in. In sobriety, James repeated the proposal a couple of days later. He showed me a beautiful engagement ring that had been passed down to him by his maternal grandmother. My automatic paranoid commitment-phobic response kicked in, then mingled with a rush of that sticky love/goo-like substance. I took a deep breath in.

I needed to think clearly, but it felt like fighting a dragon with a toothpick. I tried again. We'd only been together a relatively short time; it was too soon to be deciding on whether I wanted my child's name to be James II or George Clooney II. Darkly, I tried to see if there was a connection between his proposal and his offer to pay for Strasberg. I took a walk around Central Park to clear my head. The lake's water sucked in and out against the pylons and the crazy New York gulls kamikazed at the ground for tourists' leftover scraps. An old, rather fat couple walked hand in hand towards me. I let out a sigh as I imagined their happy twilight years together, bonding and doing whatever it was old people did together. Then the women unclasped her hand from her husband's, lifted it to her nose, formed a look of disgust then said, 'You didn't wash your hands, did you?'

He looked back at her fondly. 'No,' he answered.

Strangely that scene left me feeling abundantly hopeful – perhaps I would say 'yes'.

I knew I was falling in love with James, but I was scared to admit it, even to myself. I mean, it didn't make sense to be having these kinds of feelings about someone after such a short time, right? But love, ah, love, there are no time limits on love. It'll rear up when it damn well pleases. But love and marriage were two different things.

I had been engaged a few times before. Okay, five times. But I had always sprouted feathers and would chicken out at the last minute. I would get caught up in the whole romantic notion of marriage *à la* Bonnie and Clyde, true love, hot sex, all that, and I would shout 'Yes, yes!' to the mountaintops (my braids flying behind me). But inevitably the crash would come. I would wake up one morning and panic would thump at my chest like a psycho killer. Visions of the *Brady Bunch* would annoyingly crash in on my romantic notions of hotel-room sex, and I'd have to have 'the talk'. I mean realistically, marriage didn't seem so appealing. Married women had to do silly things like ironing and wearing clean clothes, didn't they?

Plus, I figured I would have to submit all my desires on the altar of the relationship. I don't mean I would have to check with my man to make my decisions, but in any healthy partnership you have to have equal say in all the things that affect you as a couple. Only fair, I figured. But I wasn't ready to be fair. I secretly wanted to be selfish. I had been given a taste of freedom after a series of long-term relationships and I didn't want to let go of it just yet. It filled me with alarm that I would have to check with James if I wanted to, say, go travelling, take an overseas acting job, do a musical fart, or swim naked in the ocean while pretending I was a mermaid. (That was a bit too specific, wasn't it?)

I had also been set a bad example of marriage by my parents. They were ridiculously happy, in love, best friends, and went at it in the hay even when they were too old to have any right to. What kind of an example was that to set your children? All my other friends' parents were happily unhappy, as they were supposed to be. How could I live up to the romantic notion of my parents' happy marriage?

But I had strong feelings for James. He was exciting and fun as all hell, and we'd have an adventurous and electrifying life together.

Then I reminded myself that I'd resolved, after the fifth time, not to rush into getting engaged again. I was sick of returning wedding dresses and hiding all the cleaning products in my house. I was determined to let the first blush of excitement die down and wait for my head to clear and my hormones to stop gushing before I got engaged again. I needed to listen to my past self.

I went to James' apartment, where he was sitting at the table drinking some wine.

'Baby, I'm not ready. I'm sorry,' I said.

He didn't look especially hurt, just somewhat affronted.

Men! Why, that little bugger – what kind of a response was that! I didn't want to marry him, but I wanted him to want to marry me.

I huffed.

He then looked appropriately wounded. 'I'll keep working on you,' he smiled. 'So next best thing, how about we get a place together?'

Now, that was something I could do. I liked the idea. We were always together anyway, and it would give me a chance to get to know him more before I decided on entrapment – er, I mean marriage. So, like two excited schoolkids with too much red cordial, we began the hunt for a new playground.

Within a week we had moved into a split-level, two-bedroom, two-bathroom penthouse apartment in the Upper East Side. I felt excitement chew at the very marrow of my bones: I loved setting up house. Inside, thick, beautifully scarred wooden beams supported the ceiling and an ultra-modern kitchen with marble and stainless steel completed the look. James said it was too 'downtown' and it only missed a Warhol painting and an easel in the corner. But I loved it with a passion.

After he'd carried me across the threshold, James seemed uneasy.

'What's wrong?' I asked him.

'It's too quiet,' he said, and opened up a window.

The noise of the New York streets blared up at us.

'Ah, that's better,' he said, completely seriously.

ıılılılılılı

I began to decorate the apartment. I padded around the place, sniffing the corners and working out the high-tech security system with the glee of a schoolgirl. James was working a lot, and I would wait with excitement for him to return, with flowers or a glint in his eyes that turned into a new and often diabolical plan for our evening out together. The start of Strasberg was still a month and a half away, so we filled up our spare time with partying. I thought we would have calmed down a little, with a new apartment and all, but the opposite was true. Most nights we crashed drunkenly in uncomfortable positions on the floor as sunlight stole across the floorboards and burned our dreams.

Christmas was arriving, so James and I extricated ourselves from each other and the vodka bottle and I flew to Sydney to see my family. I knew the year ahead was going to be as challenging as hell and I wanted to be ready and fighting fit for whatever it threw at me. (Okay, plus the Town Hall pool competition was on, and I wanted to refill my coffers.)

With the old places came the old memories, but this time I didn't sink into the morass I had fallen into before. Sydney was in the height of summer, full-blossomed and filled to the brim with sparkling waters and sunshine. The strange and beautiful yellow Australian light and the warm welcome of family and friends made me feel like nothing else existed. When I thought of New York, it felt unreal, like a dream, a ghost-life that ran parallel with my real one. I spent a month in Sydney, physically and mentally preparing for the Lee Strasberg Institute and missing James (who said he would cut off a single eyelash for each week that I was away – romantic and psychotic, just the way I liked 'em).

When I boarded the plane back to New York, sunburnt and refreshed, and full of lots of good advice, I felt that familiar fire in my belly. I was ready for the next adventure to begin.

8

Descent into bastardry, saved by a carrot penis and a trip to the Bahamas, plus fun on a shark slide

WHEN I ARRIVED BACK in Manhattan, I felt the familiar vibration of the city, like jacking in to a computer or taking a line of coke. The zapping cars, the energised people. I was back in my supposed ghost-life but it felt real again, vibrantly real. My senses, even though jet-lagged, woke up, and I could feel the cold wind in my brain as I sucked the air up through my freezing nostrils.

James took me on an all-night binge through the city and, once again, we ended up back at the apartment drunkenly crashed out. As the days passed, the partying started to take its toll and I was forced to have a serious talk with James. I was embarrassingly proud of my cast-iron liver but I was not even in sight of keeping up with the venerable drinker. I suggested we go on a health kick and stop partying so hard, join a gym and get ourselves together. The look of horror on his face said it all. I must say I was pretty horrified at the words coming out of my mouth too, but it just went to show how very pickled I had become. Though my real concern was with James' reaction. Around the edges of his eyes were violent traces of fear, his mouth contorted into a kind of childlike pout and his forehead furrowed in a determined way. I hadn't seen that combination of expressions on his face before and it worried me. We definitely needed to dry out.

I looked out the window and saw that Manhattan was covered with a blanket of fluffy white snow like a fairytale wonderland. The traffic noises were muffled and there was an uncanny stillness to the city. We decided to take advantage of the cold weather and go skiing. Exercise disguised as fun, or fun disguised as exercise – whichever it was, it would give us that much-needed break from drinking.

We drove through snow-covered upstate New York towards our destination, and as the car crunched onto the gravel driveway of the Mohonk Mountain House, I let out a gasp as we stared at the impressive castle before us.

The Mohonk ('Lake in the Sky') is a ginormous 266-room castle that was built in 1869 and is perched on a lake, nestled in hundreds of acres of wilderness. With its turrets outlined against the sky and its seven storeys of old-world charm, the Mohonk zoomed into my top-five hotels of all time. We were greeted by staff dressed in tuxedos and lacquered hair, who showed us to dinner in the ballroom where they served roasted pheasant and fat glasses of velvety red wine.

The next day James had set up permanent camp at the bar, so the hotel manager gave me some cross-country skis and a map of the ski trails around the property to entertain me. Armed with my skis and compass I set off. Soon enough, the castle was lost from sight and the only sounds were my laboured breathing and the crunch of ice underfoot. All around me were piles of pure white snow, bunching over bushes and occasionally shattering the silence by falling from a branch. As I reached a fork in the path, a swishing noise came up behind me. A black-suited James Bondish character screeched to a stop next to me, red-faced and sparkly eyed. He gave me directions in a sexy Russian accent to complete the circuit and zoomed off, leaving me thinking inappropriate thoughts.

Bond had warned me against taking the left route, as although it was quicker, it was for the more advanced skier. *Pschtt*, he wasn't the real Bond. I smoothed back my hair, ordered a martini from an imaginary waiter and took the left route. Soon enough, I found myself staring down an almost vertical drop. At the bottom it bent sharply out of view. What would Bond do? I swallowed and took a small rabbit hop to clear the snow at the top, tipped crazily and began the descent. I kept my knees and feet firmly together and bent down low like I'd seen skiers do on television, and it was exhilarating. The slice of ice underfoot, the glimpses of the white wonderland that zoomed past me as my eyes sprung tears and the wind blasted at my face, and my nose dripped like a tap – this was skiing!

The blind bend in the road was coming closer and closer and I began to get scared. *Not sure if this is fun anymoreeeee.* I couldn't see what was around the bend but I had far too much momentum to stop, so there was nothing for it – I crouched lower on the knife-like skis and sliced around the corner at a break-neck speed. In front of me was the dry-as-a-bone access road that led up the mountain. There was no way on earth I could stop and, like a bad movie, I heard the noise of a car coming down the mountain. On the other side of the road I could make out the continuation of the ski path, and I figured that if I was going fast enough, I could clear the gravel road and continue on down the other side. I careered like a demon down the slippery slope and suddenly felt the gristle of gravel underneath my skis. I felt my brain slamming against my skull and my jaw snapping up and down like a wind-up toy. In my peripheral vision, I saw the red shine of the vehicle coming straight towards me. Just in time, I heaved myself off the road and slammed straight into a pile of snow as the car honked angrily past. I lay there grinning maniacally as the clouds twirled above me, and gave myself a high five. I was so Bond! Shaken *and* stirred.

When I got back to the hotel, I caught up with James, who was laid out on the bed, drunk as a skunk. He heard me open the door, sprang up and scrambled towards me to kiss me, but managed just to drool.

'Babe, lie down, okay? If you have any more to drink I'll put you in a jar and sell you at a fete.'

'Shust up,' was his reply. 'I'll drank whatever I see fit, you stoopid bitch.'

'Don't call me a stupid bitch or I'll lace your alcohol with water.'

'You're lost and you're going nowhere –' he said, piercing me with his blue eyes. 'You never will – and that's a fact.'

I studied his face. 'What the hell are you –?'

'You're not very bright, are you?' he said with derision.

'Fuck you, James, seriously, just sober up.'

I got up to leave, but he barged past me and smashed himself against the door, blocking it.

'You're not going anywhere!'

He sounded like a villain from a bad sixties movie, and I took a step back.

I was shocked that he could be like this; I hadn't seen anything like it from him before. They say the truth comes out when you're drunk. Could this be what he really thought of me? Was this who he really was? But really, what right did he have to talk to me that way? Even if he was so drunk that he resembled a puddle, he had no bloody right.

I lowered my voice and tried to look tough. 'Get out of my way, James.'

He smiled, almost as if he were having fun. 'Try me.'

I walked as calmly as I could towards him and the door. When I got there, he just stood there, a strange look in his eye. I reached for the door handle but he slapped my hand out of the way. I tried again and before I knew it we were pushing and shoving each other like animals.

When I finally got out of there, I really was shaken and stirred. I went to one of the reading rooms, sat down and tried to figure out what had just happened. I mean, people argue, that's normal for any relationship, but this felt different. It had come out of nowhere. It was almost as if it were another man in there. The look in his eyes had scared me.

The next day, with a crick in my neck from sleeping in the reading-room chair, I made my way to the outdoor thermal spa where I'd been going each morning. I sat all by myself like a red-faced monkey in the hot, soothing waters surrounded by snow-laden fir trees and sweet, icy sunlight. The heat and the haze of intoxicating minerals gave me a buzz and I reclined back until only my eyes and nose were above water. Surrounding the pool was a tiny snow-covered picket fence, and blue jays twittered and splashed their beautiful deep blue colours against it. Next to the fence was a small snowman. He had been made only a few hours before and had pebbles for eyes, and a large bright orange carrot was sticking out of his groin area. I chuckled to myself and climbed out of the pool to get a closer look. He had a small rolled-up piece of paper sticking out of his forehead. I usually wouldn't think of reading somebody's private note, but there was nobody around, so I unfurled the paper and read it.

I love you. I'm sorry. Please help me, baby.

It was in James' handwriting. What did he mean by helping him? And did he think a snowman with a carrot for an erection was going to make me forgive him? Heh heh, he knew me so well.

Back at the room, I confronted him.

'Did you think a snowman with a carrot for a penis would make me forgive you?'

He grinned sheepishly and I turned my back so he didn't see my smile.

I asked him if he really thought I was going nowhere. He told me that he didn't know why he had said that. 'In any case,' he said, 'you've done a lot for your age, it can be intimidating for a man. Perhaps I was projecting,' he reflected. 'And before you ask, I do think you're bright.'

We sat in silence together.

'You wanted help?' I asked him.

He brushed it away. 'No, don't worry, a drunken, stupid moment, that was all,' he said, then suddenly turned serious. 'I have it under control.'

I tried to get him to talk about it some more, but he clammed up tighter than a Leprechaun's purse strings.

ılıllıllılı

Back in Manhattan, over the next few weeks I saw that James didn't have it under control at all. His drinking became more overt, and each time he drank he seemed to change into another person, his rants increasing in number and strength. I had begun to suspect that he was an alcoholic, and I started furtively reading books on alcoholism to try to understand the situation better.

One night he got home at three in the morning and I could hear him weeping from where I lay curled in bed. From what

I'd read, I knew that when an alcoholic had done another awful alcohol-related thing, you weren't supposed to soothe them: they had to see the destruction they caused before they could find the strength to want to change. When he finally fumbled into bed, I lay next to him in the dark and listened to his heart-wrenching moans in silence. Through venom-soaked words and tears he told me that he hated himself. He said that drinking was the only thing that kept him going. He dozed off to sleep and woke remembering nothing.

When we sat down to breakfast I asked him to talk about it with me.

'Bella, nothing's wrong.'

I glanced at his face and saw tears welling up in his eyes.

'Nothing is wrong,' he said in a monotone.

'You can talk to me, baby, really.'

James clutched at me, and his body shook like a cold motor against me. I felt a coolness, a detachment. As though my emotions were too much so my mind had shut them down like an over-worked machine. It seemed to help me see things more clearly.

'Baby, talk to me.'

He said nothing. I tried every first-year psych trick to get him to open up but nothing seemed to work. I was at a loss.

'I have the perfect idea,' he said suddenly. 'Let's go away together, where none of this matters. Where he can get better.'

I didn't think it was exactly a healthy sign that he was talking about himself in the third person, but it was a good sign that he wanted to get better. I figured a new environment would be just the trick to break him of his old habits.

⊪⊪⊪⊪⊪⊪

As we went on the net and booked two tickets to the Bahamas, it was as if a magic wand had been waved. Over the next few days, James' humour lightened, he stopped drinking so heavily, he seemed freer and more his old self. It was as though the 'other' James had completely disappeared without a trace.

If the Montelucia in Arizona was *The Shining* on acid, Atlantis – a huge Disney-type monstrosity of a resort on Paradise Island – was a Hawaiian shirt on acid. Its huge technicoloured spires and turrets outlined against the sky made it look like a great squatting monster. It cost a fortune to stay there but was so not my cup of vodka. I had fantasised about a thatched hut on a secluded beach, where James and I would heal and grow stronger together. Oh yeah, and have private beach sex. But oh no, American accountants with knee-length socks, women with orange lipstick and screaming children dressed in sailor suits were to be our companions for the next week.

James and I lumbered up from the warm sand with our non-alcoholic sodas and strolled back to Atlantis to look at the underground viewing walkway where giant fish swam and manta rays glided on silvery currents. One giant fish, a tuna I think, had me enthralled. Its sheer size got my attention at first, but as I pressed up against the glass to get a better look, I noticed the expression in its eye. It was watching me! And I could even detect curiosity. Ever so slowly I walked next to it as it swam elegantly alongside me, keeping constant eye contact. Its curious expression gave way to one of amusement. I didn't think fish even had expressions. James thought I'd gone mad and left to go and gamble. I couldn't say I blamed him. After five minutes of keeping pace with my friend the tuna, I slowed down and came to a halt. It looked back at me and swirled its silvery fins and stopped also. I turned back the way I had come and waited to see what he would do. With a quick flick of his fins, he turned around and hurried after me. We continued this game of cat and mouse until James returned and interrupted our reverie by tapping his foot loudly on the wet cement.

'Holy hell!' I murmured to James as he regarded me with concern. 'I'm communicating with a fish!'

Then, the fish opened its huge mouth, exactly as I had just done. Both James and I froze. I tried again, opening my mouth slowly then closing it again. The fish regarded me seriously for a bit then did the exact same thing.

Even James was impressed. He walked up behind me to get a better look, but I saw panic in the fish's eye and it swam off into the darkness.

James wanted to hit the blackjack table again, so I wound my way around the manicured paths of Atlantis to the infamous Shark Slide. They had erected a massive Incan pyramid amongst the palm trees and in the base was a tank teeming with large and ferocious-looking sharks. The idea was to climb to the top of the pyramid and take a waterslide all the way down through a clear plastic tube, through the sharks' enclosure and out the other side. Yes! I got to be James Bond again. I screamed down the first part of the slide, hair and water slapping at my face, feeling the weight of water urging me faster and faster – until suddenly I found myself slowing down. Possibly because of the atrocious amounts of fat fish and lobster I'd been consuming, my ass wasn't small enough to skim down the last part of the slide. So I sat there, in the plastic tube, feeling fat, water building up behind me, watching the cold and curious eye of a large shark coming straight for me. The beast was a millimetre of plastic away from me and it seemed to be coming at an incredible speed.

A tinny voice blasted over the sound system.

'Use your legs!'

'No fucking way,' I mumbled, 'this is totally cool!'

'I heard that,' came the reply.

I reluctantly bumped my way forward and made it out the other end. I had survived the shark-infested tank; and I was raring for another go.

Six slides later the attendant prohibited me from going down again. 'You must share with the children,' he said in his smooth Bahaman drawl.

ılıltlılıl

That evening, after touring the Pirate's Cove, James and I left Atlantis and went to a local bar where we immersed ourselves in rum. I'd planned on not drinking anything to set a good example, but I hadn't had a drink all week and it was our last night and the sweet Bahaman rum was doing the Alice in Wonderland thing: *drink me . . . drink me*. I complied.

I saw a girl in the bar with short black hair and a lively face. She was surrounded by a swell of admirers. She looked just like my friend Rene, and I felt a sudden pang for her company.

'She looks just like a friend of mine from Sydney. I miss my chick.'

By this stage I realised James was four sheets to the wind. He regarded her with venom. 'She's ugly and looks like a cunt.' He said the word 'cunt' as though it were cut glass in his mouth.

I turned to look at her, trying to figure out what had prompted this exceptional level of hatred.

'I expect all your friends are the same,' he added with a dogged expression.

My mouth did what my friend the tuna's had done.

'Why would you say something like –?'

'Because they are,' he said. 'All ugly and stupid. Losers. All of them. Australian fucking losers.'

Was he joking? He was being about as funny as an ulcer.

'James, number one, don't *ever* talk to me that way again. Number two, if you talk about my friends that way again, I'll . . . you'll really regret it. And three, you really are an immense prick,' I added, for lack of anything more punishing to say.

He then went off on a tirade about how one's friends reveal so much about a person.

'Yes,' I huffed, 'I am very lucky to have the friends I do, James, so –'

'Losers,' he interrupted with a mean smile.

'James, fuck you, seriously. You think it's funny? Just fuck off, will you?'

'I will, and you'll regret it, trust me,' he threatened as he stumbled his way out of the bar.

I sat back on my bar stool and took another slug of rum. What the hell? Perhaps I should have tried to laugh it off? But he was trying to make me angry on purpose. That in itself was as infuriating as hell. I realised I was a bit of an idiot for believing that he could simply switch off that side of him. I finished my drink and felt the bubble of fantasy pop. I didn't have any cash on me and wondered how I'd get back to the hotel. Eventually a kind-faced cab driver offered me a lift as he was going that way anyway. As we bumped along the road away from the bar, I saw the Rene look-alike walking past. She looked up and waved. The cab driver waved back.

'She's a friend of mine, mind if we stop?' he asked.

'Sure,' I answered, curious.

He introduced me to the girl, whose name was Ingrid, and we immediately clicked. She suggested the two of us go back to her place for a drink. Not feeling like having to face James quite yet, I accepted the kind offer from Rene's doppelgänger.

Her home was a room in a cheap hotel with red velvet curtains attached to a slender wooden pole and a bearskin rug strewn haphazardly on the linoleum floor. She placed dripping, scented candles on the floor and we set about making explosive cocktails at the bar area near the bathroom and smoked cigarettes. I told her a little about James' outburst at the bar. It felt good to get it off my chest.

'Mark my words, Bella, he's trouble,' she said.

'It was a drunken argument.'

'I bet!' she retorted. 'And I also bet you'll be saying that when he's drunkenly hitting out at the unborn child in your belly.'

Whaa? I turned to look at her.

She told me she'd suffered a miscarriage at the hands of her drunken lover. A lover she was expecting at the hotel at any moment.

'Here? Now? But why is he coming here?' I asked, alarmed. 'Are you still with him?'

'Yes,' she said.

I looked at her, confused.

'I love him,' she said, matter-of-factly.

A few minutes later, Charlie arrived. He introduced himself as the heir to a big chain of hotels and, judging by his puffed-out chest, he was fairly happy about that wee fact. He seemed more like a pompous accountant than the violent monster I'd been expecting. Nonetheless, I watched him like a hawk.

He was affectionate with Ingrid, loving and tactile. A little too much, in fact. As we were chatting, he began to inch his hand up underneath Ingrid's skirt. I averted my eyes and began to stutter about the good weather. When I looked back, she had her eyes closed and her mouth was open in ecstasy as his hands fumbled about in the dark. I went to the bathroom to do a pretend pee. When I returned, I looked around the dimly lit room and could just make out their figures on the bed. The candlelight flickered off their naked bodies and I heard a strange snorting noise in between fits of giggles. What the hell? My curiosity got the better of me and I tiptoed closer to see what was going on. He was snorting cocaine off her belly as she giggled from the tickles.

How in hell did I always get myself into these situations?

'Come join us, Bella,' chimed Ingrid as they both beckoned.

Feeling like a cast member from *Eyes Wide Shut*, I shook my head, thanked them for their hospitality and hightailed it out of there, into the street, newly painted with morning light.

I walked the cobbled streets and saw the pink light on the white buildings and a small broken sandcastle in the middle of a driveway. A kid rushed out with a bucket and spade and began to resurrect the pile of sand as he sang to himself. The markets were just opening and I strolled through the aisles fingering the shells for sale, and then on towards the harbour to watch the early morning fishing boats return. The hangover still blurred my eyes, but I could think clearly: even though I'd once again ended up in a preeetty bizarre situation, I knew there was a lesson to learn from it. I thought about going back to Atlantis and my heart sank. It wasn't just the choreographed pool aerobics for the olden goldies that had me cringing, it was having to see James.

I thought about James and his drinking, about Ingrid's unborn baby and the hotel-heir fists. I couldn't reconcile the wonderful James I knew with the one of last night. My belly was warning me of something, and it felt sinister. It wasn't just that he'd said shitty things about my friends and me, it was *how* he did it. I projected into the future and my thoughts turned bleaker than an Edgar Allan Poe poem. I didn't want to end up like Ingrid, trapped in diseased love.

When I got back to the hotel, James was nursing a glass of scotch but he seemed relatively sober. I took the opportunity to explain how I felt.

He interrupted me.

'Bella, I love you so much.'

'What?' I asked, genuinely confused. I couldn't reconcile him calling me a loser and loving me at the same time. You don't do that to people you loved. I sat down and looked at him and realised I was being naive. People did all sorts of crazy things in the name of love.

'I do,' he said. 'I know what you're about to say and I won't stop you. I don't deserve you. I was a mess. But I didn't mean any of it, really. I was in a bad mood and I just took it out on you. Please, I'm sorry. Put it down to temporary lunacy and give me another chance. I promise you, it won't ever happen again.'

I looked at his shaking hands and earnest expression. I did really care for him, and however much my belly was warning me against it, I couldn't turn that off so easily. I told him yes, we could try it, but on the condition he completely cut down on his drinking. (And bought me some flowers.)

Back in Manhattan he stayed true to his word and once again the bad James disappeared and the good James came out with guns blazing. The picture of a gentleman, he was kind and thoughtful, eager to get better and he stayed away from the bars. The argument we'd had slowly slipped away into the recesses of my memory along with James' aberrant behaviour. Life became settled again and we got along beautifully – and this time it seemed it would last.

I got a call from Lauren, the director of the short film I'd auditioned for, and she told me I'd won the role and that she'd keep me posted on the shoot dates. I was to do a New York film. Yes! First I had to learn how to act, but details, details.

Then the time for Strasberg arrived.

9

Starting Strasberg. Worshipping the Castle, the Guru and making mates

THE FIRST MORNING AT the Lee Strasberg Institute was a blur of cramping nerves and feverish expectations which increased as the day wore on. The classes were overcrowded, with thirty or so people in them, an eclectic array of cultures, ethnicities and ages. The teachers were just as diverse. I was introduced to the two people who would become my mentors, the extraordinary Method Acting teacher Robert Castle, and Ron NaVarre, the genius Tai Chi teacher who looked like a younger version of Steven Seagal, but sexier.

The thing I also noticed that first day was the other girls. They were glamorous and stick-thin, their tight jeans glued to their bones. They had that unfortunate horse-look, like their legs were growing at right-angles out of their pelvic plates. It looked painful. Feeling like a great unwieldy lard-arse next to them, I ate an extra cream bun to prove to myself I didn't care, then lumbered off to choose my classes for my first three-month term. I chose Method Acting, Movement, Character Study, Tai Chi, Great Playwrights, Film and TV, Script Analysis, Singing, Dialects and Stage Combat, all within the backdrop of the always inspiring New York City.

When I stepped through that little red door of the Strasberg Institute the scales slid from my eyes. No denial was allowed there, no putting off because of fears, no bullshit. Everything seemed to be heightened – the feeling of excitement, of dread. In Strasberg you were expected to have full access to your emotions, be honest and committed to expressing them, and work as hard as a Peruvian donkey. In the past I'd gathered what little bits of info and advice I could about acting, but it was pretty hit and miss and often hard to come by. At Strasberg, though, I knew I'd hit the mother lode.

We were introduced to the fundamentals of the Method, which was sensory work. There was a hierarchy of ten or so sense memory exercises, beginning with 'The Cup' and ending with 'Portrait'. On my first day I did 'The Cup' and felt truly ridiculous.

I had to visualise a cup of tea, then spend an hour playing with my imaginary cup. This was the height of acting? I had to touch the warm ceramic and feel the heat through my fingers, breathe in the spiciness of the tea and feel the steam on my face. Bang my fingertips on it and hear the ting sound, and the swishing of the tea as I stirred my imaginary spoon in it. Okay. I asked the teacher what it was for, and he looked at me like the idiot I obviously was, then asked me if I were a trouble-maker.

He explained to me that the Method was about three things: concentration, relaxation and sense memory. The Cup exercise was the beginning of sense memory training and also helped to improve your concentration. He said sense memory was used to better conjure up your own real-life experiences for acting, rather than faking it, or mimicking an experience. The idea is that instead of using narrative memory to remember an object or occurrence, you use your five senses, which trigger an emotion that you can then use in the scene.

I thought about the great actors I'd watched, and they did have a strong sense of concentration on screen, and also a sense that it was somehow personal to them. As though what they were doing was the realest thing in the world.

'And relaxation?' I asked.

'We're about to get to that.'

For the next two hours, we 'relaxed'. We had to sit on a chair and slowly flail our arms and legs around, pinpointing every muscle in our bodies as we did so. I peeked at the other students and they were all heavily involved, grunting and sometimes sniffing back tears.

'Emotions are locked in your physical bodies, use this relaxation technique to unlock them,' boomed the teacher.

I tried to 'unlock my emotions' but felt like a fraud. Everyone else started tearing up and making guttural noises in their throats. I decided there was nothing for it but to fake it. I squeezed out a few tears, then, inexplicably, the floodgates opened and I started wailing like a banshee. The teacher clasped me by the shoulder in a comforting embrace.

And thus began my acting training. On any given day I'd be bursting into tears at the drop of a hat, sniffing and tasting my sensory object and trying not to be a trouble-maker.

As the week wore on, I made some friends too. Eleanor, Polly and Ben, all from England. I was the honorary Australian and the fourth musketeer. Eleanor was a great beauty with high cheekbones and a hilariously dirty wit, Polly was kind with huge innocent-looking eyes, a nose ring and a lyrical cockney accent. And Ben was an affable bear with flashes of brilliant smarts. We were initially drawn together because of our similar homelands, but stayed together because of our equal desire for hardcore fun.

Then there was my Italian stallion, Gian-Luca, who shared some of my classes. I believed him to be the most handsome man on earth. He was Italian, with Botticelli curls that dangled over startlingly green eyes, a Marlon Brando face and a stunning, stunning body. I wish it had been a higher desire that drew me to him, but it wasn't, it was all lust. I'd pass him on the stairs and inevitably trip down them as I watched his retreating butt press against his blue jeans. I'd told James about my crush and he'd laughed.

'Invite him over for dinner,' he said.

'No way,' I answered. 'He has to stay in my imagination and perform all sorts of tricks for me there.'

'A lady must be given her wants,' came James' amused reply.

As time wore on, we all began to understand that the Method could be quite purist, and so were some of the teachers, even resembling a cult at times. The venerable Lee Strasberg was the ever-present ghost that we all knelt down to. I struggled a bit with the philosophy behind the Method, but was told a story by a teacher that helped me understand it better:

Laurence Olivier and Marlon Brando were the two best actors of their generation. Olivier was technical, in that he had exceptional mimicry skills; Brando was Method and used his own experiences in a scene. Olivier was asked by a pressman:

'Who is the better actor, you or Marlon Brando?'

'Brando,' he replied without missing a beat, 'not because of any false modesty, as when I am on form I am just as good as him, if not better. But Brando has consistency.'

'And that is what the Method is for,' said my teacher. 'Consistency.'

One night during a long run, Olivier was playing King Lear and all the glitterati of New York were in attendance. He was so good that night that people raved about it for years. When his admirers came to his dressing-room afterwards to congratulate him, they heard crashing noises coming from inside. They entered and were horrified to see that he was in a wild anger and was smashing up his room.

'What's the matter?' they asked him, appalled. 'You were utterly brilliant!'

'I know!' he replied in exasperation.

'Then why are you so upset?'

'Because . . . because I don't know how I did it!' he shouted into the air.

My teacher said that you can rely on inspiration for the first two times, then it falters, along with your performance. Method, on the other hand, is a sure-fire way of getting the same performance again and again. Consistency. Especially, he said, for film work, when you have to do take after take after take.

On the weekends, my English Crew and I were busy trying to take over New York, so I was glad I'd decided to enrol in Tai Chi at Strasberg, to help with my, um, stress levels and earn a bit of Zen. Tai Chi was given as a class because Lee Strasberg believed it was a good way to ground yourself as an actor, to stop superfluous thoughts and integrate your emotions and physicality. Our teacher, Ron NaVarre, was a master martial artist, healer, ballet dancer and actor. He'd created a hybrid Tai Chi class out of all of his diverse disciplines.

During our first lesson, Ron put us in physical positions that were supposed to set up communication between our bodies and emotions. He warned us that we would get emotional. The other cynical actors and I collectively rolled our eyes and I got ready to fake it again. He put us in 'Tree Position': standing, weight evenly balanced, arms bent in front as though we were hugging a tree. After twenty minutes of feeling very treeish and somewhat silly, I suddenly and inexplicably burst into a torrent of tears. Embarrassed, I tried to wipe away the deluge, and as I did, I looked around the room and hello cuckoo's nest! Everybody was going crazy. The girl next to me was wailing, the guy next to her was jumping up and down in some strange emotionally induced fit. The room was absolutely seething with frenzied emotion: some were laughing, others were bawling. It was horrible and fantastic and, in retrospect, pretty damn funny.

In another class, Ron spent two hours talking to us about 'connection'. He said that we are not alone on this earth, that everything is connected to everybody and everybody to every-thing. Actors are taught by friends and family to be selfish, to look out for number one, to screw the other actors, to shine all by themselves. But no man is an island, he said. We need other people. We are individuals, sure, like each of our fingers is an individual finger, but all four fingers and thumb are connected to our hand, which is connected to our wrist and the rest of our body, and so forth.

His speech came about because I was having dirty thoughts about him. I was in tree pose, and wondering for some reason what Ron would be like in bed. Suddenly, he moved into my 'tree area' and stood in front of me staring intently, as is his wont. A hot flush of embarrassment shot up my neck and into my cheeks. I was sure as sure could be that he could read my thoughts. I dropped my gaze like a hot potato.

'Look at me, Bella,' Ron's smooth tone commanded. 'Let it out, Bella, let whatever it is out.'

I grimaced and closed up tighter.

'What am I doing to you?' he asked, interested. 'What is the connection here?'

My eyes flicked up and met his. *Well for starters you're making me . . . shit, don't say that, say something treeish for god's sake.*

'Um, I don't know,' I managed.

'Right, class, we have a lesson to learn,' he said to the room.

We released the tree pose and listened to him talking about how important understanding the connection you have with people is.

'All sorts of connections,' he added. 'Familial, acting, relationship, sexual . . .'

I blushed brightly and looked away, but mistakenly caught the eye of the class idiot whose face lit up. Damn.

It felt good being in Ron's presence, though, maybe because he was so utterly present, perceptive and transparent, yet still grounded, like a giant oak tree. He was also patient, and you could see in his smile that he'd fought many of his own demons and won. During class each week, we would all stand respectfully and listen, like worshippers at an altar. Afterwards we would clap him spontaneously. In no other class did that ever happen.

·ıılılılılıı·

I had also signed up for a new Method class taught by the terrifying Robert Castle, a tall, imposing man with a stern face and scarily intelligent eyes. He had an otherworldly ability to see right through you and enough balls to tell you exactly what he thought. He terrified me more than anybody I'd ever met. His perceptive ability, his photographic memory, his vast knowledge on every subject under the sun and his intimidating presence made castanets out of my knees. And I wasn't the only one. At the institute, students would usually clamour to sit at the front of the room. In Robert's class, people would arrive early to scurry into the back rows, away from his all-consuming presence. As in all the other Method classes, we had to prepare and present an excerpt from a play every two or three weeks. I watched my fellow students, the second-years as well as the newbies like me, literally shake with fear when they had to perform for Castle. When they finished, his insights were so disarmingly accurate and so cleverly expressed, he had all of us in awe. I had never experienced anything like Robert Castle and, with a sense of dread and excitement, I knew in my bones that he would either make me or break me as an actor.

The time inevitably came when I had to perform in front of The Castle. The day before I had done a Lady Macbeth monologue for one of the Shakespearean teachers and it had gone badly. Like, *really* badly. I hadn't had time to learn my lines or study the piece and I was crucified by an ageing hippie with a Master's in Shakespearean literature. A cold sweat crept out of my skin at the thought of another disaster, but it turned into ice when I thought of Robert.

My scene partner, Hugh, and I were both afraid of Robert, so we'd rehearsed our scene from Teresa Rebeck's comedy *Loose Knit* time and time again until we knew the lines backward and forward and were as prepared as we could possibly be. But when the big day broke I felt like Paris Hilton with clothes on. Completely unprepared.

At the beginning of the scene, my character, a highly frustrated and damaged woman, is having a date with a new man in a restaurant. She jokingly seduces her date by softly tracing a butter knife slowly across his throat. When the lights dimmed and Robert shuffled more comfortably into his seat to watch, I took the butter knife in my hands and began to trace it gently along Hugh's throat. Robert let out an almighty roar.

'Stop! Stop!' he yelled. 'What the hell do you think you're doing?'

Petrified animals had nothing on us.

'Put the goddamn knife down!'

'But I wasn't –' I stammered.

'In Strasberg safety comes first! Use something else!'

Hugh and I looked at each other and gulped in unison. What the fuck would we do now? I had been about to soil my panties already but this fresh new hell had unnerved me so much that my hands began to shake.

Urging myself not to run off stage, I plunged back into the beginning of the scene, using the edge of my hand as a 'knife' as I tried to control the shaking. But I was so disconcerted, I couldn't remember any of my lines.

Hugh looked at me expectantly.

'Um, well, so, ah, let me see.'

I heard a roar coming from the general direction of Robert Castle.

'Have you forgotten your lines?'

He was actually going to eat me.

'Um, well, so, ah, let me see . . .' I stole a glimpse of his face. I swear I saw steam coming out of his nostrils.

'Shit. Yes. Dragon, I mean, ah. Fuck. Yes. Sorry,' I blurted out.

He was seriously about to blow his top. 'Don't apologise to me!' he yelled.

'Of course. Sorry,' I mumbled. 'I mean, oops, I'm not sorry . . . ah . . .'

'Is somebody on book? No? Okay, Bella, get your lines out now while we all sit here waiting for you,' he stormed.

I scrambled to find my bag, in which I had a copy of the play. What seemed like ten hours later, with everybody in the class glaring at me, I gingerly climbed back onto the stage.

I started again. All went well for about thirty seconds. Then, the ass fell out: I fell off the stage.

Fuck!

My character was supposed to be twirling on stage but I'd become dizzy and fallen right off the stage.

Fuck!

I avoided all unnecessary eye contact with The Dragon as *Psycho* music screeching in my head and the laughter of the class mingled. I dusted myself off, took a breath in, then climbed back on stage and continued the scene to its humiliating end.

'That's it, we're out of time, I'll critique next session,' said Robert dryly as he dismissed the class.

The classroom vacated like magic and Hugh and I were left alone on stage, frozen into position. After all of the preparation, rehearsing and the shitting ourselves, I had made a complete and utter fool of myself. New York, I had arrived. When the last of the retreating noises had disappeared, Hugh and I burst into manic laugher, which didn't stop until we were next door in the pub and a stiff scotch was poured unmercifully down our gullets. Not the best beginning I could have hoped for, but a realistic one, I figured.

That night, I went out partying in Brooklyn with Eleanor, Ben and Polly. A German guy I'd met on the subway had given me a treasure map of the 'coolest' bars in Brooklyn, which we traced with our fingers until the map was transparent and we were rollickingly drunk. We went to a bar called Galapagos that used to be an old mechanic's shop. The underground pit where the mechanics once worked had been transformed into a lagoon, and huge chairs made of steel and feathers had been placed around it like some otherworldly resort. Burlesque dancers, sword swallowers and belly dancers performed around the glistening dark water and outside there was a roaring fire that drunk artists fed with dry logs. Gian-Luca met up with us and our spilled wine seeped into the cracks of the floorboards as we all vowed to be 'friendsssh forevvvvvaaa'.

ılıltıllılıı

Gian-Luca and I had begun to hang out quite a bit, along with my English crew. He turned out to be affable, loyal and affectionate, an absolute sweetheart. He sometimes reminded me of a nuzzling infant or kitten, with that kind of butting search for something, an unselfconscious nudging for attention. His body was large, but he held himself with a kind of grace and sureness that somehow made me know I could trust him implicitly. Admittedly, I still snuck a look at his rear end once in a while, but friendship had grown up between us like a durable sapling.

I'd also begun to meet 'randoms', as we called them. If you're open to it, New York was one friendly town. You'll meet people in bars, at bus stops, in movie theatres, and end up having the most bizarre and often interesting conversations. Then, with their wisdom imparted, they would whisk off into the smog, never to be seen or heard of again.

'Part of Quantum Mechanics is the concept that a myriad of possibilities exist at any one time. Like career options, lovers or choosing between a stack of different jocks. There's a multitude of possibilities, always,' said sixty-year-old Israeli, randomer Avi Weinstein, as we waited for a train that would take us in the same direction.

'But how do we know which one to choose? Is there only one right path?' I asked.

We'd met each other while watching *What the Bleep Do We Know* at the Fourteenth Street Cinemas, and were pretending to sound like we knew what we were talking about.

'There's only one path and, with enough insight and determination, you'll find it,' he said. 'Like when you are acting, there are many choices that you could make, right? But when you happen upon the *right* one, you know it immediately, yes?' he said as our missed train whooshed past us unheeded.

I nodded.

'Why?' he probed.

'Because it feels . . . um . . . authentic,' I offered.

'Exactly!' he smiled triumphantly.

'Yes, I understand that's true for acting, but is it true for life?' I asked.

'Well, if a life is lived creatively, it is one and the same.'

I looked at him, trying to grasp all the concepts we'd been thrashing out since we'd started our talk outside the cinema two hours ago.

'I know that should make sense,' I said pensively. 'But it just doesn't,' I added with a baffled look and a raised eyebrow.

Avi threw out his belly and roared with laughter. Two nearby subway workers who had been eavesdropping chuckled as well. Then pretended they weren't.

One of the workers, with a greased-up face, spoke up, 'It's not true you know,' he said to me conspiratorially. 'There is no "right" path, only the pursuit of happiness in the moment. Remember that,' he said, looking pointedly at me, just like a greasy old Gandalf.

'Don't talk trash, Leo,' said his friend. 'At any one moment, there is only one true road in life, and either you have the guts to admit it to yourself, or you don't.'

Just then the train arrived, so we left the two subway philosophers to their earnest discussion as they pensively brushed up small pieces of trash from the ground. I loved the ease with which they joined in our conversation. I was beginning to understand it was a typically New York thing to do. There were so many over-educated foreigners forced from their homelands to start afresh in America, working hard at menial jobs as they hatched and fed their dreams. Like Avi. He had been a physicist in Tel Aviv and was now working as a cab driver trying to save money for his kids' education. 'But I'm the happiest I've been,' he told me. 'This city has taken me in, and there aren't any bullets flying over my kids' heads. New York accepts me and my family, I'm thankful for that.'

On the subway, I was squeezed in between a huge laughing black woman with *Wizard of Oz* shoes and a Hispanic in a corduroy jumpsuit who was softly singing 'Hey Jude' to his tiny girlfriend. I looked across at Avi as the cage around us rattled away through the tunnels of New York. *I really love New York*, I mouthed to him. He answered with a nodding of his head, a big grin and a slow blink of the eyes.

10

Understanding the Method to my madness, as well as his

I WOKE UP WITH a heaving hangover. I slapped together a ham sandwich then the phone rang, smashing into my amygdala. It was Zoë in Los Angeles.

On the set of *Kill Bill* in China, Zoë had spent a lot of time hanging out with Quentin Tarantino. They had established a mutual admiration society, which continued after the film was finished. They'd spent quality time together drinking and crashing on each other's sofas. I imagined Quentin Tarantino crashing on my sofa, then taking me by the hand and dancing with me to 'Son of a Preacher Man', then . . . huh? Zoë's voice on the other end of the line brought me back to reality. She was phoning to tell me that Quentin was making a new film called *Death Proof*, as part of a double feature with Robert Rodriguez that they named *Grindhouse*. And he had written in a main character he had called 'Zoë Bell': a stuntwoman from New Zealand.

'Are you kidding? That's fantastic!' I screamed.

'He's also asked me to play the part,' she said unassumingly.

'Fuck!' I screamed down the phone, for lack of anything more intelligent to say.

'Fuck!' I added.

I managed a few more words: 'Fuck, Zoë!'

After yelling and offering her all sorts of congratulations and advice, I was able to calm down and think clearly.

'Sooo . . . is there a job for me too?' I piped up.

She laughed.

'Er . . . I'm serious.'

We both laughed.

'I can try to get you in for an audition for one of the other roles,' she said cheerily.

'Noooo waaaaayyy!'

We broke into squeals of hysterical schoolgirl laughter then I choked on my ham sandwich.

Zoë said she was meeting Quentin that evening for dinner and she wanted to take my headshot and résumé with her to give him. In a haze of excitement and practice Oscar-acceptance speeches, James and I sorted through my photos, updated my résumé and sent them off within the hour.

So many positive things had happened since setting off on this crazy journey, this being one more lovely jewel on the New York necklace. It was as though my life had been on hold back home and coming to New York was the action that finally unhooked it.

ıılıılılılı

Strasberg was stimulating and challenging as all hell, although I was having problems with the Method itself. My concern was with sense memory. That if you are really, truly emotionally involved with your scene partner, if you *are* the character, you are 'in the moment' and being real and honest – what need do you have for emotional memories? Mightn't they just pollute the scene? Bring outside influence into something that should be purely about the here and now? Let's say you're doing a scene in which your boyfriend asks you to marry him. If you are using Sense Memory to remember the time in your real life when your boyfriend asked you to marry him, wouldn't the scene become about your real boyfriend, about the love or dislike you felt for him, instead of for the character in front of you? I was confused.

People in class said they used Sense Memory each time they performed. They'd work on a place (projecting an imaginary three-dimensional place from your own life that has some sort of resonance for you), a substitution (substituting a familiar object or person for an unknown one), a body overall (using your senses to feel, for example, the rain all over your body, and using the subsequent emotions that feeling elicits), a personal object (an object that has some sort of importance to you that you sensorially touch in the scene) or an animal (using the movement of an animal to garner that animal's behaviour as your own). But whenever I tried thinking about being a zebra, or the rain on my body, or my dead dog, or fumbling with an imaginary object, I lost all concentration in the scene. I knew there had to be something to it, as some of the best actors on earth were Method actors. I decided to ask one of my teachers, Mr Bustamante, who was a fabulously flamboyant man with a ready wit and an eccentric laugh.

'Bella, use the Method *in* the scene. Use your own personal experiences . . .' he said, regarding me with his wonderfully wicked smile, 'which it looks like you've had many of.'

I chortled appreciatively.

'And use them in the scene!' he continued. 'Brando did, Dean did, it worked for them!'

Another teacher, Sal, said, 'Use Sense Memory to generate a deeper connection for yourself to the scene, to make it realer for you. Don't visualise your dead dog *in* the scene, just work on the dead dog through your five senses and place it where you want it in the scene. Then, when you perform, the *feelings* that are generated by the dead dog will come up.'

'Not the dead dog itself,' he added with a little flourish.

I asked Robert Castle and he said Sense Memory was a very contentious Method issue. He said, for himself, he never used it directly while performing, but did in the rehearsal process, which he would then plug into the part of the scene where it needed it most.

I asked another teacher, Ted, and he said, 'Don't use the Method if you don't need it. Imagine Sense Memory as the diving board into the pool of emotion. If you are already swimming in the pool, you don't have to use the diving board.'

Yet another teacher went further and told me about the birth of Sense Memory. Russian director, Konstantin Stanislavsky, the father of the Method, had gone on a quest to discover the greatest talents of his generation. He watched all the stellar performers and analysed the differences between the good performances and the great ones. He then interviewed these most talented actors to discover their acting processes.

'When you screamed at your husband in the third act, I felt the hair bristle on my skin, how did you do that? How did you generate such passion?' asked Stanislavsky of an actress he'd just watched.

'I don't know,' answered the actress. 'I just felt it.'

'But how?' insisted Stanislavsky.

She sat pensively in silence. 'I think,' she said slowly, 'I had a momentary flash of anger. I still felt annoyed over my [real-life] husband not doing any housework.'

'Ah!' said Stanislavsky. And the idea behind the Method was born.

I talked to James about my Sense Memory quandaries and he suggested I slow down.

He poured more wine into his glass and regarded me.

'You don't want to overdo it, honey,' he said.

His eyes were red with the wine.

'You should stop Strasberg, in fact.'

Huh?

'And do what?' I asked.

He looked down at the meal I had prepared for him. 'Cook for me,' he said without smiling.

I didn't think he really meant it, but normally I would have risen to the bait and he would have had the argument he obviously wanted. I could sense in my bones that Bad James was getting ready to enter the ring. I laughed hollowly, then hurriedly made ready to leave for a school networking party. When I turned at the door to look back at him, he was staring at me, a wobbly and cruel expression in his eyes.

When I got home that night, James was tangled between the sofa and a chair, the alcohol fumes wafting through the room. I tried to wake him to move him into the bedroom but he lashed out with his fist at the invisible intruder. I left him there and went to sleep in the other room.

⠀⠀⠀⠀⠀ılıllıllılı

Over pizza the next day, Gian-Luca folded his napkin in half, then in half again. 'Bella, if you were my old friend, I would tell you to leave James. I would make you see. But that is presumptuous so I can't do that,' he said in his lilting English. He resumed eating his pizza and stared out the frosted window.

The next week in Tai Chi, the Guru Ron NaVarre talked about

bottled emotion. He said that when you have emotions you don't want to experience, you ball them up and stuff them away into a recess to deal with later. He said to visualise the emotion as a ball of tangled energy residing in the pit of your stomach. It ricochets around inside your body, touching and affecting everything. That niggling feeling won't let you relax, or sleep or concentrate properly. No matter how much you think of other things, or how far you push it down inside of you, that emotion will continue to bounce around, rising up at inopportune times. As a natural response, over time, you cover this ball of suppressed emotion with a force field of fear, to keep it in place, to stop it jumping about, to tell yourself that the emotion is somehow dangerous, it will harm you, to leave it alone. Later, when you finally go to deal with it, you find this layer of fear waiting for you. You become afraid to feel the emotion. He said you must remember that there is only a layer of fear to get through until you find the real concern that needs to be addressed – often never as bad as the fear makes you believe it is.

My fears with James were becoming ever-present. I'd try to force them away, swallow them, rationalise them. But they grew stronger the more I tried to deny them, just as Ron had prophesied. James had spun into a downward spiral and had begun to drink more and more and was steadily getting worse. I had stopped going out with him in the evenings because of the aberrant and vicious temper he'd suddenly fly into when he was drunk. I had put off acknowledging it, partly because he wouldn't talk about it when he was sober and partly because I was becoming scared of him when he drank. I wasn't living with the James I knew any more, but some malevolent person I had to watch and respond to like a dangerous stormy ocean.

One night James came home at four in the morning, his

cheeks covered in the silvery trails of tears and his clothes and mouth glistening with alcohol. He'd given his Rolex to a limo driver as collateral while he went to an ATM and the driver had zoomed off into the night with it. Then, as he was stuffing the cash into his pockets, he'd tripped and fallen. So drunk he was unable to stand, he had just lain there, on the cold concrete, watching the crisp hundred-dollar bills scatter into the air and hug themselves around lamp-posts. He couldn't remember how he'd got home.

He was building himself up into a state of fury. 'Those cunning assholes, try and rob me again and I'll – I'll –' He turned to look at me, taking me in with slitted eyes. 'Where were *you* last night?' he accused.

'What are you saying?' I asked, returning his cat's eyes.

'You knew I'd be in that area.'

I stared back at him. 'Are you fucking kidding me?'

He gave me a look, so pregnant with contempt and suspicion that I was convinced I had indeed planned the robbery and was as guilty as he evidently thought.

Then I snapped out of it. 'Fuck you, James.'

'You're that sort of person,' he said, as his alcohol-soaked spittle flew at me. 'I knew I couldn't trust people like you.'

A tremendous anger began to burn at my face. I felt its fiery tendrils ready to wrap around his paranoid fantasies and squeeze the life out of them. But from experience my tongue had learned to grow thick out of self-protection and I remained stonily silent. I'd grown used to his blanket drink-induced accusations of paranoia. You could argue until you were blue in the face, you could show him proof after proof, you could rage, you could cry, but nothing seemed to stop them.

I could see a cool, sharp glint of intelligence in his eyes, like a snake's. That combination of rage and consciousness scared the shit out of me. He took in my fright. Then a slow creep of satisfaction came into his eyes.

'I still have you,' he said in a low whisper.

I shuddered and realised then that it was all about control, or lack of it. He felt absolutely out of control and it scared him to the marrow. He didn't have any control over his life, his drinking or his drunken actions, so when he saw the fright in my face, to him it was a kind of achievement. He had control of something. Even if it was only his scared girlfriend.

I realised, too, that James was your classic Jekyll and Hyde. Neither side acknowledged the other, and one was as wonderful as the other was disturbed. Even his appearance changed. When he was sober his face would be soft and his eyes would twinkle merrily. He'd have a kind of sexy, mischievous radiance. But when he was drunk and belligerent, his eyes would widen to an unnatural size and stare blankly and his jaw would hang loosely. Wearing this strange mask, he would be in the middle of a rant – 'Bella, you are worthless' – and suddenly he'd snarl at me. There's no easy way to describe that snarl, but that's what it was: an animal's snarl. The skin on his face would bunch and twist up to the upper middle of his nose, his eyes would flash narrowly, and his mouth would turn down in a grimace. It would come from nowhere and in a lightning flash would be gone. The first time he did it I was utterly taken aback, and every time since then it had affected me like a snake bite. I think it was hatred, of himself. So much of it was bubbling away inside his skin that it spilled over onto his face without him having any control over it. When he was sober, his eyes would be clear and affectionate – and horrified, deeply sorrowful even, about the things he'd done.

I used to be so dismissive of the women I saw – strong, seemingly intelligent women – partnered to verbally or even physically abusive men. I couldn't understand how they stood for it. I could now, clearly. Apart from the drunken pockets of abuse, it was about increments. The abuse doesn't happen over-night, it is insidious: small put-downs, a smirk at a dress you are wearing, a comment on your weight. All seemingly negligible, so you let them pass. Like a lobster placed in a pot of cold water on the stove, you don't think anything is particularly wrong at first. But then the heat gets turned up. His insults become overt, he asserts more control, and in the face of ever-increasing arguments you give way to his demands to keep the peace. The lobster, by this time, is disjointed from the heat, and ready to be cooked.

My confidence had gradually been broken down. I felt con-fused a lot of the time, tense, waiting. I was vigilant around him, studying his moods like an animal sniffing out the forecast for the day.

If James was all bad, I would have been able to turn on my heels and leave, but just when I thought I couldn't bear it any longer, he'd flip back into the James that I knew.

Like that night, once he'd slept a little, he woke and began to rock back and forth, his wild eyes full of pain, his cheeks wet and swollen. 'I did it again, I did it again.' He looked like a little boy, scared shitless, panicked, guilty, hurting. 'I hate myself, I'm so sorry! What can I do?' he pleaded. He began to pace, then began to punch at himself, at his chest, at his temples and at his eye sockets, pulling at his hair as he swiped his forearm through the shelves, making everything smash to the floor.

Comforting him wouldn't work. I had to try something more drastic. I used a visualisation that Ron had used once. I told him he was drowning in a river. A river of self-loathing. Alcohol was a rotten, poisoned log that he clung to, enabling him to momen-tarily lift his head above the river of self-hate. But the more he grasped the poisoned log, the more the poison would seep into his skin.

It was a bleak and awful analogy but his eyes became child-like and alive and I knew it was sinking in.

'I have no hope,' he said like a boy.

I took him back to the visualisation and told him that on the furthest bank of the river, he could see a small pinprick of light. He nodded.

'That's hope. You can see it does exist. It is just small right now, frail. It needs to be strengthened. Only you can do that.' I told him to imagine that pinprick of light as his future, happy, alive, without the crutch of alcohol. To imagine it getting bigger and brighter.

James nodded. This time *he* brought up going to rehab and said he would do it; he would book in. He went to sleep it off in the other room. I knew that in the morning he'd wake inside that river of hate, but I hoped he wouldn't forget the light waiting for him.

11

Digging for happiness through alcoholism and the swirly swirly carpet (or how I learned to stop worrying and love my chicken drumstick)

O NE DAY IN CLASS, the Guru singled me out.

'Bella, you have trouble receiving,' he said as he studied my face.

'What do you mean?' I asked slowly.

'You're a warm-hearted giver, but you have trouble receiving from others.' He stopped and thought about it. 'It gives you pain,' he concluded.

I looked at him blankly.

'You don't open up very easily because you're afraid of being hurt. Somebody hurt you.'

'Yep,' I laughed, 'an older sister with a harder right hook than mine.'

'Perhaps.' He smiled. 'You're afraid of attention being on you, you're afraid of receiving attention.'

'Not a very good look for an actor, huh?'

He gave me one of his searching looks. 'You probably give

to others because it makes you happy, yes?'

'I guess so –'

'And it also shifts focus off you, doesn't it?'

I looked at him, embarrassed somehow.

'You subconsciously deflect, any way you can. You use your intellect, your emotions, your body, to deflect attention away from you.'

I felt my nerve-endings writhe, the hairs on the back of my neck stiffen.

'Why would I do that?'

'Something made you feel you had to and your body has hard-wired that response into your brain, it has become habit.'

'So I'm fucked, doc?'

He looked at me in alarm.

Shit, I'd forgotten that Americans didn't generally curse. 'Shit, sorry,' I added.

He chose to ignore it.

'But it's not *you*, Bella,' he continued.

We looked at each other in silence and I felt my mind being pierced by him.

'So, what should I do?' I asked.

He looked at me for a long time. His soft grey-blue gaze resting on me made me feel like crying. I felt vulnerable and scared and excited. Amongst all these emotions I felt immensely grateful. Here was this incredible stranger helping me, teaching me about myself, when I couldn't.

'You begin now,' he said. 'Don't worry about going back and analysing your past.'

I nodded.

'Begin now. From this day onward, simply embrace and receive. Not just people, but places and things and thoughts. Don't block anything out. Try talking about yourself even when the listener is not attentive. Practise. You deserve to be heard and felt. Don't shy away from it.'

Even though I had a sneaking suspicion he had just called me boring, I felt like the sun had dried the scales on my eyes so that the silvery edges had curled up and exposed me.

I was deeply thankful for his interest in me and I wanted to return the favour. To both our amusement, I offered to exchange skills and edit his new novel for him.

'You're deflecting again, Bella,' he said as his eyes twinkled. 'But yeah, that would be great,' he added.

ıılılılılı

After Ron's class, I took a short-cut home through a shopping mart, my thoughts about his words and my life thrashing about inside. I looked up out of my reverie and saw a woman staring at me with deep concern. My face was the betrayer. Everything was written on it. I felt so thin-skinned sometimes, as though my innermost thoughts and secret emotions were etched in neon and flashing across my features for everybody to see. It made me feel raw and vulnerable and, right then, scared. I puckered my face into a smooth-straight mask and went out onto the street with my protection firmly in place.

I realised I felt scared of opening my heart. Of being hurt by somebody, of being judged, of being found wanting. I knew the feeling of exposed flesh. Images of James' face swam out at me from my confusion. Of a hot, soft heart, like the underbelly of an animal, all softness and vulnerability until the attack. Your protector's licks become the predator's teeth ripping into the most sensitive parts of you. But you eventually heal. Then, that stubborn human need for connection, for the ecstasy of love and acceptance, grows in your belly and forces you to open up again with stubborn hope. Perhaps the joy lasts a little, perhaps a lot.

All the while, the teeth are sharpening their inevitable points. Again and again, the cycle continues. Eventually it takes longer to heal. Soon I would become more hesitant to open up – but still, still, that damned unearthly desire for submission to love would make me yield again, like a bruised limb rising to the challenge and bracing itself against the coming blows.

In all my ten million or so relationships, I'd never thought as negatively as this before. I was aware that something was beginning to change in me and I didn't like where it was going.

ııılıılılılı

The time for my birthday came around. I'd organised a dinner with friends at our house for the first Friday night after the actual day, as I had class that evening. But when I got home from school, James was all dressed up in his tuxedo.

'Are we going somewhere?' I asked.

He regarded me sideways, then looked away. 'Well, actually, I can't invite you to this, ah, benefit tonight, it's a work thing.'

'I told you I had class anyway.' I looked at him. 'You do remember it's my birthday today though, don't you?'

'Yes, I know darling, sorry. I'll make it up to you.'

'Fine,' I answered, silently wishing he'd fall down the stairs.

I walked down Broadway to get an early dinner: pecan and caramel ice-cream. I practised 'embracing, accepting and receiving'. I felt like a dick.

That evening I went to class and Hugh and I did the scene from *Loose Knit* again for Robert Castle. Robert had accidentally-on-purpose forgotten to critique my last horrendous falling-off-the-stage experience, so I was feeling kindly towards him. I had prepared like a bat outta hell, gotten into character hours before, visualised the scene, did relaxation and Sense Memory exercises and planned on staying well away from the edge of the stage. I was terrified beyond words. I thought I had got over feeling anxiety before a performance, but evidently not. I walked onto the stage and could see my hands shaking with the ferocity of a boat's sail in a gale. Despite the Parkinson's thing, the scene felt good, and soon enough the lights dimmed and it was over. Then, there was an unnerving silence.

Robert regarded me for a long time. His expression was a mixture of intense concentration, doubt and excitement.

He opened his mouth to speak and I felt my stomach plunge.

But he closed his mouth again. Then he began to furrow his brow with concentration once more. After what felt like a year of silence, he finally spoke.

'I don't know if you stumbled onto that, or if you're an exceptionally talented actor,' he said.

Exceptionally talented actor. Exceptionally talented actor.

He regarded me seriously again. 'Too soon to decide,' he said at last. Then he looked around. 'Next scene!' he yelled at the classroom.

ılılılılı

James arrived home from his benefit in the early hours as the grey dawn began to smother the city. He was trashed like I'd never seen him before. I was asleep wearing a pair of pink flannel pyjamas when he came in.

He crashed into the room and ripped the blankets off me.

'What the hell are you wearing?' he yelled, wobbling precariously. 'You don't even look after yourself!'

I snatched my blanket back from his hands, but he lost his balance and fell into a heap on the bed.

'You bitch,' he roared as he lunged towards me.

I jumped out of bed and ran up the stairs to the sitting room.

He followed me and started yelling abuse. I tried pleading with him, threatening him, appeasing him, yelling back at him. Nothing worked. It was like trying to control a tornado. I made my way back to the bedroom and slammed the door behind me.

Then I heard him pounding down the stairs. I reached for the lock and turned it. There was a tremendous banging against the door. He was throwing himself against it like a wild animal, screaming and yelling for me to open it up. He started trying to kick the door down. I didn't know what to do. It felt like I was in the middle of a nightmare with my legs stubbornly refusing to run.

'James! James! Stop. I'm going to open the door. But only if you calm down, okay?'

I opened the door and he fell into the room and landed spread-eagled on the carpet. He writhed a little then abruptly fell asleep on the floor.

I tiptoed around him and went back into the sitting room to try to steady my shakes. I had become so exhausted, both emotionally and physically, that I didn't even have the energy to be afraid any more. I had to leave him. I walked back into the bedroom, into my closet and grabbed a few of my clothes. I didn't know where I would go, what I would do, or where I would stay for the rest of the night even. He woke up as I was packing and began to plead like a wronged little boy. His knees sank into the carpet and he begged me not to go. He punched his head with his fist and yelled that he despised himself. Then he got up and blocked the front door and said he would hurt himself if I left. I stood there in the hallway with my bags packed and looked at this pleading man in front of me prostrating himself against the door. Everything around me slowed down to half-speed. I was an island and James, the walls, the carpet, were all a swirling mass of colours and movement. My vision blurred and I couldn't move. All my energy, all my thoughts, my heart drained out of me into the swirling carpet. I laid my bags down and with blank eyes moved into the living room and went to sleep on the sofa.

Later in the day I woke with the same deadened apathy I'd experienced earlier. My body felt like a monolithic monster; my arms and legs like they were being pulled down by an invisible current and I couldn't move them. Thoughts tried to form themselves but this strange and drugged dullness obscured everything. A spark of fear lit up somewhere deep inside. When I looked around, I noticed that James had cleaned the apartment and he was sitting on a chair facing me.

'I'm going to go into Alcoholics Anonymous,' he said. 'I know I have to and I'm prepared to do it, if you can be with me.' Tears started to splash down his cheeks. 'I'm so fucking sorry,' he said, as the tears began to rush down his face.

I looked at him. 'I want to help you. But you have to understand. I don't have any fight left in me, James. This will have to be it because I just can't do it any more.'

'I know it,' he said. 'It's all I can think about. I can't lose us, Bella. I can't,' he continued as a fresh river of tears streamed down his face. 'I see you look at me like the monster I am and I don't blame you. Because I am one,' he said with wild, teary eyes. 'I can't escape it, it's inside me, so I drink and then I fulfil my nature.' His eyes grew far away. 'I can beat it, Bella, I can.'

I could often detect a speck of deep pain dancing in the blue of James' eyes. When I looked at his eyes then, I could see that speck growing, ballooning and breaking out onto the surface, obscuring everything. He was finally facing his monster.

That day we logged on to the Johns Hopkins University website and did a test on alcoholism. If you answered yes to three out of the twenty questions you were classed an alcoholic.

James scored seventeen. I found a local AA meeting and booked him in. I compiled a list of rehabilitation clinics and we went through them together. I allowed myself to feel hopeful. That day, when my mum called to say hello I told her the truth. I hadn't told many people about James' behaviour. I don't exactly know why – perhaps through some screwed-up sense of protecting him, maybe pride. I hadn't told Rosie as it would just cause her to impotently worry, but now I had something hopeful to tell her. It was an immense relief to get it off my chest and she handled it so amazingly well that I wished I'd been more open with her before.

The next day was Friday, my faux birthday. A friend of mine from Sydney, Chris, a fellow actor with a chiselled jaw, piercing blue eyes and ridiculously white teeth had been staying with James and me, and we'd been traipsing New York together as we plotted and hatched our actorly dreams. That night Chris and I set to work cooking a delicious spaghetti bolognaise with fresh herbs and bought crusty French bread and good red wine. Twelve of my friends came over to the apartment and we sat around laughing and eating. It was a window of relief from the last few days. At one stage during the night I looked around for James but he had disappeared. I found him in his study with a cup of tea and a scared face.

'What are you doing in here?'

'I can't go out there. I can't socialise without alcohol, Bella.'

'No worries. Let's just tell them to go and we'll go watch a movie,' I said, offering him my hand.

'No, go out there and have fun, it's your birthday. Really,' he said, as he took my hand and led me back into the sitting room.

After dessert, James and the rest of us hired some cars that whisked us away into the gleaming city to continue the celebrations. We ended up, through a friend's invite, at a Russian bathhouse on Fulton Street, down in the Financial District. By day it was an innocuous-looking day spa; at night it turned into a debauched playground. Inside, there was a full-length heated swimming pool packed with drenched party-goers, a sauna jammed with fleshy, raucously sloshed Russians, a tanning room that doubled as a coke room, and 'the Backroom'.

The others were kicking on into the next day but I could see James was beginning to become agitated so I took him home. We collapsed into our bed and lay entwined in each other's arms until the lights dimmed and morning arrived. As I lay in the crook of his arm, I felt his body trembling and sweating and I stroked the wet hair from his forehead as he mumbled in his sleep. I stayed with James over the next few days as his body detoxified. I hired funny movies and he tried valiantly to laugh his way through them. I ordered food and he struggled to keep it down. I could see the energy it took out of him; his strained eyes and hound-dog expression. But he didn't drink. A softness came back into his face and I felt myself slipping back into the warm waters of his company. But soon enough I had to return to school.

When I got home later that day though, I saw that the apartment was a total shambles and James was slumped at the table. He looked up at me as I entered. His eyes had that vicious drunken look again. I figured we were in for a long night.

I asked him fearfully if he still intended to check into the rehab clinic.

His face turned dark and he sneered.

'It has nothing to do with you. You call me a monster and I'm supposed to just accept that! You drive me to drink! Look at you, your face all ugly and stupid-looking like a slave. Who the fuck are *you* to ask this of *me*?' He looked at me unsteadily, projecting with all his damaged might.

I saw his expression and knew instinctively that this face was a part of him now. Stopping drinking for a few days would never change that.

'Who the hell do you think you are, huh? Mother Teresa? You think you can save the world, starting with me?' he asked, needling me deeper. 'It's none of your business, you hear me?'

After months of all the peacekeeping, the fear, the relenting and denial, something in me finally snapped.

'Yes!' I yelled. 'It is my business! Don't you know how much this is affecting me? Don't you even know!' I was screaming so much, I could feel the whistle of air through my clenched throat as it tried to open and vomit out the words.

I broke. I finally broke. Adrenaline surged through me and I began shaking violently. I didn't know what was happening to me. I had to keep my hands moving or else this black lake of emotion would rise up and consume me. I grabbed my bags and started jamming my clothes and books in. I broke. I just broke. I was shaking and crying like a mad woman, blinded by emotion – emotion that I had pushed down for months. It was exploding inside me and all around. I couldn't control it. I couldn't stop moving. It hurt, deep and unrelenting, and it was finally coming out.

With my face and neck wet with tears, the words began coming out. I looked him straight in the eye and tried to make him see. 'It affects me, James. It *affects* me. It *affects* me . . . James, *it affects me.*' I felt like a robot stuck on that one sentence, but everything was jammed into that sentence. All of my hurt pumped into that one sentence. 'It affects me, James. I cannot do it any more. I don't know who you are any more.' I could see he wasn't listening. '*It affects me, James.*'

As I was saying it, it was becoming clearer and clearer to me that it was the undeniable truth. I wasn't immune, as I had thought; I didn't have it under control; it was affecting me badly, all of it. His alcoholism, the constant changes, my foolhardy hope, my deteriorating self-esteem, my attempts at denying it all.

But his eyes were dead and drunk. There was no compassion there, no glimmer of understanding.

'It's none of your business, you stupid thing. Look at how you're acting!'

I felt all the rage drain out of me.

'It is my business, James, don't you see?' But they were empty words, a part of our diseased ritual. I realised I didn't need to convince him, I had already convinced myself.

He seemed to sense this change in me. 'If you leave me, you will never be anything,' he said.

Another surge of adrenaline pumped through my body. I felt the familiar closing of myself. Protective shields up. I don't know why, but I walked into the bathroom and took up a hairbrush to stop my hands shaking and began slowly brushing my hair. I was in some sort of a daze, shut down like a burnt-out computer. James came up behind me and watched me in the mirror as I pulled the brush through my tangles. He smiled and said, as was his game, 'It's no use. You'll always look the way you do.'

I became strangely calm. I had heard it before, but this time was different. The truth of my realisation was cut somewhere primitive inside me. With this last whack the tree was freefalling. I turned to him and said in a monotone, 'It's over.'

He blinked. Then came at me with such vicious intention that I pushed my arms out to fend him off.

'Chris, Chris!' I yelled at the guest bedroom door, behind which my sheepish friend had hidden himself away during the whole thing.

James moved closer to me, like a boxer, circling.

'Chris! Please!' I yelled at the closed door.

In that second, I understood both Chris and James with blinding clarity. James was in so much pain that anything was possible, and Chris . . . Chris, I discovered, was a coward.

Chris peeked out.

'I don't want to be involved,' he said.

James looked at me, then at Chris and back again. His face stretched in a kind of sudden realisation.

'I get it! You two are trying to rob me! I hit her and you are her witness,' he yelled accusingly at Chris. 'Then you take me to the High Court and sue me for all my money! No, no, no. I'll say she hit *me*! I know what you're up to, you've been planning this for years. I won't have it, I tell you! I won't have it!' Spit was flying from his mouth as he screamed.

I didn't know whether I should call an ambulance or not. Was it an alcohol-induced psychosis? Maybe he was on drugs? It felt like my brain was going to explode.

I don't clearly remember what happened next; I was dazed and confused. Angry, scared and numb all at the same time. I grabbed my bags. James was pleading and threatening somewhere in the background. I heard the front door close behind me.

Out on the footpath, as I tried to stop the shaking and waited for Chris to catch up, I took in the situation. What was I going to do? I had nowhere to live, I didn't know where I would sleep, and had only a few clothes with me. I looked down at my hands, and for some inexplicable reason I was holding a roasted chicken drumstick.

New York gleamed up before me and suddenly I felt a jolt of wellbeing, like a moment of sunlight in the middle of a vicious storm. I looked around at the glowing city and felt a soothing kindness emanating from the buildings and the streets themselves. New York has that quality; you can be down on your knees but the city always seems to be there for you, ready to pick you up again. Standing under a street lamp with my chicken drumstick, I was touched by its magic.

When Chris arrived red-faced, I gave him some of my chicken drumstick and we hurried up Fulton Street towards the subway station. After we had been walking for a while I glanced across at him. He had a panicked look on his face and the chicken drumstick was bunching out his cheeks and sticking out at odd angles from the corners of his mouth. He returned my look and, with surprise, we both burst into gales of nervous hyena-like laughter, chicken spraying everywhere. It was a necessary release from the all-consuming stress of the night. Here I was, in New York City, hurrying like a fugitive from a crazed millionaire, my friend and I stuffing chicken into our panicked faces as we stumbled under the weight of hastily packed odds and ends. Life truly was utterly ridiculous.

12

Homeless and hating men (except Quentin Tarantino)

WITH NEXT TO NO money, Chris and I made our way to the Hotel Devon on West 94th Street to share a room. It was only a couple of metres wide and contained a double bed, a cranky old heater and a vase with an imitation flower sticking defiantly out of it.

My friend Eleanor came over to comfort me. She painted my nails and sang show tunes off-key to try to cheer me up. Eleanor and Chris had been seeing each other for a week already, and after a while I began to notice they were looking horny and frustrated. Although I wasn't excited about the prospect of wet sheets, I offered to take an abnormally long shower in the bathroom down the corridor while they resolved their lust. A shy but excited 'Yes please' came from them both. After I was waterlogged to near hypothermia and I couldn't find a spot on my body that wasn't polished to a shine, I dried off and went back to the room. I heard a crescendo of screams emanating from behind the door so I withdrew to the corridor and read and reread the back of the shampoo bottle until the noises subsided. I crept up and pressed my ear against the door. It seemed silent. Then, two things happened at once. Eleanor let out a soprano orgasm while Chris grunted in tenor – and our neighbour came out of his room and spotted me pressed up against the door listening to two people coming in unison behind it. He stared at me horrified for a few seconds as my jaw dropped to the ground. Then he turned on his heels and marched back into his room, slamming the door behind him. I slapped myself on the back. I was now officially the resident pervert of the Hotel Devon.

The next day, Eleanor and I talked all morning snuggled up in bed eating chocolate while Chris sat on the carpet at the end of the bed doing his usual meditational granola chanting. It was an enormous relief to talk about what had happened. Only the powerful desire for a greasy breakfast (and a respite from Chris' chanting) motivated us to drag ourselves outside into the freezing cold.

I spent the rest of the day with Eleanor; it was a balm to forget what had just happened and what I had to do. Back at the hotel, I began to stress about the coming week, about classes, where I was to live and what James was doing. As the reality of the situation bore down upon me, I felt constantly on the verge of tears, frustrated, scared.

Chris looked at me as if I were an idiot and told me to stop being so stressed because it was interrupting his chanting. I remembered his cowardice in the apartment and shuddered. I told him he was being insensitive and from there we got into a row.

I tried to bring an end to it. 'Chris, we're both tired and stressed, so why don't we just take it easy and not make it worse, yeah?'

'Fuck off. Just don't talk to me. Just because you're going through a hard time, it doesn't mean you have to take it out on me.'

I looked at him, stunned.

'Please, Chris, not you too. For god's sake, please don't.' I was aware I sounded like a soapy actor but it was all I had left in me.

He repeated it. 'Don't talk to me.'

'We can't spend the evening ignoring each other in our tiny cupboard, the wallpaper will melt off.'

'I don't care what you have to say. Just don't talk to me.' Hostility was emanating from his face like a chemical.

I realised in a flash that it was because I was no use to him any more. I didn't have a place for him to stay, or free food he could eat. People had said that about Chris but I'd always stood up for him. Silly me.

Eleanor looked at Chris horrified, as though he were some strange and disgusting bug she'd just stepped on. As we packed the last of my bags, Chris raised his eyebrows suggestively and asked Eleanor if she would stay with him at the hotel that night. I guess you had to give him credit for trying. She looked at him as though he were a bug again. We gathered up my belongings and hightailed it out of there – although not before we'd cancelled his use of my credit card at the hotel.

We got on the subway to Brooklyn, where I was going to spend a few nights with Eleanor and Ben. There was an old black woman in a green hat sitting opposite me. I watched her kind old weathered face staring pensively off into space. A thought flashed through her eyes, then with quick, birdlike movements, she turned to her husband sitting next to her and kissed him lovingly on the cheek. Such a beautiful and unexpected display of love. I felt a burden lift off my shoulders, off my heart. I felt my brain clearing and becoming sharp and alive. I caught the smiling eyes of the old woman and felt our connection. With every rattle of the train taking me further away from the world that I knew, I believed that I had made the right decision.

ılıllıllılı

Eleanor and Ben were living in a tiny cheap room in the Brooklyn YMCA, a kind of halfway house for nutters and drug dealers. It had thin walls and syringes lined the old carpets in the hallways, but their room was filled with empty beer bottles and kindness. I pretended I was a drug dealer. Fun for about half an hour. My phone rang. It was Zoë.

'Dude, Quentin loved your headshot, and, wait for it, he said he really wants to meet you. He'll audition you for Abernathy, one of the kick-ass chicks. Said it didn't matter about your Aussie accent, he could work with it.'

So there I was, four months into my New York experience, a relationship in ruins, homeless, with a chance to star in a Tarantino film. I felt strangely hopeful.

The next night we raided a two-dollar store for popcorn, chocolate and Sierra Mist to take to the YMCA Oscar party. We got into our pyjamas, ordered pizza and watched the glitz and glamour as the crazies hollered and mumbled to themselves in the hall outside our door.

After the awards, the news came on. A few days earlier a young graduate student who had been partying in Soho had been abducted, raped, strangled and found dumped in Brooklyn. There were no new leads. Then some live coverage started: two women had just been stabbed in their sleep about ten minutes down the road from where we sat, frozen to the TV. Another woman had just been fatally injured in a hit-and-run in outer Brooklyn. The borough seemed to be caving in on itself.

We slept side by side on two single beds pushed together, all three of us twisted into bizarre shapes as the TV rattled to itself and the world outside fed on itself and its wards.

I spent the following week or so crashing on friends' sofas and feeling utterly fusty. My socks were as stiff as my drinks and smelled like a public toilet. My undies were in emergency mode and I was so dosed up on deodorant my armpits smelled like a sickly florist. I caught a subway to Hugh's house to rehearse our new scene. He lived in a beautiful apartment on East 90th Street, with elegant rugs and trimmings. He asked me to take my shoes off as I entered. We both pretended there was no dead animal in the room.

I tried to fight through my feelings about James. He'd been my best friend and his absence created a void that made me feel stranded and not sure what to do with my hands. I couldn't reconcile loving one side of him as much as I did and loathing the other half just as passionately. Most of the time I punched thoughts of him from my mind like one of those hole-punchers. It felt too dangerous to think about it, about me and him, what we had become.

And I was beginning to feel the stress. I had nowhere to live, had been wearing the same clothes for days, was washing my underwear in the sink, had put on weight, had to choose my classes for next term, was stressed about the Tarantino audition, the ATM only gave me half my money, it was snowing a blizzard, my mother was sick, my father hadn't telephoned me when he said he would, I had an assessment due at Strasberg, a scene due the next day with Robert that I had only just been given, and James was constantly circling inside my head like some malevolent carrion-eating bird. Fuck bum shit. Then, to top it all off, I received a trumped-up bill for two thousand dollars for the hire of a mobile phone that I'd hired for just one month. I thought fondly of going around to Rentacell and putting strychnine in their water fountains. I probably made twenty (short!) calls in the period, but they'd tacked on extra hidden costs in taxes, levies and provisions. I had been scammed badly and had to buckle my belt and downgrade to 59-cent sardines instead of the more lavish $1.25 cans.

I was struggling through my days exhausted because at night I found myself unable to sleep. My head would come alive with thoughts of James, Strasberg, apartment hunting, money – or lack of it – the murdered graduate student, rehearsals, life. The next day I would crawl out of whatever bed I'd been in the night before, my *One Hundred Years of Solitude* insomnia pulling curtains over my senses. Late, and in a haze, I would grab the clothes nearest to me and pull my hair back into a messy ponytail. Dag central. On the street the well-dressed matrons would flick their eyes at me and find me wanting. I went to school in this unkempt state and got embarrassed stares and subtle ignorings. My mismatched socks were glared at. Sometimes, though, I rallied myself, looking crap could be a good thing: you can blend into the background and become invisible and watch the world like you are its only audience, witnessing its secret and fascinating games. (I got that off the back of a cereal box.)

Growing fairly tired of wearing the same clothes and trying to find life solutions on the back of other people's Coco Pops cartons, I figured I'd better try to find a place of my own. People had been scaring me with hellish stories of apartment hunting in New York City. A girlfriend of mine said it took her three months to find a place even bordering on appropriate. Factors such as location, cost, broker's fees and flatmates all came into play. Gian-Luca paid four thousand dollars upfront to a broker to find an apartment. Another friend paid a six-thousand-dollar fee to a broker to secure a rent-controlled apartment, which he insisted would work out cheaper in the long run. I used the infallible Craigslist. Finding the room I did was a stroke of luck, as it was the first place I saw – and ended up being much, much more than a place to live.

It was a room in a two-bedroom apartment in the East Village and had been advertised by a nice and rather handsome Israeli named Axel. The place was a little run-down and my room was small, but the energy was good and my new room had two tall windows that flooded the floorboards with winter sun. We bargained on the price and decided to split the two-thousand-dollar rent right down the middle. I handed over my deposit and felt a flood of relief: a new adventure was about to begin, but this time it would be on my terms.

13

Immersed in Strasberg, a fern named Bob, my first NY film (and bums and chocolate. Don't ask. Yet.)

OVERNIGHT I SEEMED TO transform into Happy Smurf. I was in my little 1920s walk-up brownstone apartment only ten minutes from Strasberg, on a tree-lined street crowded with Indian restaurants. I could concentrate on Strasberg and I could breathe again – despite the chicken tikka masala wafting in through the windows. To get to the apartment you had to walk up thirty-four chipped stone steps and along a graffitied hallway and the woman upstairs woke every morning at five and emptied her chest of phlegm for the next thirty minutes. She sounded like a rattlesnake with a cold, and each morning I was convinced it would be her last. But I had my own room, and the perfect mix of location, company and privacy. The apartment had polished wooden floorboards and was decorated for a bachelor, with overflowing ashtrays, a faux leather couch, La-Z-Boy chair, a huge TV and no paintings or prints on the wall. Ah, the bareness of men. A cave, designed for function not form. I was ready and willing to lift my leg and make it my own.

Up the road was the infamous Coyote Ugly, as well as Polish bakeries, colourful flower shops spilling onto the sidewalks, swish sushi bars, old-school pubs, cool chic bars, funky tattoo parlours and underground video stores. There were hundreds of boutique restaurants too – Tibetan, Israeli, Ethiopian, Indian – with delicious smells emanating from behind their small, heated doorways. The East Village was truly the Mad Hatter's tea party, and I merged into the stream of crazies with relish.

My new flatmate, Axel, had arrived in New York from Israel two years ago to try his luck as a drummer in the indy music scene. He had deep chocolaty brown eyes fringed with long black lashes, white creamy skin and a straight nose that fitted perfectly onto his handsome face. He was over six foot four and his hands were big enough that mugs and cutlery seemed to disappear inside them. He was twenty-five years old, looked a sexy thirty, and acted like a naughty nineteen. Axel slept until late in the afternoon, when he left for his shift managing BB Kings, the blues bar at Times Square. I loved watching his retreating figure, and not only because he had a fine ass, but because I got the privacy I'd been yearning for.

I felt stronger by the day as the inordinate amount of joy I got from buying a small house plant (named Bob), or finding bright red sheets for my comfy bed, became balm for my soul. Even though my lack of self-confidence still paper-cut itself through me at times, I could sense that I was at last beginning the process of healing after James and was on my way to becoming sane again.

ıılılılılılı

One of my favourite people at Strasberg was a German student named Tom Schilling. He was a tiny, handsome man with

serious blue eyes and a deep plentiful laugh. I thought he was
the most talented actor there. He was shy as hell until you got to
know him, but once you did, he would open up like a butterfly
and you'd bask in his crazy humour, smarts and affectionate
nature. He had made a film in Germany and won a Best Actor
award for his performance; part of his prize was a three-month
scholarship to Strasberg. I liked Tom immensely and we soon
became good friends.

One evening he came back to my apartment to rehearse a
scene. He entered and looked around doubtfully.

'Well, it's . . . so shall we start?' he stammered.

'I know it's a slum, but it's my slum!' I laughed.

We rehearsed for a few hours and stopped to make some food.
The heating wasn't working, so I was dressed in my snow coat,
gloves and scarf, trying to unhook the pull ring off a sardine can
as I measured out equal amounts of Sprite into cracked mugs. I
stopped mid-pour as my current situation sank in. I turned to
look at Tom and his amused eyes confirmed it. We burst out
laughing; the kind that escalates and hurts until you are bent
over and have something coming out your nose. From my luxurious apartment and penchant for Dom, to this battle of the
sardine tin. A bubble of joy rose in my stomach and splashed
onto my face in a wide grin.

'I love it,' I grinned.

'I know,' Tom nodded, smiling.

ıılılılılılı

In a Tai Chi class soon after I moved to the East Village I told
Ron that I wouldn't be doing any physical movement that day
because of a sore back I had from my couch-surfing days. He said
that visualisation was the key to curing my pain. He told the class
about the Dalai Lama's personal doctor: the Dalai Doctor, or

the DD for short. As an example of the power of focus and how emotion affects the body, the DD staged an experiment where he would diagnose a patient just by looking at them and literally reading them. The regular doctors collectively rolled their eyes. After an hour spent looking into the patient's eyes, he pronounced his diagnosis: 'She's thirty-five years old, her relationship with her parents is passive–aggressive, she used to have kidney disease then was cured, and the cancer in her spine is spreading.'

And he was completely correct.

Ron said that DD had an incredibly defined sense of focus and an understanding of how the body is affected by our emotions and daily lives. He said it wasn't 'hocus pocus', but simply tapping in to how it is and how it has always been.

I asked the Guru how one got into 'Tai Chi II' and he looked at me and smiled.

'It's by invitation only.'

I stood there smiling like an idiot. 'Will we also learn how to fly?' I said, before I realised I was speaking aloud.

'What?'

'Reading people's thoughts, levitating – same ball park, right?'

He looked at me.

'Funny-joke-har-har?' I offered.

'I don't think you're ready for Tai Chi II yet, Bella.'

Damn.

I had a new life goal. I would get into Tai Chi II and learn how to read people's thoughts (and possibly levitate) if it killed me, or any number of innocent bystanders.

ıılılılılı

In the next class Ron told us that we all have inbuilt defence mechanisms originating from childhood and we had to discover what they were to better understand ourselves. One guy in the class said his defence mechanism was to laugh things away; another girl said she would get angry. I wasn't sure what mine was, I figured it was probably eating illegal quantities of chocolate, but wasn't sure.

James was calling and emailing me quite a bit, but I still would have preferred to play contact sport with a Rottweiler than actually have to talk to him. I understood then what my defence mechanism was: to cut off. To deny. To ignore the problem by not thinking or talking about it. I was, as my mum would say, a 'bottler'. I would deny, deny, deny that anything was wrong then when my denial pot was full, I'd explode at the least appropriate time. Very healthy stuff.

When I finally returned one of his emails to arrange a time to pick up the rest of my things, he sent me an email saying he was at the country house and would reply when he returned. So much of me wanted to entirely forget that relationship. Him and the person I'd become. I wanted to isolate it in my brain, freeze-dry it, chop it out and use it as a doorstop or something. Then go sailing on the Riviera. Not that I was in denial or anything.

Mmm, the Riviera.

Something else we learned at school around this time, in Robert Castle's class, had a big impact on me: a bizarre exercise called Affective Memory. It was the only technique developed by Strasberg that was primarily concerned with making you cry like a baby. You were supposed to go back to the worst part of your life, relive it sensorially, then use those high salient emotions for your scene. Robert's version of the exercise was to remember a time in your life three or more years ago when somebody betrayed you. It could be a big betrayal or a small one.

'Go back to that time and see the time of day and time of year,' he instructed the class.

Hmm. Okay, easy enough: a small one. I shut my eyes and

envisioned myself with a former lover who confessed he'd kissed an ex-girlfriend of his when we first began to date.

'Look around at the environment. There is a smell in the room, perhaps of the person, or the food you were eating at the time. Smell it. Remember it and keep smelling it. Stay with that for a while, then concentrate on taste. It could be the food or beverage you had at the time, or just the metallic zing of fear. Feel that taste in your mouth: does it pucker your mouth, feel smooth? Next, concentrate on the sounds around you. Traffic? Ocean? The voice of the person?'

I smelled the dusty, fruity-smelling furniture of the country inn that he'd confessed in, but nothing came up. I tasted the tannin-y old red wine we'd been drinking. Nothing. I heard the whip-crack of the whipbird in the bush in the background and his smooth low voice as he told me. Nope. Still nothing. Cool. I reckoned that I wasn't affected by the memory as it was so long ago; I'd already dealt with it like a sensible mature adult and moved on. Ha! I was ready to smugly sit there as the class erupted in a maddening disharmony of crying. Until I got to 'touch'. Robert stood in front of me and said, 'Touch him.'

I imagined touching him.

'No, Bella, use your hands.'

I reached out and touched my ex's wrist. I felt his warm, soft skin and the little golden hairs on his arm. Then something shifted inside me – and I abruptly erupted into a deluge of tears. And I couldn't stop them; they came from somewhere deep and primal and I joined the hysterical sobs of my other classmates. Cuckoo Land, I had arrived.

If something years ago could still affect me that much, per-haps I had to be more attentive to my recent unhappiness, to stop those bad emotions from congealing inside me and living in my body for years to come.

When I got home I sat on the sofa and felt the familiar thoughts of James rise in my head, and then the familiar banishing process. But this time I made myself go there. Suddenly, there came a startling range of emotions: fear and anger and confusion and hurt and regret and sadness and love. It felt like an explosion, like a train smashing into a building, like a bullet biting into wood. I understood then that my denial had given these emotions superhuman strength, and the more I'd stopped myself thinking of James and the situation, the more fuel I had given them.

Afterwards, I was released in a way that was wholly new to me. Like I'd literally purged the demons from inside me and could see them dancing and grimacing as they dissolved with shrieks into the air. A huge weight that I hadn't even acknowledged existed drained from me and left me feeling lighter, stronger. Less wet. The matchsticks holding up my eyelids were kicked out, and I was awake.

Not that it lasted long.

ılıllıllılı

The next week I had to perform again for Robert Castle and was nervous as hell. I sat down next to Gian-Luca and tried not to whimper. Gian-Luca patted my hair and my arm without speaking. He showed such genuine unaffected closeness, compassion and understanding that my dread slipped away into the air. I adored his maleness, his tender maleness. Friendship like that seems to be something you can never find if you search for it; it will find you only in the best moments. I punched him in the arm to return the affection.

The scene I was to do was from *Waiting for Leftie* by Clifford Odets. I played the impassioned Edna, who encourages her husband to go on strike. When I finished the scene, my classmates said they liked it but Robert wasn't quite so forthcoming.

He said I 'carried too much tension in my shoulders' and was somewhat 'commercial'. I didn't know what the hell he meant by 'commercial' but I resolved to think badly of him just in case. But, as I made a small effigy of him in my mind, I thought at least I didn't fall off the stage. Or set fire to something. Or curse. In fact, looking at it that way, it was a total success.

That same afternoon I had the fabulous Tim Crouse for Film and TV class. He set up a simple scenario for me to perform. Having broken up with my lover three weeks ago, I've just arrived home after having a brute of a day. Then the realisation dawns on me that I have put the past to rest and can happily move on. It sounded pretty familiar. I loved being back in front of the camera, I felt instantly at ease, back on home turf where I knew my way around and what the hell I was doing. After class I asked Tim what 'commercial' meant. He didn't know either. But he did say he was impressed with my scene in front of the camera.

'Thanks, Tim,' I said gratefully. 'I was kinda working from personal experience.'

'I gathered that,' he replied, his eyes soft.

Well, that was one positive about the whole James thing: it was making me a better actor.

It was funny, though: after Robert's comments I was feeling unhappy, confused and frustrated; after Tim's comments I was feeling enthused, excited and proud. It was completely pathetic. I wished I had a strong sense of self like others seemed to. I was so easily crushed by Robert and so easily lifted up by Tim that day, even I could see how ridiculous I was.

ılıllılıı

When I got home, I opened a beer, cut my hand, put a wad of toilet paper on it and slumped down onto the sofa. Then my friends bashed on the door.

'Chick! Let's go get smashed,' yelled Eleanor through the door.

'I don't get "smashed". I get "tiddly",' I yelled back unconvincingly.

'Whatever. Let's go.'

Like in the movie, bras and panties lined the walls of Coyote Ugly, like a colourful seedy brothel. Twenty-one-year-old birthday girls with three-inch cork heels kissed each other while their boyfriends stood around smiling nervously. They jumped on top of the bar and gyrated to early Madonna as their menfolk affected relaxed postures and hard pricks. We left and tried to find Karma, an infamous joint where you can still smoke cigarettes, but Ben was sulking from earlier in the evening when we'd made him eat a raw onion to atone for the sins of all mankind, so I went back to my apartment to watch Ali G instead.

At two am Axel arrived home from work. He appeared in my doorway to chat, as was his habit, leaning like a cowboy against the door frame. I looked up at him and realised there was something new in the way he looked at me from beneath his beautiful black eyelashes. Gulp. I felt a strange prickling sensation coming from the lower regions of my body. Oh hell. No, no, it was probably just my unwashed pyjama pants. I looked down at them, at the bright pink flannel pants with garish red dots interspersed with food stains. I looked like a bag lady. We only really saw each other early in the morning when he got home from work, and I was always looking like crap. I don't know why that bugged me, but it had begun to. I looked up at him. Who was I kidding? Damn, he was ridiculously good-looking. Anybody with skin that could goose-bump would be attracted to this six-foot model-esque man with big sensuous hands and a stunningly svelte body. 'Nooooo!'

'Did I just say that out loud?'

'Yes,' he answered with a confused smile.

Once he'd gone back to his own room, I phoned Rene to get advice.

'Babe, I've just escaped from a relationship, I'm committed to my I-hate-men phase and I know you should never screw the crew, *and* not one single part of me wants another stupid relationship. There is not one single reason I should be getting excited about Axel!'

'Isn't that what you said about James too?'

'Damn.'

'Are you falling for him?'

'God no. He's twenty-five years old, he doesn't know the difference between a Republican and a Democrat and he thinks Manhattan is a country.'

'So? Then what?'

'He's heartbreakingly good-looking and makes me feel like a dirty old woman.'

'Bells, just repeat after me: "I, Bella, am here to study to become a kick-ass actor not to get into bed with a twenty-five-year-old and end up working at McDonald's barefoot and pregnant." '

'What if said twenty-five-year-old's ass was as irresistible as a karaoke mic after the second martini?'

'That tempting?'

'Yes, even more, like, like . . . a twenty-four-hour chocolate shop!'

'Asses and chocolate should never be used in the same sentence.'

We both shuddered in unison. 'Ew, not what I meant . . . okay, so what if I said twenty-five-year-old looks very, *very* good? Like Luke Gracey from high school kind of good?'

I could hear her brain clicking over. 'Good-looking, not very bright, thus good for one thing. Hmm. Well then, my dear, you are well and truly rooted. Enjoy it while you can.'

ıılıılılıılı

The next week, on my way home from class to meet Axel for our apartment 'cleaning day', my thoughts began to fondle him again. Damn. I bit down on the ice-cream cone I was eating to wake me up. But other than a dose of brain-freeze, it didn't seem to work very well.

In the apartment, Axel and I worked together in a slow dance amidst the bright dust mites and the smell of soap bubbles, and scrubbed the apartment from top to bottom. We cleaned the floors and surfaces to a bright wet sheen, rearranged the furniture and adorned the walls with photos and paintings. We then stood, hands on hips, surveying the damage. My suggestions of covering the doors in magazine cut-outs was met with laughter, but we managed to make the place into something we thought was 'cool and cosy'. Plus, I had got through the whole afternoon with only one ass-check-out. Things were on the up-and-up. The ice-cream torture must have had something to it, after all.

That evening, after Axel left for work, I went to see Cate Blanchett in the Sydney Theatre Company's production of *Hedda Gabler* at the BAM Theatre in Brooklyn. The theatre was built in 1904 and is nestled on a back street in a formerly bad part of Brooklyn. When they renovated it, the designers tipped their hats to its weathered history and left the dilapidated feel of the building. An old painting of a giant Pegasus and a gladiator remain on the curved ceiling under the light rigs. Scaffolding is holding up the beautifully carved walls.

Cate Blanchett was magnificent. I sat in the front row a metre from her. It sounds dicky, I know, but I felt so privileged to see this extraordinary actress so close up. Her Hedda was like a caged animal, tempestuous, sad, conniving – wonderful. I noticed the way the actors used their entire bodies on stage; there were no tense shoulders in that cast. There was one particular moment when Hugo Weaving put his hand on Cate Blanchett's shoulder, caressing her neck. Her face was a thunderstorm of emotion; tears were splashing off her magnificent cheekbones as her tiny body trembled and shook. It was absolute perfection. She was a real scene-stealer, too: even when she was standing silently in the background, she commanded the audience's attention. And I noticed Hugo's hands. They were shaking with nerves. I remembered my awful nervous shaking hands when I performed in front of Robert, and here was this seasoned, brilliant actor, still nervous to go on stage. I could die happy.

ıılııllılıı

When I left the theatre, I got a call from Lauren-the-Director, from the commitment-phobe/chair-throwing audition I had done months ago.

'Bella, sorry, I lost your number, and have just tracked it down.'

'No problem, I didn't have yours either, but it's great to hear from you,' I answered, trying to sound upbeat and American-ish. In truth I'd forgotten all about it.

She told me that her film had been cancelled because the investors had pulled out, but that another director, Rich Gartrell, had seen my audition tape and wanted me for his new film. *Safe Room* was Rich's NYU thesis film, twenty minutes long and set during a biological warfare attack on New York City. I was to play the 'Carrie Bradshaw-ish' lead. Wasn't quite Hedda, but happily it was very much paid. The only catch was that they wanted to shoot my first scene the next day.

That night, as I lay in bed, I thought of Cate and her

magnificent performance. I thought of the shoot the next day and was excited. It was my first New York film, and it was a chance to test out the Method. Cate began her career at the Sydney Theatre Company; I was to start my NY film career in a low-budget student film as a poor man's Carrie Bradshaw, not that I was comparing us or anything. It was all about, um, per-spective, I thought, as I happily sank into sleep.

ıılııllıllıı

I was woken by the Rattler upstairs and made pancakes to the sound of her death splutters. I rummaged through my closet for something 'Carrie Bradshaw-ish' to wear and, feeling ridiculous, caught a cab to the East River Promenade where Rich and the other crew members were setting up a scene. It was freezing, below zero, with icy winds speeding off the water and digging like needles beneath my Carrie costume, first into my bones and finally into the nerves of my face. My whole body was shaking and my lips had swollen so much I couldn't talk properly. We had to change the dialogue from 'Nice night, isn't it?' to 'Very cold, isn't it?' But I couldn't speak properly because my jaw was shivering so much. So I began some Strasberg mouth exercises, chewing like a demented cow and blowing out air. The camera operator took a step back and avoided eye contact with me. At one point I heard a shout and turned to receive a paparazzi-style camera lens pushed into my face as the stranger captured my confused expression. A typically New York moment as he took a gamble on whether I was famous or not.

On the way home I thought how strange most actors' lives are. We're always on the 'brink'. One good audition, one good role scored, and our lives of sardine-eating and op-shopping are replaced by working with De Niro, fame and success.

At the first stage, there are literally millions of young hopefuls.

A square-chinned boy or rosy-eyed girl gets told they should be in the movies. The bright lights of Hollywood and the exciting celebrity gossip magazines make it seem glamorous and wonderful. With a bit of luck, their good looks bag them a TV commercial. But many discover it is harder than they thought and drop off.

The stubborn ones and the ones with a bit of natural talent go on to the next stage. Here the rejections and boring day jobs dissuade many.

The next culling stage is the realisation that apart from talent and looks, a lot – and I mean a *lot* – of it comes down to blind luck. To base your life as well as happiness on blind luck is hard at best and terrifying at worst. So some throw in the acting towel for creature comforts and a lashing of warming stability.

The following level is filled with people who, to use a cliché, love acting so much they can't survive as a balanced person without it. There are a lot of talented people there, some of them quite nuts. They would still be actors even if they weren't paid. They are happiest performing, discovering a character, or rehearsing. These people continue, and some make it while others don't. They have low incomes but love their jobs: the 'happy starving artist' paradigm.

The ones who get a 'break' go on to the next level and become working actors. They have worked diligently to get to where they are (or happen to have a mum who's in the business). This is the stage where people earn a decent living out of the game and don't have to have a day job. They love acting, are talented and have luck on their side. The trifecta.

The ones who rise to the final level are the Extremes. The extremely beautiful, the extremely well connected, the extremely loveable and/or the extremely talented. They are the celebrities with fast cars and faster paycheques. (Then, the stage after that, they go off the wall with their celebrity status and play with monkeys and small boys, but that's a whole other story.)

Screw that, I thought, as I kicked an empty can along the street. I wanted to go straight to the Extremes. Bypass all the steps and get offered a blockbuster movie deal where my stunt double would make me look really cool and I'd get to throw high kicks into the air and French-kiss George Clooney, then get incredibly famous and be able to afford the necessities of life like champagne and foie gras. Oh, and have enough money to buy a space shuttle so I could fly out to the moons of Jupiter. My needs were simple.

It *was* possible, though, to bypass all those steps and go straight to the fondling of the monkey part. We've all heard the stories: a young actor plucked from obscurity and given the role of a life-time – advancing to fame and fortune like a rocket ship to the moon. Perhaps my upcoming audition for Quentin Tarantino would be my rocket ship to the monkey fondle? It was bizarre to think that if I got the role in his new film, my whole life would change. I wanted to work with Tarantino badly. I loved the strength and pizzazz of his female characters, and damn in hell it would be a blast. I didn't know when the audition for his new film was, but I was getting nervous.

14

Living in the moment with well-muscled energy, as Castle decrees my worth, despite my becoming a drug kingpin

SPRING STARTED TO PEEK out from behind the mighty veil of winter. Glorious warm sunshine; people smiling under sunglasses and hats. The giant scarecrow tree outside my window birthed sprays of vivid white blossoms, making me feel like a romantic child back on Waiheke Island.

I took a break from learning lines for an upcoming performance for Robert Castle, and stared out my bedroom window at the sunny street below, watching people luxuriating in the warm air. I wondered what they were thinking about? Fame and fortune? I doubted it. Who could possibly be as narcissistic as I was? I imagined them each enclosed in a soapy shimmering bubble filled with their own secret loves and fantasies, frets and thoughts. Worlds so private and yet so palpable.

I was struggling to get inside Laura's mind. Laura is a character from *The Glass Menagerie* by Tennessee Williams and I was to play her for Robert Castle. Laura, I realised, is queen of the bubble people. She is permanently in her own bubble world, pathologically so. Her invisible nail-hard balloon of air conceals and protects her from other people and herself. But her bubble was threatening to harden and block out the world for good.

I'd done all the research I could for Laura and I was at last getting some insight into her painfully shy world. It was a stretch for me to play her, but I was intent on being challenged and showing Robert what I could do. I'd prepared, planned and researched as much as I normally did, but still, I felt the cold prick of fear like evil little strength-sapping needles.

I'd been placed with a scene partner named Craig, who had only shown up to two rehearsals. We'd got into an argument over it the night before and hadn't made up. I was pissed off at him, yet my character had to be wildly in love with him. It was going to be a disaster.

Yet, when the time came, and the cocoon of the hot stage lights did their magic, I felt Laura's bubble grow around me and my lungs began filling up with her. My problems with Craig vanished as I drowned in Laura's acute shyness, her terror, her fragility. That delicate balance between the actor's self and the character's self got broken. I forgot Bella and became Laura. And it felt amazing; like I was swimming in the fluid of her secret bubble world. At one point when her precious glass unicorn figurine got smashed, I felt such grief that my head began spinning and I lost control of my legs and dropped to the floor. I looked out from behind her eyes and saw what she saw, felt what she felt, and my heart was full of her. I fell in love with her.

I knew in that moment that it had nothing to do with blockbuster movies, or fondling monkeys or rocket ships to the moon. It was about the bliss and discovery of what I felt in that moment. Nothing on earth could beat that. Okay, maybe sex, but it was a close second.

When the scene finished I didn't move much because my mind was reeling. The audience wasn't moving either, they just sat there in the dark. I tried to gather myself and walk off stage, but Laura was so much a part of me, the attempt to pull away from her felt like dragging a momentous weight. I didn't want to leave her, I wanted to stay in her skin longer.

Robert cleared his throat. 'I have absolutely nothing to say about that performance, Bella.'

I was still so inside Laura's insecure skin that my first reaction was that he must have loathed it, loathed me. My heart began plummeting down from a very high place. It was hurtling towards the ground.

'Oh,' I managed.

I respected Robert's judgement so much that despite all I'd learned, if he'd told me I was a mediocre actor and should try something other than acting, I probably would have.

'It was perfect,' he said.

My eyes widened to saucers.

'You're a very talented actress, Bella. I took some time to be sure, but I haven't seen somebody of your calibre in quite a while.'

A cold chill crept up my spine. This was important. This changed things in a very real way. I'd had accolades before, but this was *Robert Castle*. He never gave compliments like this, to anyone.

I felt that no matter what happened, I'd just passed a test that had given me a solid and astounding security that I'd never experienced before as an actor: Robert's comments; the lingering warmth of Laura still nestled inside me; that sensation of taking a hit of acting-heroin and knowing my life was devoted to it. It was good. Really good. This was my very own rocket to the moon.

But, acting being the fickle mistress she is, I was in for a new experience soon afterwards. That week, Tom and I partnered up to do a scene in Mr Bustamante's class. We camped out at my place, smoking cigarettes and rehearsing together into the wee hours. Okay, truthfully, we spent more time camping and smoking cigarettes. So when the time came to actually perform, we were both a little unprepared. Tom had the idea of taking a double shot of vodka before the performance. I agreed half-heartedly as I once knew an actor, a good one, who used to take lines of coke before any performance. But it degenerated to the stage where he couldn't perform unless he'd painted his nostrils white. His career had flown down the toilet and out into the sea. Last I heard he was on a small island in the Pacific drinking kava with an underage girl. But what the hell, you had to try everything once, and a tropical island didn't sound that bad.

I walked out onto the stage in my bare feet and felt the floorboards warm from the overhead stage lights. I was sure everybody could see the alcohol fumes emanating like dragon's breath from my mouth. I heard shuffling in the room as the audience got comfortable. I drunkenly spied Tom, sitting on stage, in character, writing something in his notebook. I walked towards him – then suddenly, my nose started aching, my knee started bleeding and small yellow birds were circling my head.

Tom ran over and picked me up off the floor.

'Oh Lucinda, aye do love yooo dear one,' he said unsteadily, yet still in character, as he brushed me off.

I wobbled up. 'Thank yee, dear brother, for that . . . mosht lovely of helpfulness-es.'

Afterwards Mr Bustamante looked at Tom and I sideways as he critiqued us; and we tried to stop swaying. Although Bustamante did say my fall looked realistic.

Tom nudged me.

'Yes, yes, thank you, I'd worked really, um . . . hard on that,' I said, trying to avoid eye contact.

I was a lying scumbag, and if there was a god she would strike me down, but there wasn't one, so I was saved. Not exactly another rocket ship to the moon.

My other classes, thankfully, weren't going so badly. I'd put a lot of work into learning the craft of acting and it was really beginning to pay off, well, that and the vodka shots. Robert's comments were still embedded in my heart, alive and sparkly. It was fantastic to feel confident about something. It seemed that when you concentrated on something (acting) other than your problem (self-confidence), then you got the thing you wanted in the first place. Life could be so tricky sometimes.

On the flip-side, the more we all worked our asses off at Strasberg, the more we felt entitled to let loose. We had a lot of promoter friends who got us free entry into the clubs as well as free drinks, so we partied a fair bit. Okay, a lot. One of the places we went to fairly regularly was PM nightclub at the Meatpacking District. It's a hot-spot for models and coke dealers and was always crawling with beautiful, stick-insect women, their heads gliding a foot above the crowd. One night, I spied a girl who seemed completely out of place. She wasn't one of the artistic model-types, rather, er, a playboy-type. She stood by herself and nursed a red-coloured drink in her clawed-up hands. I followed her eager gaze as she stared like an excluded child at a group of models who were laughing and being pawed at by a group of admirers. One of the models glanced over at her and took in Playboy Girl's outfit, eager-to-please expression and exploding fake breasts and promptly bent over in a fit of derisive laughter. Playboy Girl's face crumpled like a Coke can underneath a semi-trailer.

I made my way over to where she stood and invited her to our table and introduced her around. She was softly spoken and kept thanking me profusely. I introduced her to Gian-Luca to see if they hit it off, but she kept gravitating back to me.

'I don't have many female friends,' she whispered in her little girl's voice.

'They're just jealous of your huge boobs,' I laughed.

Her shoulders shook with giggles. She told me she'd only had her breasts done a little while ago and they were still sore, then asked me to touch them to see if I could tell whether they were fake or not. Then, quick as lightening, she took my hand and placed it on her boobs, placed her hand on top of mine and squeezed it – hard. Not letting go of her Vulcan clasp, she let out a little squeal, fluttered her eyelashes onto her forehead then asked me out on a date.

The penny dropped.

She hurriedly clasped my other hand and looked into my eyes. 'I understand,' she said, studying my face. 'You're not that way. Mostly I wouldn't take no for an answer. I can do that, you know. Make somebody do anything. But you're so nice to me, so I'll just sit here quietly next to you.'

Okaaaay.

Gian-Luca, who had been watching, leaned over. 'Does that usually work?' he asked with interest.

She smiled mysteriously. 'Girls are curious to try new things, you know, you've got to let them try a bit first.'

Gian-Luca shook his head. 'I fucking love New York,' he murmured to himself, evidently very impressed.

All the same, it made me start thinking about sex again. I sat at the Coffee Bean a week later with a good friend, a talented German actress named Natalie who had the face of an angel and the wit of a sailor. The subject had turned to sex with the ex.

'Would you with James?'

'No.'

'Do you ever miss him?'

'Yes. I miss our conversations, our connection. I don't miss his drunkenness. Hell, after all this time it still feels confusing. I do know one thing, though. The thought of being in a relationship makes me want to eat my stilettos.'

She studied my face. 'Buuuut?' she prompted as a smile started itching at her mouth.

I returned her smile. 'I'm starting to feel a bit randy.'

A lady with mean little eyes and a lemon-twisted mouth leaned in to eavesdrop on our conversation.

'So are you masturbating a lot?' asked Natalie, loud enough for her to hear. 'Because I am,' she added even louder, 'cucumbers, deodorant bottles, nipple clamps . . .'

Lemon Lady stood up, fanned herself, glared at us and left the café. Natalie laughed.

I wasn't quite into the whole fresh-smelling-vegetable-clamp thing but I could definitely feel my body coming alive again. But apart from Axel, who was off bounds, I wasn't really attracted to anyone. I would have to squish my feelings up into a healthy little ball and let them explode all over some unsuspecting fellow when he arrived from whatever dimension he was currently in.

'Good choice,' agreed Natalie.

I set out on my way home through Stuyvesant Park. During the winter it had been a dark and dirty needle park that I hurried through, the ground black from clumped snow, dirt and rubbish. But when spring arrived it transformed into a colourful playground, like Oscar Wilde's Secret Garden, with the frenzied growth of multicoloured flowers and green grass, and people reclining on the wooden benches staring wide-eyed at the symphony of rebirth around them. Kids, open armed, twirled the pavements, catching the rain of blossoms falling from the sky.

I went up to Saint Marks and watched punk skateboarders do ollies and flips up and down First Avenue. People were sitting and gossiping on the large flat stairs leading up to the brownstones, shopkeepers stood on the corners chatting with locals, everybody with a coffee or sandwich in hand. A lovely neighbourhood feeling.

New York was really beginning to feel like home for me, and I recognised people I knew as I walked the streets. My acquaintances had become dear friends and my slum was done up beautifully and had been sprayed with my scent. I knew the best places to shop, or the bars I could smoke in. I had slowly made a small dent in the city and it felt like the impossible was starting to happen. I was satisfied and happy. But, if the past was anything to go by, a new adventure would be just around the corner, with a shotgun.

ılıllılılı

One afternoon, I looked out the window and everything had gone silent in the city. It was two o'clock in the afternoon and an amazing dark glow had settled everywhere, that quiet hush of the city as it prepares itself for a storm. Then a strange, otherworldy wind began to blow and I could hear a lonesome dog barking. Rain pellets began slamming down and the wind began to hurl itself against the buildings. The white blossoms from the scarecrow tree outside my window were ripped off their stalks and thrown in the air like confetti. I loved the start of a storm that comes out of a blue sky like a secret war building on the horizon.

Plus, rainstorms insist on making one indulge. I put on a pair of PJs, stuffed myself into some slippers, wrapped myself up warmly in a fleecy blanket, got a bucket of cold ice-cream to create temperature balance, and grabbed the TV remote control.

I clicked through the channels with an ice-cream spoon jutting out of my mouth and landed on an interview with Tarantino. I listened delighted as he obsessed about movies to the point of distraction. The interviewer asked a question and he spouted an intelligent, passionate but totally unrelated answer. I was getting pretty excited at the thought of meeting him. Tarantino's casting director had contacted me the week before saying it wouldn't be too long, but I hoped the day of the audition would come before I did myself an injury.

ıılılılılılı

Natalie decided she'd take my mind off the audition by challenging me to one of her dares. Besides, she had to get me back for daring her to do a Meg Ryan over an especially delicious cocktail. I had to dance through Central Park pretending I was a 'dyslexic wood nymph'. In the pouring rain. Who was I to resist? However, the only thing I got was a cold.

I came home, ate half a roasted chicken and pieces of brie with my fingers, then washed it all down with my faithful lemonade. Then I sat watching *The Office* until Axel walked through the door.

He saw the crumpled tissues scattered around me and got almost angry. He remonstrated that I should be wearing socks and demanded to know my symptoms then made me take some vitamins, drink some green tea and put my feet up. Gulp. So not only was he really good-looking, he was also really lovely. Not good. I reminded myself that relationships were bad and only ended in disaster and strange bonding moments with chicken drumsticks. I had to continue to stay away, despite his hotness.

Through a haze of cold and flu tablets, Axel and I had a heart-to-heart. He told me that he didn't know what he wanted in life, that he was drifting around, not serious about anything. I asked about his music and he told me that he didn't feel confident enough to pursue it full-time. I told him that life was short and that he should go for it. Then he asked me about my past relationships and I tried to change the subject.

'Come on, at least tell me what you're looking for in a man, then.'

'Well-muscled . . .' I began.

He looked at me, somewhat taken aback.

'Er, well-muscled . . . energy. It's (ahem) an Australian term.'

'Well-muscled energy?' he repeated slowly.

'Yeah, for, er, life. You know. Flexing for life. Ah, like energy that is strong. Strong-muscled life-energy.'

'Do you mean motivated?'

'Sure. Ah, yes. Ah ha,' I nodded.

‎ illtllilllth

The next day Axel went to the studio to rehearse and sent me a text saying, 'Thanks for the pep talk last night.' I tried not to think of his beautiful big hands drumming away, his lean, well-muscled body sweating from the exertion. I splashed cold water on my face then called my friend Polly for advice.

'Bella, just do what I do –'

'What? Neuro-linguistics programming? Cognitive Behavioural Therapy?'

'Er, no. Every time you think of Axel naked or in a compromising position – think of your mum on the bog.'

'Brilliant.'

Just to reinforce her message, the next day at school, Polly gave me an old Christmas card with magazine cut-outs of a ceramic toilet and a giant poo. Stick figures of my mother and Axel were drawn in the margins. We had a substitute teacher named Hilde in class that day, and, prompted by our giggles, she asked to see the card. Feeling like a sixth-grader I passed her the card with my head held low. I heard a great cackling sound and looked up to see her doubled over in laughter.

'I don't even want to *know* what the fuck this is all about,' she managed through her laughter.

Hilde was great. She had a huge energy and personality that somehow fitted into her tiny, tiny frame. She looked like a loveable clown with her purple tie-dyed pants, and was by turns hilarious and self-deprecating and kept saying things like, 'Talk to me like I'm retarded.' I asked her advice on a role I was working on for class, in which I was supposed to have been married to the other character for ten years. She answered with a story about her and Robert Duvall. They were filming *Metamorphosis*, playing husband and wife, married for five years. Never having met Duvall before the first day of filming, she wanted to create a connection with him that would conjure up the knowing smiles and worn words that only married couples truly have. She asked Duvall if he would try something with her and to wait for her in his dressing-room. Being that they were both Method-trained actors he didn't look at her sideways, but did what she asked. Hilde entered his dressing-room a little while later and found him sitting in the dark. She sat down next to him and together they sat side by side in the dark and in silence. Eventually, he reached across and placed his hand on top of hers. They sat companionably like that for half an hour until the assistant called them on to set. Then, without a word spoken, they got up and did their first scene together. It worked a treat. On screen they looked exactly like a couple that had brushed their teeth together for five years. Gotta love acting tricks.

As I was listening to Hilde, I felt a warm rush of joy go up my back and land on the top of my head. Then, like an egg breaking, it washed down my face and landed on my cheeks, which puffed out in a smile. I had only really just begun Strasberg and I was enrolled for one year, but I realised then it wasn't enough. I was Oliver Twist and I wanted more. That afternoon I signed on the dotted line for a second year. I figured practicalities like money and living arrangements could be decided on later and by somebody else. Gulp. As I signed my life away, Ruth, one of the admin workers, told me I would then be eligible for an OPT.

'An OP what?'

'OPT. Optional Practical Training. After you complete Strasberg you can get an OPT visa which would let you live and work as an actress in America for a full year after you graduate.'

'Hell yeah!'

'I think "yeah" would do just as nicely, Bella.'

'Shit, sorry. I mean, *damn*, sorry.' Fuck, I really had to stop swearing.

Score. Another year of Strasberg and a visa at the end of it.

Then all I needed to do was figure out how in hell I would pay for it. Perhaps I could find a good drug kingpin position on Craigslist or I could ask some of my sexy actress friends if I could pimp them out. Hmmm. So many options.

One option that was definitely closed to me was getting a well-paid job as a professional singer. Jellyfish wearing lipstick would be more congruous. Admittedly, not that I didn't try. I diligently went to singing class with the lovely Michael Bayer with fantasies of million-dollar record deals. For the class presentation I had stupidly chosen to sing 'Miss Celie's Blues', a stunning old number from *The Colour Purple*. For one, I wasn't black, and two, I couldn't sing, so why in hell I chose that I'll never know. I sang like a rusty nail, wet chalk down a blackboard, like a goddamned horror movie. I'd been practising all week, and apart from some irate neighbours, nothing good had come from it. I really sucked. And to do it in front of Michael and the whole class. There were magical mystical moments in the shower when I swear I sounded like Aretha Franklin, and I become a pretty mean air guitarist too, but even that, I admitted reluctantly, was probably delusional.

When the day finally arrived, my knees were weak and my insides were shaking like a leaf on a tree. Pure unadulterated humiliation was waiting for me around the corner. My Machiavellian tendencies were in full swing – I needed to get out of it. I considered changing into slippery soled shoes as I climbed the precarious staircase up to the fourth-floor singing room. A slight break of the leg in three places would do the trick. Perhaps I could find some New York acid and go mad. They wouldn't let a mad woman sing, would they?

I sat in class waiting my turn, every nerve in my body screaming: 'Run! Get out of here!' Michael looked at me sympathetically then told me to climb on to the stage. I swallowed thickly and reminded myself that this was what I was here for: to learn, to push my comfort zones. I bit down on the cold silver bullet between my teeth and walked the long mile to the stage. I felt my skin pucker and my throat clamp down in fear. Everything became vivid – I could smell the wooden boards of the stage, the stench of somebody's perspiration in the front row and the whirring of the air-conditioner as though it were a helicopter. I took a breath of air into my lungs and felt the rush of noise as they expelled. I was singing! And damn, it sounded bad. I snuck a quick glance at the audience and a few had sunk down into their seats, hands covering their mouths. Bamboo spikes in fingernails had nothing on me. As I wailed my way through the song, I became more and more angry with myself. What the hell was I doing? I wasn't a singer. I had a sudden thought: I wasn't a singer, but I was an actor. Perhaps I could just *act* my way through this unadulterated humiliation? 'Okay. I was a black woman named Celie and I was singing the blues.' I felt the familiar glove-like feeling of a new character slipping under my skin. I was becoming Celie. My hips started to sway like a large black woman's and I felt a groove flow through me and then, then, I began to belt it out. I was singing! Loud. And it was even worse than before. People were plugging their ears with anything handy. The only thing I could do to make the badness go away was to stop singing. Which I did. Much to the relief of the audience, and Michael, and myself, and anyone within earshot.

I remembered how James used to tell me what a beautiful voice I had when I sang in the shower. Bless. Tone-deaf people should stick together.

ıılıılıılıı

That night James phoned me while I was out at PM nightclub. He sounded a bit lonely. Forgetting to be stand-offish after my two vodkas, we chatted and joked like we used to in the early days. I told him about my singing debut and he laughed and told me he'd always known I was a strangulated cat.

'So why did you tell me, and I quote, "Bella, you sing like a lovely magic elf"?'

'Have you ever heard a magic elf sing well?'

'Point taken.'

Later in the conversation, he asked me to go with him to Oslo, Norway, for six days, leaving in two days. Damn, he knew my weaknesses too well. It was strange, though – while I didn't consider going, I realised I didn't have any anger towards him any more. It was because I was safe and my heart had healed from him and he couldn't hurt me any more. I could afford to see him without the veil of the past, in a new and different light.

He put on his sexy voice: 'Please come with me.'

His smooth, sexy tones didn't sway my decision, but they did make me think about sex again. Damn, and I was doing so well. There was nothing for it. I had to get laid.

15

My ho period commences: the twenty-five-year-old, the German, the salty sailor, Abernathy and the bulldozer lady

THE WHOLE ENGLISH GANG – Eleanor, Polly and Ben – were to leave Strasberg and go back to London to work on their careers. I was sorry to see them go. We organised a party for their last night and met up with all the crazies they'd met, shagged and loved, and bar-crawled like munted ants, hollering and shouting to the rooftops, 'Goodbye, goodbye New York!', to which the replies came fast and furiously. 'Fuck you and goodbye!' I wished them luck and love then gave them each a miniature bottle of vodka for the flight home.

When I got home at two, Axel had just returned from a party. He looked half-sloshed and handsome as hell. He turned the music up on our tinny CD player and we began to dance. Then, he stopped and turned to me.

'Dance for *me*,' he said.

I did my Travolta dance, and it wasn't pleasant.

'You look like a cross between a hooker and a farmer,' he said, laughing.

'Har bloomin' har,' I replied elegantly. 'Let's see you do it.'

'Try and make me,' he said, a wicked look in his eye.

Game on. I approached him and grabbed his shirt. He swiped it out of my grasp and before I knew it we were in an all-out tussle – shirts lifted in the struggle, bodies pressed together as we rolled around on the floor. When I tried to grasp at his flailing arms, a little groan escaped his lips. We both looked down – and he had a huge erection. Too late! The inevitable was about to happen, the slow build-up that we'd been containing was in danger of flooding the room.

'So I see some part of your body likes to dance,' I said, trying not to smile.

He stood, pulled me up from the floor and picked me up in his arms, then opened my bedroom door with a shove of his knee and threw me onto the bed like a goddamn caveman. I lay there, breathing hard as he stood above me looking down. *My mum on the bog, my mum on the bog.* He paused a second, then jumped on top of me and ripped off my T-shirt with his big hands. My breasts smoothing against his bare chest made his throat close up and that tight groan escape his mouth again.

I woke the next morning on the hard wooden floor with Axel's arms curled tightly around me, his deep regular breathing in my ear. The room looked like a bomb had hit it and my bed was broken completely in two. Well, that was one way to break my drought.

I got dressed and took a Q subway to meet the German Crew at Brighton Beach, on Coney Island – a long stretch of grey sand filled with Russian restaurants. Tom, Natalie, Dieter (a handsome German Strasbergian friend with blonde hair and a penchant for the ladies) and a few others listened to an iPod as it pumped out sounds and we danced and mock-fought along the water's edge, pretending we had feather boas and top hats as we spat sand out of our mouths and postured. Bloody actors. We took our bows and settled back onto the blanket and sipped our beers.

'So was it good?' asked Natalie.

'Was what good?'

She gave me a shrewd look. 'You got laid last night, didn't you?'

'How did you –?'

'Babe, you've been beaming like an idiot all morning.'

I beamed like an idiot, then denied all knowledge of it, then promptly spilled the beans.

Coming back from the beach, we fell asleep to the gentle rattle of the train and woke at Union Square, where I left the others and met up with Gian-Luca for a movie at the Regal and pizza at L'amore Pizza. When I got home, Axel was out so I was thankfully spared the whole pretending-we-weren't-avoiding-each-other-while-surreptitiously-trying-to-gauge-the-other's-thoughts-on-the-matter thing.

ıllıllıllılı

Overnight my English Crew was completely replaced by the German Crew. We partied around New York, discussing acting and actors in earnest, waking at one of our apartments, usually underneath a table, with hangovers and heinous cravings for fried eggs and bacon. One night we were at my place arguing and coughing over red wine, as was our norm. As the light grew grey outside the window, Natalie began talking in her sleep, crashed out on the sofa, and Tom and Dieter were crumpled into a heap on my bed, snoring contentedly. Axel arrived home from his shift and poked his head into my room.

'Group sex?' he asked, watching me slowly gather bottles from between the snoring people and dump them in the bin.

'Nah, just group alcoholism,' I answered, my head already pounding.

'Well, looks like your room is full,' he said. 'You'll just have to sleep in my bed.'

I looked at him and my stomach did a little flip. I slept next to him, his leg brushing alluringly against mine as I kept to my side of the bed. In the morning I woke with something hard pushed against my back.

A part of me was like a little girl when it came to sex. I got all flummoxed and wasn't sure about the ins and outs (literally). Watching a 1960s porno (featuring a dwarf and a blue-eye-shadowed vixen) when I was fifteen hadn't helped to clarify things.

But the other part, I guess the ho part of me, relished the passion, the intimacy. When you lovingly and confidently know every freckle, every line on your lover's body. When those unbearable heights are reached, when both your minds and bodies explode in unison. Having now done the samba for the first time since James, I could feel the adult/ho part in me emerging again. I was looking at Axel as if in a whole new light. Every move he made as he washed the dishes or played the drums made me desire him. The way his shirt folded against his arms, the way his T-shirt slipped up and exposed the soft hairs on his belly. I tried to block him from my thoughts but he would pop up like a jack-in-the-box with surprising regularity. I'd catch a glimpse of his beautiful tall frame or his soft brown eyes resting on me, then my body would startle awake and an air bubble would get caught somewhere inside me. When his soft, insistent lips had been on my skin, I'd felt myself awakening. I had felt his touch somewhere deep inside me, in a primal, dizzying way.

Even Strasberg wasn't safe from my ho-iness. I had to perform

Top Girls by Carol Churchill with Natalie in one of my classes. My costume was a silk green top that had a slit all the way from the neckline to four inches above my belly button. Apparently the fabric got caught and for the entire scene my breasts were exposed. Bare. Uncovered. Just hanging in the wind. I'll just repeat that for the cheap seats – *I exposed my breasts for twenty minutes to thirty-one of the crème de la crème of acting students as well as a fifty-year-old Shakespearean acting teacher with diabetes.* Hell! And what's worse is that nobody told me. During the scene Natalie broke a crystal glass by accident and the teacher stopped the performance to yell 'watch out for the glass', but I gather he wasn't comfortable enough to stop the scene to yell: 'Bella, your tits are hanging out, for public safety and morality, put the fuckers back in!'

My mum, Rosie, arrived to visit, which thankfully took my mind off sex and possible indictment for public exposure. She still had the same beautiful comforting hugs and words of wisdom the she would pluck out of the air like expectant jewels. It was such a delight to have her. She was staying at her friend's house but would sometimes stay over at mine. I would bring her tea in the morning; her lovely face, crumpled from sleep, would smile, and I would lie next to her chatting amiably about things until our mugs were empty. Then she would set off to explore the neighbourhood and I'd be off to Strasberg.

One night, as I was teaching my mum how to say 'mudda fucker' to cab drivers that cut her off, I got a call. It was from Tarantino's people. I was to come in and audition in two days' time.

'Shit, great! I mean, ah, "great". Um, what's the address?'

'Wiltshire Boulevard.'

'Isn't that in Los Angeles?'

'Yes,' came the response.

Oh dear.

After a bit of wrangling, we worked out that they would meet me a few days later in New York, as they had other people to see there anyway.

Of course I wanted get the role on the film, but just to work with Tarantino for even twenty minutes in the audition had my knickers in a knot.

I read the script for *Death Proof* in one sitting and loved it. It was an homage to the slasher genre, but with strong kick-ass female characters. Abernathy, the character I was to audition for, was witty and eccentric. A Hollywood make-up artist, she falls in love with the director of the movie she is working on, and, as the intended victim of the slasher's desires, she gets into hot water fairly frequently. She'd be a hell of a lot of fun to play.

I heard through the grapevine that they were looking for a big-name star for the Abernathy character to complement the unknowns like Zoë. Not good. But I figured even if I wasn't famous enough for the part, if I could just get Quentin to see my work there was still a chance he would consider casting me.

The next day the casting people called me again to set up a date and time. It slipped out that Tarantino couldn't be at my audition. I was a little disappointed to say the least. Okay, I was a lot disappointed. Okay, the weight of it was like systematically crushing each part of my body until I was a small whimpering puddle. Then my bubble burst. Who was I? I had been getting all hopeful about winning the part when realistically he was probably doing Zoë a favour and wouldn't even see my audition tape. Not that I blamed him – I mean, really, who was I to him?

Then I remembered a piece of advice a teacher once gave me: 'Treat an audition like a mini performance: have fun with it and enjoy being that character for however long you can. Then hope.' And I was going to. Blind hope can be a very nice thing.

I began my usual preparations. For a full week, I walked, talked and thought of nothing else but Abernathy. Extremist, who me? Even before Strasberg I'd got a kick out of researching and preparing for a character, but Strasberg had given me such an armoury of techniques to analyse a role and prepare that I felt as cool as Batman. Though without the pointy ears, just the cool gadgets part.

I started the process of breaking down the script. What clues could I get about who she was? Where was she from? What did she like, dislike? How was her childhood, her relationship with her parents? Did she like herself? What were her views on life, on men, on friendship? Physically, what was she like? How did she walk, talk, hold herself? I read and re-read the script until I had gathered all the facts I could find, then I set about writing a character back-story for her.

I was to do four scenes for the audition, so I needed to work on them individually, then as a whole. I broke down each scene to find where the beats were, what the nucleus was, what my objective and intentions were, and added sensory work. I researched make-up artistry and read articles on why people fall in love with their bosses. Then I learned my lines. I played with her physicality and experimented with voice and posture. I discussed her at length with anybody who would listen, got my hair cut and tried on a dozen outfits.

When the day of my audition arrived, I was as sick as a dog. Whenever I sneezed, projectile fluid flew from my nose and embedded itself against the wall. The night before, James had called me at three in the morning drunk, to tell me he missed me. My mum and all my friends had texted me throughout the night to wish me luck. Axel came home at five am and force-fed me stinging nasal drops that burned my sinuses for the next hour. Not the best of nights.

Despite all that, and other than a shake in my cowboy boots, I felt confident and cool with my ridiculously expensive haircut and new red lipstick. I took a cab to the Tribeca Grand to meet with the casting director, Mary.

The lobby of the elegant hotel was tightly packed with groups of filmmakers and actors waving champagne glasses and checking out the competition. I had forgotten the Tribeca Grand was the official headquarters of De Niro's Tribeca Film Festival, which was opening that night.

I was told that Mary was running late and to take a seat in the bar and wait for her. The bar? Civilised. I watched the throngs of filmmakers on the make and tried not to think of the audition so I wouldn't curl up into a foetal position and wrinkle my outfit.

I scanned the menu for the cheapest item and ordered a grapefruit juice. The waiter-cum-actor considered me for a bit then asked if I would like a splash of gin in it. And here I was thinking I was looking cool and relaxed. Evidently not.

'So, you want some?' he needlessly prompted.

I felt so Greta Garbo cool, reclining on a chaise longue in the Tribeca Grand, waiting to audition, mentally rolling a sexy waiter in the hay. I couldn't resist a half-smile.

'Surprise me, handsome,' I purred.

He smiled and bowed, brought back a tall yellow liquid and watched from across the room as I sipped it. When I asked for the bill he smiled and said, 'It's on the house, lovely lady.'

Ah, a good start to the afternoon.

I went back to the foyer and sat down with two other actresses who were going for the same part as me, though they were both the sweet blonde type. I felt out of place with my thumbs in my jeans and a snarl. My bladder was bursting but I could get called at any moment, so I asked one of the blondes to mind my seat while I rushed to the marbled bathroom, flogging some popcorn off the buffet table on my way.

With my stolen popcorn and a little buzz from the grapefruit juice that may or may not have had gin in it, I waited my turn. An hour later, JC, an affable short gay man with tight ringlets, took me upstairs to a tiny hotel room where Mary was waiting. She was middle-aged with a kind smile but daunting eyes. She said she loved my top, then offered me a seat.

The room was tiny, I mean broom-cupboard size, with elegant furnishings and a view of the street below.

So this was the big time, huh? In a tiny hotel room with my legs cramped under a veneered coffee table, brushing stolen popcorn from the corners of my mouth.

I asked if I could take my shoes off.

'Of course, go ahead, darling,' replied Mary. I unzipped my boots and a faint but noticeable smell emanated.

I looked up and blushed.

'Don't mention it,' said Mary as we both tried not to smile.

I was off to a pretty shaky start.

The ice broken, we got down to business and started in on the first scene. Other than nerves the size of the Rainbow Serpent busting up my concentration and making me screw up the first line, it went well.

Then, to see if I could take direction, Mary asked me to do it again, this time at a faster tempo.

As I machine-gunned the lines out, she kept yelling 'faster, faster'. Speedy Gonzales had nothing on me. I got to a crucial part – when my character shows her vulnerabilities – and slowed down a bit. I said the line slowly with relish, then sped up again.

Mary smiled and nodded her head approvingly. 'You're a good actor,' she said.

Then we started the next scene. In the middle of it I saw JC in my peripheral vision, camera pressed against his eye, having some sort of fit. His whole body was shuddering. I couldn't stop the scene, so I tried to continue as best I could. On closer scrutiny, I realised he was pissing himself laughing. Mary, who was reading the other character's lines with me, also began laughing like a jackal. A sudden cold fear gripped me. Was I so terrible they were laughing *at* me? Before I released something from my bowels, I remembered in time: the scene itself was hilarious. I'd worked on the comedy with such minutia and on such a technical level, I'd forgotten how funny the end product was. Both Mary and JC had seen this scene over a hundred times and they were belly laughing at my interpretation – woo hoo. I gave myself a mental high-five and pressed on. When I finished, the room erupted and we burst out laughing and started back-slapping each other. 'Well done,' enthused Mary. It was a thoroughly enjoyable time. I loved the character I auditioned for and had a blast being able to play her.

I gathered Mary was impressed with my work, but I also gathered that all of Hollywood was trying out for the part. When I picked up my things to leave, Mary smiled strangely at me, shook my hand and told me they would be in contact within the month.

Oh baby! I'd just done my first New York professional audition – and she didn't swear at me or call the cops on me. She even said I was a good actress and liked my top. I'd really felt good in there, in control. Professional. Confident. I loved the whole process: the research, the character development and finally the performance. That day I realised for the first time that I could hold my own with the big girls. My nervousness hadn't screwed up my performance like it had on other occasions, and that was the key. The confidence I'd gained from Strasberg and Robert made me that much more comfortable and my work that much tighter.

I bought myself a Twix bar from a street stand to celebrate. ' "You're a good actor." ' ' "We'll be in contact." ' A homeless guy looked at me in sympathy as I mumbled embryonic words and grinned to myself.

ılılıılılılı

Axel came hurrying to meet me after the audition. He arrived looking extraordinary, dressed as if for a date. He really was the most amazing looking man. It was weird walking next to him, all dressed up like that. Women couldn't help but stare. Not the sly glances of attraction, but the bold 'holy crap, you are hot' kind of looks that are strangely unthreatening because of their brashness. I felt myself swoon a little as his tall figure walked next to mine. He was filled with unassuming grace, surety and sex. Every time his arm brushed mine, I felt a maelstrom ripple up my arm, through my chest and straight to my groin. His very presence was turning me into a scarlet woman.

That evening we finally talked about the night we had made the rafters shake and he told me he was beginning to have feelings for me. That was really the last thing I wanted. I knew I was beginning to think fairly highly of him, and that only meant trouble. I knew my limitations far too well. If I got into a relationship, I wouldn't have time for Strasberg. My mind would wander to him instead of my lessons. My teacher's voice would end up droning in the background as I thought of Axel's thighs. I wanted to concentrate on acting this year, not men. I was learning more than I ever had and I didn't want to screw that up. Axel said I could have both school and a relationship, but seeing as I could get distracted by a puff of air I figured I had to stay on the safe side. He said he would respect my decision.

ılılıılılılı

I had always wanted to play Martha in *Who's Afraid of Virginia Woolf*, the role made famous by Elizabeth Taylor. It was a huge part to undertake, with complex characterisation and the ever-present shadow of Taylor to get by. Martha was diabolical in nature: scheming, argumentative, highly intelligent, ruthless, scared, vulnerable and in love. I asked Robert, with fear in my belly, if I was ready to take on the role, and happily he said yes. I would perform it in his class. I started my preparations and read through the pages almost reverentially. Martha was the most clever, well-conceived character I'd ever read. Reading her felt like walking into the awe-inspiring Pantheon or bracing from fresh sea air. The three-dimensional characterisation, the subtle themes, the brutal honesty, the pathos. Like all great artworks, it left you feeling slightly breathless. I spent two weeks with the research and slowly I began to bury myself in Martha's uncompromising and damaged heart.

For me, the word for Martha was *Storm*. Just like the one I'd watched from my bedroom window. The storm and Martha were inseparable, cut from the same cloth. Both utterly powerful in their volume, yet even more deadly in their silence. She needed to be as dangerous as the storm with an underbelly of Laura-like vulnerability. One evening, I sat down with my scene partner, Ferdinand, to go over the lines.

'Mart-aa ayeivebought fleyers.'

'Sorry, didn't quite catch that, Ferdinand.'

'Mart-aa ayeivebought fleyers,' he repeated.

'Oh, you've bought me flowers?'

'Yed datswhat I saiyd.'

Okay, time to re-think my scene partner. I was assigned to Ferdinand by a random draw. He was there for half a term on a Spanish scholarship. I'm sure he was a good actor, but I couldn't understand a damn word he said.

We agonised over the lines for four hours, but there was no way I could play Martha when my George sounded like Salvador Dali on acid. I felt somehow relieved that I'd have to turn the part down. Alarm bells started ringing and I felt a stone sink into my stomach. Bullshit. Ferdinand was just an excuse.

The truth was that I was terrified that *I* wouldn't do Martha justice. She was such a mighty character, what if I screwed her up? What if I couldn't capture her storm? I loathed seeing actors take on roles they weren't ready for and turn them into parodies. I couldn't take that risk.

In class one day, I had seen one of the most atrocious things. Like the *Mona Lisa* with slashes across her face, the Sistine Chapel bulldozed to rubble: I'd seen a chick massacre Blanche.

A Streetcar Named Desire is the Holy Grail, especially for Method actors. Brando's and Leigh's performances in the movie, directed by renowned Method director Elia Kazan, is what we all aspire to.

Before my time, at Strasberg you could only attempt to do a scene out of *Streetcar* if you had studied the Method for two years and were given permission by one of the teachers who had worked with Strasberg himself. That sounded a little over the top, even to me, but that day in class I saw only too clearly why those rules used to be in place.

Blanche, one of the all-time great female characters that actresses dream of, the female actor's Hamlet, was turned into an eye-rolling strumpet. For a Southern belle type character in the 1940s, the student had chosen a hot-pink cheerleader-type costume with leopard-print stilettos. *Leopard-print stilettos.*

Blanche is a woman famed for her dreamy indiscretions, her enormous pathos, her fragility and tigress-like strength. She is a catalogue of complexity, an extraordinarily challenging character. And she does not look like a hooker. To see this student display her range of emotions by rolling her eyes for sad and grimacing for happy made it hard to watch, but, like a witness to a car wreck, I had been enthralled. Every single thing was magnificently wrong. I'd looked down at my hands and seen half-moons imprinted on my palms.

When she'd finished there had been a deathly hush in the room. The teacher, Ted, looked uncomfortable, then cleared his throat. The student sat on stage, grinning broadly, looking very pleased with herself.

'So how did that feel?' asked Ted.

She started to gush. 'Amazing! It felt so good. I was really in the moment!'

Ted looked confused. The class looked confused. She thought she'd done an outstanding job. She truly didn't realise that she'd played one of the all-time great scenes and made it look like a *Saturday Night Live* clip.

What if I did that to Martha? Could I take that risk? Of fucking her up, I mean. Then being unaware of it, like that student? The answer was no. No, I couldn't take the risk. I didn't care if Robert thought I was ready, I reckoned if I was doubting it, that was enough. Martha was safe from harm for the time being.

But one day, I vowed (with my fist in the air), before I left Strasberg I would play Martha. (Drum roll subsides into soppy music.) Until then, I would just continue to play her in my bedroom as my imaginary crowds roared with delight.

Equally as terrifying, that day PMS hit me. Axel came home and saw me slumped on the sofa munching on Twizzlers.

'What are they?' he asked, trying to avoid the deranged look in my eye.

'Twizzlers, an ingenious American product of raspberry-flavoured liquorice sticks. They're brilliant. They cover all the necessary food groups: red, chewy and sugary. Mmm. Never being one for excess, I bought eight packets of them but it saved money on lipstick as my mouth is always red.'

He looked at me like the mad woman I was.

Women have been let off murder charges because of those three little letters – need I say more. I am a total freak when the time comes. I am either crying over mobile phone commercials or manically discussing something stupid like Twizzlers.

Axel repeated the are-you-mad look and I retaliated by silently scoffing three anti-PMS pills crammed with Efamol.

He quickly left the house for the evening while I continued to scoff mouthfuls of Efamol and Twizzlers. Well, at least it was a good way to keep the distance between us.

That week I went to see Dieter performing in a play in Midtown. The play was fun and Dieter was superb as a transvestite gangster. When it was over, Dieter and I made our way to Karma to meet with some friends where we bopped to hip hop and felt decidedly white. Dieter told me he'd left his keys at home and asked if he could crash at mine. I was unsure if this was the whole truth as, strangely, it had happened on more than one occasion before. On the other times, though, we'd had friends with us, but that night we were to be alone.

When we arrived home, I blew up the airbed for him in the sitting room. As we were fooling around with the bed, one thing led to another, as it does, and Dieter drew close to kiss me . . . Fade to black (but not total black, more a greyish colour, as we didn't actually become 'unionised', as I once heard a wizened old evangelist call it on late-night TV). Taking a break from deflating the bed with our activities, Dieter excused himself to go to the bathroom and, naked, managed to somehow lock himself in there. As I, half-naked, was trying to drunkenly push the door open with my hip in between giggles, I heard the front door creak open. Axel walked in and took in the scene.

The room became a vacuum as my drunken mind tried to decode the significance of the situation.

Axel looked at me, anger building behind his eyes. 'Try kicking it down,' he said, as dry as a bone. Before I could answer, he turned on his heels, went into his bedroom and slammed the door.

Oh shit, oh shit.

I tried to regain my balance, but toppled over and ended up on the floor just as Dieter broke through the door and tripped over me in a naked Twister moment. Axel poked his head out of the door to see what the loud noise was. Dieter and I embarrassedly disentangled, Axel went back into his room, and I hurriedly got dressed.

The next day, Axel looked like a thunderstorm.

But we weren't in a relationship, I thought, as I tried my hardest to be self-pitying. It wasn't working. I felt as guilty as he did whenever his Jewish mama called. I figured I'd have to use the old faithful: never mention it again and hope that he didn't either.

That evening, I had agreed to meet James for a drink. He was perhaps thinner in the face, but his eyes still had that same magical intensity. We chatted and joked amicably and it felt easy and good being in his presence again. I'd forgotten how funny and bright he was. The good side of James was very good. He would really make somebody a great partner if he got himself together. But soon enough the conversation turned towards the past and our relationship. He wanted to get back together. He said if I got back with him, he'd get me an agent. I turned to look at him. My offended silence was met with a further offer: he would get me auditions through his contacts. I slammed back my Stella and glared at him.

'I'm going, James. Nice to see you again,' I said stiffly, trying to hold back my anger.

He looked confused. That always irritated me about James. He'd try to buy people and not have the first clue how offensive or rude it was.

'I'm sorry, okay, please wait, just sit for a sec.'

He explained that he hadn't stopped loving me and still wanted to get married. In the next breath he told me his friend Carol-Lee had moved to New York from Orlando and was staying with him at our old apartment. How perfect, I thought as I gritted my teeth. He told me how she'd asked him to marry her and how she'd even bought him a ring.

'She . . . You're kidding, right?'

He took in my expression. 'No, but I shouldn't have said anything, that was my lousy attempt at making you jealous.'

'I'm not jealous, you know.'

'I know.'

'I'm not.'

'Okay, you're not,' he answered, his eyes twinkling.

'Stop being an asshole.'

'Okay, I promise tonight I'll abstain from any asshole-ness, and if I dare step over any line, real or imaginary, you have my full permission to relive a classic movie moment and dump a drink on my head.'

'I'll hold you to that.'

He turned to the bartender. 'Please keep a full glass of Moët right here,' he said, pointing at the wooden bar-top. 'In case my friend here feels the need.'

The rest of the evening he was good to his word and was as charming as a fox, our banter a verbal tennis match of puns and innuendos. I had missed James. When good things happened, my first instinct was still to call him, but then I'd remember. I often felt him near me, though, his eyes still burning their bright blue somewhere inside me. That night, he asked me again to return to him, and in a Stella-fuelled moment, bathed in an hour of his full-force charm, I considered it. I wished I could have said yes, I wished things were different and I could have succumbed to the feelings I still had. But however much I wanted the charming James in front of me, I knew there was another one, a darker one, waiting, just around the corner. I told him no, there was no possibility of it.

But he didn't get to where he was by giving up, so, like a salty sailor, he expertly changed tack after scrutinising my mood as if it were the wind. He charmed, he threatened, he reasoned. I managed to stay just ahead of him until he walked me home and asked me to kiss him. I shook my head.

'Bella, I know we can't be together now, I see it in your eyes, so at least give me one last kiss goodnight.'

His face crumpled so painfully into his neck like a heart-broken child's that I was swayed by his seemingly genuine feeling. I leaned over and pecked him goodnight. Then, like in a B-grade movie, I heard a familiar voice coming out of the gloom.

'I thought it was you,' said Axel, his eyes boring holes in me from his great height.

Shit shit shit!

Axel looked like he was going to blow and James looked unpleasantly smug as they made inane small talk and I blushed like a beetroot.

I vowed then and there to never see James again, never sleep with Axel again, and, most importantly, get out of there that very second.

'I have to go,' I blurted out.

They both looked at me expectantly.

'Wee. I have to wee!' I stammered. 'Bye.'

I heard James' amused voice mumble something about 'imaginative exit'. But I was already halfway up the stairs.

ıılıliılılı

Later that evening Axel and I had it out. He was as mad as hell because of the interlude with Dieter and couldn't believe that I'd let James kiss me. I admit it did look pretty bad. But, I reasoned, I *was* in my Ho Period. As he got angrier and angrier I realised he didn't have any right to be. Yes, he'd told me he'd developed feelings for me, but I had said no, so really, what right did he have to give me so much crap? My mind fumbled onto the obvious answer but I chose to ignore it.

I decided to stay the hell away from anything that resembled the opposite sex as the 'twilight zone' loomed anytime anything happened. I was Crazy Bulldozer Lady, crashing into everything and screwing everything up. I figured I had to de-complicate the mess I was in, so I emphasised to Axel that I just wasn't ready for anything serious, then I sought out Dieter and explained the same thing to him. Dieter took it well, but Axel wasn't quite so forthcoming at first.

I knew intellectually I had made the right decision, but the strange sensations I continued to get in my belly told me a different story. My instincts were telling me to allow myself to slip into the soft, warm glow of his sexy presence, but my head was willing me to remain staunch. The eternal battle between the head and the groin.

Then one day, as we were cleaning the apartment together and the sun shone in through the windows and the music blared, I felt the tension between us escalate. We drank cold beer and looked sideways at each other as we chatted and tidied up. That evening, he invited me out to see his friends' band. It was glam hard-rock, hilarious stuff – the young men posturing and screaming teenage obscenities into the microphone. The music was infectious, and the long, flowing hair hurled at the audience, the exaggerated pouts and snarls and the hot-rod tattoos all screamed high-school rock band. I liked them – enthusiastic and sweet – although I doubt they would have liked that description. We left late and walked home. A few blocks from our place, Axel suddenly slipped his big hand into mine. I continued walking. Then he slipped his arm around my waist and I felt his warmth through the fabric of my shirt. We walked on without speaking with a heady, nervous excitement steadily building. Then he tightened his grip, as though he were staking a claim, and damn in hell if I didn't like it, a lot. I felt myself release into him as he took me home.

16

My ho period climaxes despite choosing my focus, getting balanced and discussing politics with a gnome (with lovely elbow patches)

THE DAY AFTER SEEING the rock band, Axel and I had unravelled our legs from the twisted sheets, got up out of my rumpled bed and, tripping over the top mattress which had become askew, pulled on fresh clothes and walked downstairs, my body still aching from him. We sat in Café Teresa and ordered roast duck with apples and drank tall glasses of Polish beer. Our hands glided across each other's thighs, our skin wanting contact. My hunger was huge; we wolfed down the meats and breads and then returned to my room, which smelled like sex. Exhausted but insatiable, we continued through the evening until we fell asleep, our limbs entwined. When we woke the next morning, we lay in each other's arms. Axel's lovely face suddenly creased into a wide smile and a chuckle came from his belly. I looked at him and raised an eyebrow. He squeezed me tight and said simply, 'You make me happy.'

But we were pretty clear about where we stood. We were being, um, 'primal' with each other, no strings attached. And damn in hell if it didn't feel good.

My mother had a good friend she'd visit in New York whenever she came, and one day she invited me along to meet her. She also invited Susan, a relative from New Zealand, who had been living in New York for years. Susan has that rare and comfortable quality of being a highly successful person but without any hint of affectation at all. Her great intelligence, humour, warmth and tenacity had won her a place, just third beneath Kofi Annan, in the United Nations in New York.

Susan picked us up outside Dunkin' Donuts at seven, and we wove our way through Friday-night traffic to Tribeca. The apartment we were heading to was Marilyn French's. I had Googled her already and was amazed to see over 500,000 entries. She was the famous feminist author of the crucial best-selling novel *The Women's Room*, as well as a bunch of other books. She was also Harvard-educated and considered to be one of the foremost modern-day authorities on Shakespeare. She was in her seventies and still, I figured, a force to be reckoned with.

I felt a surge of electricity at meeting a person who had changed history as we knew it. As we exited the elevator on the 48th floor, we were greeted by Marilyn's exquisite view of New York City twinkling crazily at night and the Hudson River long and dark below. Light grey slacks and a jumper fitted over her tiny seventy-eight-year-old frame, and her shrewd and quite beautiful eyes, rimmed in blue eye-shadow, peeped out to appraise me.

'Yep, you are your mother's daughter,' she said, as she held me at arm's length to survey me.

Once drinks were served and we nestled into her plump and elegant sofas, the conversation turned to feminism. Each of those three powerful women were extraordinary in their own right. But getting them together in one room and listening to them talk was a real eye-opener. They spoke with humour and intelligence about the trials they had fought to change history, to shake up the status quo and to fight for those who couldn't. I felt in awe and inspired and deathly afraid that I would say something stupid, which of course I did.

When there was an expectant lull in the conversation, I offered my own experience of sexism.

'My generation of women were raised by trailblazers like you guys and now we (heh heh) are probably the sexist ones.'

I waited for a polite chuckle, but none came so I bulldozed on.

'On a personal level . . .' I said, trying to sound intelligent, 'I haven't encountered much sexism. Because of you guys, we are gifted with the legacy of feeling strong and proud of our feminine state. In fact, I think this generation of women are the sexist ones. We have it all: career, the confidence to change the world, economical freedom and, last on the list, we can have our little fluff on the side . . .'

I looked at their faces and realised I was making an absolute dickhead of myself. Polite slurping of liquids and shuffling on cushions was my only response. I felt like a prize fool. I'm sure I had offended all three, but wasn't exactly sure how. I poured myself another glass of wine and vowed to keep my mouth shut.

I sat transfixed, listening for their gems of wisdom as they talked about their battles and the things they'd learned along the way. Marilyn said that, sitting at the end of her life, she realised what had been, and still is, the most important thing for her.

Changing the world? Fighting evil?

'My family,' she said simply.

Susan told us an amazing story about how early on in her career with the UN, she and another group of women had marched into their boss' office to demand equal rights for women. They explained how the UN could better set an example for women everywhere by first changing their own policies. Boss Man nodded in sympathy then said, 'Yes, but come back later and we'll discuss it then. Okay, *girls*.'

Susan and the others were suitably flabbergasted.

'But, next time, girls,' he patronised, 'try wearing something more feminine. It might just work better for you.'

'Did you bop him one?' I asked incredulously before I remembered my vow of silence.

'No, Bella,' said Susan rather amusedly.

ıllıllıllıl

While Rosie, Sue and Marilyn were busy trying to save the world, I was busy at working on how to adapt my acting techniques to selling products on television. I couldn't sell a condom to a safe-sex worker so I was already worried.

The last TV commercial I'd done was for Fudge hair products back in Sydney, years ago. There were four thin supermodel types and me. From the outset I was feeling fat. We were being shot in front of a green screen and they were to digitally superimpose a big cartoon Roger Ramjet type character that we were to giggle at appreciatively. When the director yelled 'Action' we were to imagine the character coming in our bedroom window. After the first take, the director asked me to flatten my stomach.

'Just breathe in a little, dear,' he suggested unhelpfully.

The next take I was told to get 'bigger'. So I did. I camped it up and did a parody of a Valley girl and oohed and ahhed and shook my curls and pursed my glossy lips. That'll show him, I thought wickedly.

'Excellent, Bella!' exclaimed the director. 'Girls, that's how you're supposed to do it!'

It was truly ridiculous and I felt like Ashton Kutcher on *That '70s Show*, but the director was happy and I could afford to buy a new 'Chicks Are Cool' T-shirt that I'd had my eye on.

In class, the practice commercial was for Lime Away, a weird little product that lifts stains from your bathtub. I hated it. I felt so ridiculous holding up the product next to my cheek and smiling inanely through my gritted teeth. That was what my image of marriage was. There was my mother, Marilyn and Susan working hard to change the world for the better, and there I was learning how to sell a bathroom product. I suddenly saw myself from an outer perspective and lost all control, and laughed so madly that I screwed up my lines and had to leave the room to regain my composure. But even when I came back in, I still wished for the floor to swallow me up. 'Lime Away – and then I discovered Lime Away!' I was on my hands and knees scrubbing, pushing my tush in the air as I Limed Away. I knew I looked ridiculous, and my befuddled, slightly pissed-off expression was like that of a cat that has just been dunked in cold water.

'It's all experience, Bella,' said Tim, trying to hide a smile.

I sprayed him with some of my Lime Away.

The next class was Tai Chi and Ron taught us about focus. He said that you need to choose your focus, because if you don't, somebody else will choose it for you. When your partner comes home in a teeth-grinding mood, for instance, their focus is firmly planted on whatever awful thing happened to them that day. A flood of negative emotion surrounds them, and eventually you. They rant and rave at you about their awful day and you try to empathise and help them out. But eventually you start feeling pissed-off, too, nodding your head and agreeing 'yes, the world is awful'. They have just transferred their bad energy to you. They feel better because they got rid of it and you feel worse for having accepted it. When people offload onto you, he said, you must maintain a neutral state, keep your focus on maintaining that state and sympathise (rather than empathise) with their problem.

A student asked him how energy can be physically transferred that way and how that relates to focus. Ron replied that energy is a physical thing, and demonstrated by holding his arm out and asking one of the big footballer types in the class to try to bend it. Ron tensed his arm, using physical force, not 'energetic' force. His bicep bulged trying to physically resist the footballer's strength. The footballer managed to bend Ron's arm at the elbow. Then, Ron relaxed into himself and he moved his focus off the process of trying to keep his arm straight to visualising the energy flowing through him like a steam train. The energy originated in his belly, he said, and extended outward from his arms into the next room. Once again, the footballer tried to bend Ron's arm at the elbow, but he couldn't even budge it. And to all our amazement – especially the irate footballer's – Ron's bicep was soft and flaccid. He wasn't even *physically* trying. This, he demonstrated, was the might of focus.

If you change your focus or your intention, he continued, everything else changes. But you have to be specific to get specific results. As in acting, he said. The general intention to be a 'good' actor is not enough, you have to be specific about your focus. For example, with character work you can't describe your character as simply 'sad', you have to get into more detail: What kind of sadness do they feel, and why?

That afternoon, Ron asked to see me after class.

'You've put a lot of work in, Bella.' He smiled. 'So, are you ready to learn how to fly?'

'That was a joke, right?'

'Yes, Bella. Welcome to Tai Chi II.'

Yes! My months of breathing into the ground, bending like

a tree, 'extending into the universe' (and not thinking dirty thoughts about Ron) had paid off. I was now a member of the elite group Tai Chi II, Masters of the Universe.

I ran all the way home and told Axel about it.

'Um. So. You are excited because . . . ?' he asked, confused.

'Because I can learn to move like a drop of water and read people's thoughts and, and, and learn all the secrets of the universe. Which will help me to take over the world, you know, that sort of thing.'

Axel moved out of my reach, went to the cupboard, removed some Efamol tablets, put them at my feet and slowly backed away.

James suddenly broke into my thoughts. He would understand. He would laugh because he'd understand it was a joke, then he would beam at me and tell me he was proud, because he knew it wasn't only a joke.

The fridge was stocked with good food, the apartment was freshly cleaned and warm and the noise from the street below my window was bustling with positive energy. I had just showered, put on clean clothes and felt that kind of satisfaction that makes you want to write bad poetry. Strasberg had been challenging as all hell and I was exhausted from burning the candle at both ends, my lungs overworked from the Marlboros and my liver in need of a detox. I heard the front door open and saw my beautiful mum come in for a visit. We sat together in the sun and talked fondly until it was time to order a car to take her to the airport and back home to Australia. Her trip had been a long one and even though we hadn't seen each other every day, it had been a beautiful thing to know she was close by.

As my mum left, so did spring, and on came summer in all its glory. Overnight it had become hot, damn hot. Hot like a chilli-eating contest, as hot as Brad Pitt doing the splits in the nude. Hang on, that's kind of gross. Anyway, the tar on the pavements had begun to melt and when you walked anywhere your feet would make this strange suck-pop sound as they got stuck to the pavement. There was absolutely no warm-up, summer hurled itself at the city like a mad thing. Skin became silky with sweat and you could feel your arms slide as you walked. You didn't seem to think so much in summer, it was nice. Animalistic, primitive.

Axel took fairly good advantage of the whole hot/animalistic summer thing, and we had lots of mind-blowing, acrobatical, nautical, kitchen-table-ical sex. He was sexy, primal, had hands like a watchmaker and was always hard. The perfect man. I realised, though, for the first period of being together, we hadn't kissed. We just had sex, like blind, brutish animals. One summer night, though, as we assumed the post-coital position, our lips began to brush. Then a kind of buzzing electricity began to storm in-between us and we both of us took on the mad look of a sex offender. Still, we resisted (cue porn music). We held back. But then, then, we let the glorious moment come when all of our willpower was used up. Ahhh. And we kissed for the first time. That kiss was a death kiss. My whole body died in the rush of it, my self became merged with his in that single kiss. I wasn't the same again, I was new, awake. He was alive in me.

Soon enough, never one for moderation, the skin on my lips was red and sore from kissing. When we passed each other in the apartment, we'd kiss; when we sat, we'd kiss; when we ate, smoked, talked, walked – smooch. I hadn't kissed so much since practising on my hand in high school. Our bodies had such magnetism that our minds became obedient and passive slaves to their passions (I always wanted to say that).

It's difficult to describe the sex though. It was as if my self didn't exist any more. Thoughts and ideas and self were gone and I was left with skin and tongue and wetness. Every moment, every tiny second was brimming, full, overflowing, ready to burst over itself and the pretty red sheets. His big hands settling, stroking my arches, my curves, following the lines of me, time standing still in complete full-throated ease. Almost painful in its complete pleasure.

I'd find myself watching him while he slept: his mouth open, his eyelashes pushed against his clear white skin. He was heart-breakingly beautiful. His slight stubble gave him a sexy manly look, which contrasted magically with his angelic skin. I could see his profile when I'd tilt up from the crook of his arm, so lovely, so perfect. His neck would crane forward, his torso strong, thumping, pushing against mine to recapture me. 'Oh no, please don't (giggle).'

I was officially a complete ho. My days began to revolve around Axel's lips, the thought of his skin, the line of his shoulder as it swooped down to the small of his back and onto his ass. Everything else became hazy and unclear, leaving just the burning clarity of feeling him next to me. My friends said I was lust-struck and I was.

ıılılılılı

It was the fourth of July so I climbed to the rooftop of my building to watch the exploding fireworks. When I pushed the rusty roof-deck door open, I could see only darkness. Then, when my eyes grew accustomed, I saw that all the nearby rooftops were crowded with standing shadowy figures. It gave me a fright. Like it was some apocalyptic vision with silent black sentinels, heads tilted upward, waiting for a sign. I could see the Empire State and Chrysler buildings done up with red, white and blue lights, and distant fireworks were booming in the smoky night sky. Once the fireworks started closer to my building, the strange figures hurled themselves into the air and became animated and yelled from building to building, holding up sparklers towards the inky sky.

I felt deliriously, stupidly happy standing up there. They were really incredible fireworks, not the fizzlers of my childhood, but huge multi-coloured, booming fireworks: smiley faces and tubes of dazzling colour and bright blue fists smashing at the sky. That night, the people seemed to reclaim the city: the people had grown bigger than the buildings. I stood up there, my summer dress blowing, and I felt like the world was my oyster. My cheeks hurt from grinning and my skirt twirled high above my head in the wind. I felt crazily happy and damn lucky to be a part of this amazing city. To my right I could see the old buildings with their clanking air-conditioners and heat ducts and wires sticking out at odd angles into the smoky sky: the old New York. To my left was the new New York – the high towers of the shining downtown skyscrapers festooned with bright lights and flags. The two sides of this incredible city merged together under the fireworks. Yeah, I can take this city, I thought, as I stumbled and nearly fell off the roof.

'You better watch yourself,' came a voice from the darkness.

I turned around and saw what looked like a gnome. Late forties, short, an olive-green corduroy jacket with leather elbow patches. I wondered if he was magic.

'Thanks,' I mumbled. 'Yeah, I got a bit too excited.'

He looked off into the exploding night sky and seemed full of thoughts.

'Beautiful, isn't it,' he said, almost to himself. 'It really does make you feel good.' He looked down at his feet, then sat. 'And that's what it was designed for,' he said almost sadly.

'What do you mean?'

'It's all for show. Patriotism. America is all for show. Keep the masses happy with bright lights . . .' he said, trailing off. 'Do you realise the majority of foreigners despise America? Despise us.'

I studied him more closely.

'They think we're wasteful. Wasteful consumers. Uneducated. Base. Arrogant warmongers.'

'You have lovely elbow patches,' I added, for lack of anything better to say.

He smiled slowly, fondly and sadly like a tired old horse.

'But can we really blame them? Fundamentalist religions, church and state combined, corporate greed. Forsaking lives for the mighty dollar.'

He sighed and got lost in his own thoughts. He seemed to carry the burdens of the world on the shoulder-pads of his corduroy jacket and seemed somehow hurt and forgiving all at the same time.

'But it's all a hoax,' he said, 'the biggest hoax on earth.' He turned back to look at the night sky and its thundering fireworks. 'But they are very beautiful, aren't they.'

After a while he spoke up again. 'I was brought up to believe in the values we espouse. Freedom of speech, liberty, justice for all. And you know what I learned?' He sat there looking out into the distance. 'That even my belief was a construct of the system.'

He suddenly looked at me closer then smiled softly. 'You look like my daughter. I'm sorry, a young girl needn't be burdened with an old man's crimes.'

I wanted to hug him and tell him everything would be all right, but restrained myself in case he thought I was a nutcase.

After a while, he exhaled and stood up.

'Well,' he said, 'I'm tired. That's enough for tonight.' He regarded me kindly for a moment. 'Thank you for listening.' And with that he went back into the darkness.

On that rooftop I'd felt so filled with New York City, so

delighted by it and humbled by it. I realised with a start that what I'd felt was a kind of city-patriotism. I had felt patriotic. Usually that word filled me with dread: like when I went downstairs and turned on the TV, Tom Selleck was reading out part of the Independence Proclamation as part of the nightly news July 4th special. He valiantly surged on, his voice thickening as actor's tears welled in his eyes. Patriotism. I got an immediate sense of distrust.

History has shown us that leaders can manipulate the community with their own interpretation of patriotism: sanctifying war, murder, exclusionism. The gnome was right. America was like oral sex, vastly different depending on which end you looked at it. I knew about the wars on foreign soil and about the poverty, the non-existent healthcare system. There were things about America that were truly appalling. Yet, I couldn't seem to reconcile the America I knew existed with the pride and exuberance I still felt for New York.

I'd always thought that New York was different. That people in New York were the types who arrived here because they didn't fit into the places they were born to. Or who questioned the status quo or just wanted to tread a different path. They would gravitate to New York because their difference was accepted and even celebrated here. I knew that people were really and truly, almost terrifyingly, alive in New York.

I flicked through the channels on the TV and landed on another news program. There's always that last segment on a nightly news program, the feel-good segment, like the funny/strange guy juggling, a hot-dog-eating competition – 'Oh those Texans' – or the kitten that was just born: 'Cute, isn't it, Jen.' That night they showed a patriotic Pakistani guy with his face painted red, white and blue, yelling into the air and singing the national anthem. The female newscaster said, after a well-rehearsed laugh, 'What a patriotic fellow!' The male newscaster smiled like he was in a toothpaste commercial and said, 'I love America.' I shuddered. They both seemed so disingenuous. It did feel like a hoax, a show somehow. I wondered if the announcers were privy to it, or victim to it.

I went down onto the street and breathed in the city. Crap, New York wasn't duped by the corporations or government, the people in this city were too sexy and tough to fall for all that. Nobody could pull one over on a New Yorker, I reckoned, then stopped mid-thought.

I suspected I was being naive. It probably didn't have anything to do with being a New Yorker, or geography, it was happening to all of us, everywhere. Capitalism. Misguided patriotism, rampant consumerism. The biggest hoax on earth.

As I was bleakly contemplating, I spied my neighbour leaning against the door. We chatted about his job in real estate and his current vacuum of motivation. I tried my best to make him feel better. Damn in hell I wish I hadn't. My rent got increased. Apparently he got so motivated by our conversation that he tried to convince our landlord into selling the building to his company. The landlord didn't sell it to him, but figured if the building was in such hot demand he could raise the rent on us all. Which he did.

Other than the increase in rent, which impacted on my ability to ever eat food again, I was feeling pretty happy. I realised it was because I was turning into, shock horror, a balanced person. All the four elements were in equilibrium. The physical, emotional, mental and spiritual.

At Strasberg, physically I was working harder than ever before (okay, kudos also has to be given to Axel the sex machine); emotionally I was as activated as a yeast infection; intellectually I was as stimulated as a fat man locked in a candy store; and good ol' Guru Ron was providing for all my spiritual needs. Ah, happiness. It was sometimes exhilarating, sometimes scary, but it was always a pure rush for the addict I had become. It felt like before Strasberg I had been a dried, salty sea sponge, brittle and discoloured, but I'd soaked up so much information there that I'd become a wet Sponge Bob Square Pants. But it wasn't all cocktails and weird little cartoon characters as once in class, after a student had an exceptionally large breakdown, Robert Castle told us: 'It's not easy, I know that, but just like a fireman running into a burning building, it's an actor's *job* to explore their emotions, however painful, and if you want to be an actor, this is what you have to do. If you can't do it, don't be an actor. You have to have ready access to *all* your emotions, *all* the time, even the ones you dread. Especially the ones you dread. I make no apologies for pushing you; you have to be at the top of your game in every way. A lawyer has his law books, a carpenter has his tools, you only have your self – your mind, your body, your emotions – so keep them sharp, work on them, perfect them. Balance them.'

I knew that when my life was balanced I was happier as a person, but from what Robert said, balance was also useful for becoming a better actor. Score: two birds with one stone.

And he was right. It was tough-going a lot of the time, but the more I worked on all those four elements of balance, as an actor and as a person, the happier I became. Was I at last becoming one of those happy, normal people I'd seen on TV?

17

Cupid and the green-eyed monster cometh (or trying to stay staunch with drugs in my system from ancient Israeli stomach-ache remedy)

THE HEAT REALLY HAD become ridiculous. The crime rate soared as people figured the only response to the summer heat was to pop a cap in somebody's ass. Tempers flared, the city stank, and we were expected to have whole city blackouts as restaurants froze their patrons with overworked air-conditioners. The subways were ghastly too. To create cool, heat had to be generated, and the poor old subway was where all the city's heat ended up. A simple train ride uptown turned into a painful sauna as sweat pooled, clothes become scratchy, make-up melted and breathing became painful. But there was a plus side: hemlines went up and shirts came off. By day it felt just like a summer's day back on Bondi, and at night the bars and streets were crowded with summer party-goers as a feeling of anticipation and celebration began to form an excited bubble around the city.

In Midtown one day, with the searing sun ricocheting between the buildings, I took shelter in beautiful Bryant Park and sank down into a chair. A rather nice-looking young American guy ambled up to me and asked if he could share my table.

'Sure, help yourself.'

'Thank you,' he replied, then added, 'Hot, isn't it?'

'Yeah,' I answered, smiling politely.

We got to chatting and got along quite well. We talked about relationships, politics and New York, about his work as a pilot and my acting. Then out of nowhere he let out an exasperated *rrrrr* noise from his throat.

'What's the matter?'

He turned to me suddenly. 'I'm sorry, I really like you and I want to ask you something . . . but I can't.'

He looked as if he was about to cry.

'Go ahead,' I said, 'it's okay.'

He took a deep breath. 'I know you're going to think this is –' he cleared his throat – 'ah, somewhat weird. But there are things I want to do with a woman. I like to do things with faeces.'

I froze into place.

'I know I am a freak,' he said quickly, 'but I just can't find anybody willing to do it with me.'

Why me? Did I look like a poo pusher?

'So you saw me and thought I was a likely candidate?' I blurted out incredulously.

'No, it's not that, I just knew you wouldn't judge me and thought maybe you'd give me some advice.'

Who was I? The Doctor Phil of Poo? Now, I agreed with him, he was a freak – but the strange thing was that I could tell he wasn't crazy or one of those men who like to shock women for the sake of it. He was a normal guy with a pretty abnormal appetite.

'Shit, Gary – I mean, damn, Gary, I really don't know what

to say about that. Perhaps there is a club or something you could join.'

His eyes lit up. 'Really, where?'

'I don't really know. Er, perhaps you could advertise.'

It was probably the most bizarre conversation I'd ever had.

'Where?' he insisted.

'I don't know . . . um . . . how about Craigslist?'

'Is, er, that something you would be interested in experimenting with?' he asked tentatively.

'Messing with *merde*? No, Gary.'

I didn't like where the conversation was heading so I made my excuses to leave.

'Well, er, good luck with . . . um . . . the whole faeces thing, Gary.'

'Thanks, Bella, I really do appreciate it.'

I got up to leave and, as I was walking away, he called after me and beckoned me back.

'What is it?'

'Um . . . I think it's that time of the month and . . . ah . . . it's all over the back of your dress,' he said haltingly.

For god's sake. First poo, then blood. It was turning into a really disgusting day. I hailed a cab with my handbag covering my ass and arrived home to Axel who unhelpfully laughed for an hour about my shitty adventure.

᠁

I was a walking tomato sauce bottle. I had been trying a new contraception, a small plastic ring that you put up inside that secretes hormones throughout the month. It had gone well for the first week; I started feeling nauseous the second week, then suicidal the third week. The hormones pumping into my body were making me alternate between laughing hysterically one minute and crying big fat tears the next. Now I'd started bleeding. The packet said bleeding was bad; I said bleeding was bad. So I took the damn thing out. But I continued to bleed. Finally, I went to the only doctor I could afford. The Lower East Side Free Medical Clinic.

After the doctor listened to my symptoms and examined me and I heard all about her son's mental problems, she said with a vague intonation: 'You're bleeding.' She then looked up at me surprised. 'Why?'

'Er . . .'

Perhaps she was hard of hearing? She looked at me expectantly so I repeated my symptoms and reminded her that she'd just examined me. She scratched her forehead.

'Nope. I have no idea.'

I replied with an eyebrow raise.

'Okay, well, if that's it, you can go now,' she said brightly.

'Are we finished?' I asked.

'Yep.'

'Um, I've had my period for more than two weeks, so perhaps we could investigate just that tiny bit more . . .' I paused. '*I am bleeding from my vagina, doctor.*'

'Vagina. Vagina, funny word, that, isn't it?'

'Yes.'

'Yeah, I suppose you're right. We should look into it further,' she said after some thought. 'Okay, put your clothes back on, and I'm going in here to think. I always find the bathroom easier to think in.'

I watched her retreating figure with alarm.

Five minutes later she came back into the room.

'What do *you* think it is?' she asked as if she'd just found the cure for cancer.

'Well . . .' I began slowly, 'I don't know, that's kind of why I'm here.'

She looked disappointed. 'Well, that makes two of us.'

I eyed the door, but restrained myself. A regular doctor would cost a few hundred dollars and I was on a tight student budget so I had to stick it out with cuckoo lady. I offered her some alternatives.

'Perhaps it's an infection from the ring? Could I be allergic to it? Maybe the ring was faulty? Perhaps I'm pregnant?'

She looked like a kid in a candy store, trying to figure out which lolly she wanted to pick.

'Yes, that one. Yes, yes!' she exclaimed. 'You're on to something,' she added conspiratorially.

She gave me a pregnancy test and it was negative.

'Well, I have no idea now!' she said exasperated as loose strands of her hair flew over her face like a mad professor's. 'Let's just put you on some pills, huh? That'll do the trick.'

'What kind of pills?'

'I don't know. Maybe pelvic inflammatory disease pills,' she said, furrowing her brow.

I looked around for the hidden cameras.

'I don't think so, doctor. I think perhaps I'd better get diagnosed before we start with treatment, yeah?'

'By god, you're right!' she said with an appreciative smile. 'You should be the doctor!' she added emphatically.

I quietly agreed with her.

When I got back home, Axel insisted on paying for me to go to a real doctor and spent the afternoon researching my symptoms on the Internet. Shucks. It turned out that the ring just didn't agree with me, and a few days later I was back to normal.

ıılıtılılıılı

The time soon came for Tom and Natalie to go home to Germany. I was really going to mourn the loss of them, despite their Germanness. There was a party for them at a downtown loft where we banged on guitars and drank schnapps until the wee hours. We hugged and started crying, then pretended we weren't. Watching them and talking with them, I knew, despite the distance, we'd be lifelong friends and continue to indulge in bad jokes until we were all old and grey and had bad comb-overs. I loved that thought.

Natalie gave Axel the thumbs-up as we analysed him over our schnapps. She said he had a lot of sex appeal. I agreed wholeheartedly.

'You guys have a lot of sexual tension together,' she said. 'Watching you two together is kind of like watching a porno.'

I chuckled.

'But I also detect more than just friends with benefits,' she said sagely.

I stopped chuckling.

Natalie's parting quip was to not get pregnant with him.

'What? No way, I don't even love . . .'

And it was true. I knew I was beginning to fall for Axel, not that I'd ever tell him that, mind you. But the line between lust and love had started to blur. He'd send me texts, 'I need your smell, your voice, just to fall asleep, or even to breathe.' I liked stroking his forehead when he slept. I liked him looking up at me in bed, grappling with powerful, loving emotions, trying to conquer them with manly restraint and failing beautifully. I was feeling foolish and girly, like a love-struck teenager. Where was the world-weary woman I used to look at in the mirror? Lying like that with Axel, everything was felt; I was falling in love with him. It was the last thing I expected and the most powerful thing to resist.

In those unspoken moments, I couldn't have imagined being happier, and they felt golden and everlasting. But with a jolt,

I remembered feeling that exact way before, a few times. All relationships start that way. The first blush of love, the intoxication of an uncomplicated future together, thoughts of love and babies and cuddles and sex and laughs. Lying there, a sudden sadness overcame me, knowing that everything was finite, even our seemingly everlasting golden moments.

Like that day I was waiting for a taxi cab on First Avenue. Next to me was a bundle of dirty rags, with two thin white legs sticking out. A homeless man had passed out, his beer bottle still grasped in his big paw. Sleep, the intoxicant of the damned. A loud Italian shouted into his cell phone and a young black mother hit her child's small arm for spilling lemonade on her pants. It suddenly struck me – all three of them were afraid. Afraid of being alone. I could even see it in the unconscious face of the homeless man. I suddenly felt terrifyingly alone too. Somehow both scared and exhilarated at being so truly, terrifyingly alone. The brief moments of togetherness, like with Axel, just stall the inevitable. The discovery of being alone, absorbing that knowledge into your skin, does something to you. But when you scrape away the fear of alone and accept it, you find power underneath it, strength.

I suppose that's why I liked going to Sun Nail Tan on First Avenue. All the clients there are getting cleansed and scrubbed and polished and poked; such intimate things happening to a roomful of strangers reminds me of how connected we all really are. That day, I entered Sun Nail Tan, with its smells of ammonia and nail varnish and, as was the tradition, the owner, a stocky Chinese woman who looked like a kindly bulldog, let out a shout.

'Ah, she's back! Waxy waxy,' she threatened and wagged her finger at me.

I greeted her with a grin and tried to avoid her eye. I was

the local entertainment at Sun Tan Nail. They called me 'The Amazon' because of my legs – not that they are particularly Amazonian, but compared to the owner's lovely stumps, they look like flag poles. My resistance to pain, being almost as bad as my resistance to chocolate, also had them in stitches. They would fight over who got to be privy to my apparently hilarious inability to handle any kind of pain whatsoever.

Apart from the hot wax torture I endured, I loved going to Sun Nail Tan. The overly familiar staff members, the affectionate and eccentric owner, the smells of varnish and the female kindness.

'Amazon, take down your pants!' the Bulldog bellowed, then with the skill of a wild woman she stung and ripped and sloshed and smacked at me until I was completely leg and bikini hair free.

I don't know why I kept enduring that fresh hell with that crazy Chinese woman, but somehow I liked it. I liked the familiarity, the absence of affectation. The sense of secret women's business. The connection between strangers.

Bulldog flipped me over like a sumo wrestler and smacked me on the bottom with a triumphant grin. 'There! Boys are happy now.'

As I limped off, vowing to save for electrolysis, she hugged me around the waist then prodded my stomach. 'Eat more!' she commanded, then marched off to inflict her special kind of torture on another unsuspecting soul.

With my new silky legs, I rushed home to see Axel.

We would hang out, talk, watch movies. Before, I had been a pretty hard worker at Strasberg, but since Axel and I had started blurring the line of sex and love, I'd started to do the bare minimum, enough to get by but not enough to really improve. I had to pull my finger out.

I had a sit-down talk with Axel and explained how important Strasberg was to me and how I had to concentrate on acting and not men. Anyhow, I told him, his Jewish mother would have a coronary if he ever married a gentile. I was basically saving her life. He managed a smile.

'Okay, Bella, okay,' he said, 'I'll back off for a bit.'

Over the next few weeks he stayed true to his word and I hated it. The days wore on and my resolve crumbled under the weight of his tall frame. I missed his big hands resting unselfconsciously on my thigh and his sexy lingering gaze directed at me. My plan hadn't worked out too well as my classwork didn't improve either, because I was thinking about him even more. Damn and blast in hell. But I had to hold staunch to my resolutions. I was in New York to be an actor, not fall in love (however well muscled his biceps were). Plus, a wonderful by-product was that if I broke up with him now, I wouldn't get hurt by him in the future. Quite brilliant really, I thought, as I inhaled more chocolate.

I called Zoë for a catch-up, and when I told her about Axel, she pretty much repeated the same thing Polly had directed me to do. But instead of *'My mum on the bog'* it was, *'I will hold staunch, I will hold staunch.'*

One night, I went into my room chanting my mantra in my head, but I felt a hollow ache in my chest and a queasiness in my belly. Then my belly actually started cramping as it released guttural, blood-curdling noises. Axel came into my room with an old Israeli stomach-ache remedy. He had heated olive oil in a pan, which he gently dripped onto my belly, his big hands massaging me.

I will hold staunch, I will hold staunch.

He wrapped my abdomen gently in a woollen scarf to keep the heat in and looked down at me with his beautiful brown eyes. My staunchness utterly failed me. We kissed each other goodnight on the lips and both of us trembled. My mantra flew out the window as he pressed his face into my neck and we tightly wound our arms around each other. I could feel our hearts beating furiously on either side of the woollen scarf. Being in that cave, that oasis, that womb of love, the joy never goes. The bliss, the heightened feelings of love and sex. The smell of his skin near mine, his strong arms tightly gripping me. Our lips searching for contact. I would have given away the world at that moment.

'I'm sorry I hurt you,' I told him as we lay entwined.

It took me what felt like years to say the next sentence. 'It's unfair of me, but I have to say it . . .'

He gripped me tighter. His cheek was pressed against mine and his skin was smooth, freshly shaven. I raised my lips up to his ear and felt my chest pulsating, getting ready to explode. I felt this huge wave of love for him and I wanted to let it out to wash all over both of us. I wanted to open the floodgates and tell him that I loved him. But my voice wouldn't work, I couldn't do it. Was it fear or sanity?

He held me tighter and tighter until I couldn't breathe, then he realised he was squashing me so released me with a laugh.

My face touched his face and I finally told him. I said those three tricky words.

'I love you.'

It felt so good to tell him, but it was laced with real fear too.

He pressed his face to mine and his arms and legs gripped me in a bear hug. He kept repeating, 'Baby. Baby. Baby. Baby.'

Eventually he whispered: 'I can't say it.'

I felt my stomach plunge through the floor and slam into the ground four storeys below. I hurriedly tried to save face and stammered that 'It was silly . . . silly of me to say it . . . and the worst possible timing and . . .'

His face was blank so I continued on like a blathering idiot.

'Entirely stupid of me to say, I understand. Completely. But you know, no, I'm sorry, I didn't mean it, well, yes, but I'm just being selfish and you don't have to –'

'Bella. Bella . . . stop. Okay?' he commanded.

I stopped, but couldn't meet his gaze.

'I fell in love with you months ago.'

Bliss.

ıllıılllıı

It felt so good, Mother Nature pumping her drugs full tilt into my system. The world of lovers. The irrationality of it. The junky's desire for his arms around me. The blush of love. I felt it in every pore, in every bone, in the flush on my face, when I saw his shirt draped over a chair.

We grabbed a light blanket, some cold Tsingtao beer and vanilla body oil and ran up to the hot tarred roof. We lay in the sun, our glistening limbs entwined, sweat pooling in the little hollow in-between his rib cage. We hungrily looked into each other's eyes and we kissed. And kissed, and couldn't stop kissing. A suction fish had nothing on me. My mouth was red and hurting but I couldn't stop. Those moments are inexplicable, they pop out of an accumulation of secret glances and touches and make you feel like an addicted, lovesick, well . . . suction fish. We hugged each other so tightly, chests flattened, legs entwined, with some uncompromising claim that I could hardly breathe. We wanted to become a part of each other. When we had to break for air, slight panic set in and didn't subside until we were firmly back in each other's arms. We must have looked like a couple of idiots, smothered in oil, rolling around between empty beer bottles under the New York sun. But I didn't care. I didn't care at all.

Back in our apartment, he came out of the shower refreshed,

his blue jeans fitting his sexy body perfectly, his white Polo Ralph Lauren jocks peeking over the edge of the waistband. His sculpted chest, his slight stubble. Dave Matthews Band pounded from the speakers as he drummed in rhythm on my thighs, making coffee and singing. He was pure sex.

But it wasn't only sex, he noticed the little things about me, too. He knew that when I curled my toes up under my feet, I was feeling uncomfortable. Or when I smiled through the left side of my mouth I'd done something naughty. He could read me like a book and it felt good to be known and loved in spite of it.

I became embarrassingly high-school romantic, too. I surprised him with immaculately prepared dinners over candlelight, and he filled the apartment with balloons and wrote bad poetry. It would be embarrassing if it wasn't for the delightful madness of new-born love.

My motivation for school also sky-rocketed. I didn't even have to make myself concentrate. I felt such a joyous light-heartedness that I wanted to rip into school and work my heart out.

My friends would ask me about Axel and how we were doing. I'd break out into a wide grin, confess I thought I was in love, then freeze and suddenly feel panicked. I suppose I shouldn't have felt that way. But love brings with it so many things.

For instance, one night he'd gone out after his shift with some waitresses from his work, including one who phoned him up regularly to chat and flirt. I thought fondly of maiming her. Then thought about my jail cell to be. I resolved to try to get over my jealousy.

I asked Guru Ron a thinly veiled question in class the next day.

'So, I have this character I'm about to play . . .'

'Yes, Bella,' he answered. I swear I saw him roll his eyes.

'Well, she was never jealous before. Ever. But she's met this guy and suddenly she's a green-eyed freak. So what is beneath jealousy and how do we resolve it?' I added quickly.

'First off, you do not "resolve" it. You allow it. You do not fight it, you breathe into it. Be brave enough to feel and allow it and not repress it. Remember, emotions are not right or wrong, they just are.'

'Yeah, but . . .' I started.

He gave me one of his intense gazes so I shut up.

'Jealousy is often the desire to control somebody or something,' he said after a while. 'To possess them. It's about needing to feel in control.'

Damn.

He regarded me again, his gaze reaching my very cells.

'Often, too often,' he said, 'we've been taught not to feel a particular emotion, thus we repress it and are afraid of it. For example, when I got angry as a child, my father used to punish me, so I learned very early not to feel anger. Then, because I had denied my anger for so long, my anger, over the years, became stronger . . .'

His voice droned into the background as I thought about my paternal grandmother. She was an exciting, scary woman. Full of life and charm, and also, somehow, an insidious threat: that if you were found lacking, her intense attention would be withdrawn from you like a blade, leaving you gasping, and firmly put in your place. My sister was a beautiful child with bright golden curls set around a cherub's face with huge blue eyes. I, on the other hand, was a bit of an ugly duckling. I had scraggly hair, freckles and an unformed face, as my grandmother thought it prudent to remind me. She once picked us up at the airport in her furs and sparkly rings. She grasped my sister by the cheeks and exclaimed how beautiful she was. I stood there expectantly, grinning, waiting my turn. Then she turned to me, looked me up and down and said dryly, 'You need a haircut.' I guess if that happened now, I would high-five her and say 'Good one, Grandma!' But as a little kid, it pretty well demolished me.

I began to dread staying with her. In a restaurant once, in front of her many friends, she began espousing the charms of my sister and once again making fun of my freckles and bad hair. But on that day, I snapped like a candy-cane. I upped my Danny DeVito legs and didn't even say 'excuse me' (I was a real rebel) and stormed off to the bathroom. Gotta love a good storm-off. But it didn't exactly have the required effect, as all I could hear was the sound of her laughter and her wineglass clinking. 'Ahhh, little Bella is jealous of her sister!' she sang gaily to the room. I remember turning around, courage balling my fists, and retorting with a big mean: 'Yes, Nonna, I am!' Which only made her laugh harder. I felt ashamed of myself. I think Dr Freud would say it was then that I decided to repress jealousy at all costs.

I had a lot of male friends and I couldn't stand it when I'd have to explain to my partner again and again that they were just *friends*. Nothing more. It irritated me. But there I was, doing the same thing to Axel. I resolved to push down my jealousy into the bottom of my tennis shoes and kill it with my foot odour.

18

Terrorism in New York

I T WAS THE TIME for summer vacation. Woo hoo! I could sleep in, forget about learning lines and doing effective memories; I could go to the beach, dance naked around the house and eat copious quantities of ice-cream and pineapples. Random, yet exciting. The second week of the holiday I got a call from Gian-Luca, who told me he'd heard that if we took the summer off, we'd be ineligible for the OPT.

I went in to Strasberg to double-check and the kind-faced office staff confirmed that the government had changed the restrictions and we couldn't take the summer off. Gian-Luca had to cancel his flight back home and I had to give up my dreams of naked pineapple dancing.

I did get a couple of days of hard-core New Yorking in, though. I went to the Gay and Lesbian Mardi Gras parade that snaked along Fifth Avenue. From the fun of Oxford Street in Sydney I was excited to see how the New York version would compare.

Although the actual parade lasted eight hours, it seemed like a put-together school play compared to the glitz of Sydney. The marchers were wielding home-made signs, with textas and safety-pinned costumes, and included a large chicken with a strap-on cock. I saw an old trolley bus go by with a sign that read: 'We Are Aged Gay Gentlemen'. There was a tiny bird-like white-haired old man with a fedora and an old grey suit that had been pressed and re-pressed a hundred times. He had shiny black shoes and a cane that he hobbled along the float with, supporting his bow legs. He was emphatically clasping hands with another old man with startlingly dyed-black hair. They held a sign written in crayon: 'We've Been Together 48 years!' The old fedora guy was grinning so much, it looked as if his face would split open. He kept pointing at the sign with his knotted old finger and pushing his chest and arms out with pride. I watched the lovely old couple who had been through so much to keep their love alive and felt a bubble of emotion rise up and threaten to form into a tear and embarrass me. But looking around at the cheering crowd, I saw a few misty-eyed people so let one slip out in the confusion.

My lovely father, Danny, flew in from Sydney for a quick visit on his way to Ecuador to see my sister. I'd missed the old codger a lot and it was damn wonderful to see him. On the Saturday, we went to the Bronx Zoo. It was a beautiful day and the animals seemed ridiculously happy and playful. The river swept the boundary so you could meander along it, the brightly painted birds squawking in the trees above. There was a giant white polar bear that played for hours in his pool, attacking a bright blue ball and generally being very naughty and sweet. Danny convinced me to join the queue of kids waiting for a camel ride and took pictures of me as I grinned inanely. It was glorious spending a whole day with my father. We both have a keen sense of adventure and we talked incessantly about acting as the lovely smells of the zoo wafted around with the heat. He was always so full of enthusiasm for the subject and told wild inspirational stories which had me champing at the bit. I could still smell the wet hay on my skin as we made our way back to Manhattan.

The next day, my friend Alex, an all-American twenty-something guy with a charming smile and mischievous personality, and I were hanging out after class, smoking cigarettes and thinking up new and diabolical ways of making money, when Sour Receptionist Chick interrupted our plot-hatching to tell us about some auditions for a play that were being held that afternoon at Strasberg.

Fresh from my father's inspirational acting stories, I urged Alex to sign up with me. So, completely ignorant of what we were auditioning for, we filled out the forms and signed on the dotted line. Under 'special skills', Alex scrawled 'women'. I left mine blank.

The other actors had had their scripts for weeks in advance so we had some catching up to do. It sounded like suicide by audition. I was just about to pack up my bags and whimper out of there when I saw Gretchen. Greetccheen. She was a thoroughly annoying twenty-six-year-old stiletto-wielding yank with an impossibly pretty face and an abnormally impossible personality. In one of our classes she said to me after I'd performed, 'Try doing it in character next time, Bellllla.' I could have ripped her smug nose off. Every girl has to have an arch nemesis and she was mine.

Soooo, I thought. *Greetccheen's auditioning, huh?* I made a snap decision: I would win this part over her dead body, or her broken stilettos if need be.

We made eye contact from across the room.

Grrrrr.

I don't think it was exactly what my dad had in mind when he gave me his 'acting and motivation' pep-talk at the zoo, but baby steps, baby steps.

Apparently the director was some kind of famous Russian, trained at the Moscow Art Theatre, his résumé reading like a who's who of the theatre and film industry. I was also told that the day before there had been a mouse in the theatre and he had refused to go inside until somebody had chased it out. He sounded talented and eccentric, just my kind of fella. After scanning the script for five minutes, I found myself in front of him. He was tall, preppy-looking, rather intriguing and his eyes were humorous and intelligent. I did a performance for him, and when I'd finished he leaned back on his chair and grinned.

'You're a good actress,' he said.

'Thank you,' I answered, then paused.

'Is there something else?' he asked me.

I wanted to ask him about the mouse.

'Er, I heard, you –'

'What?' he said rather sternly.

I stood there. 'Er . . . nothing. Thanks.'

He looked at me like I was a nut job.

When I walked out of the audition I saw Gretchen snap to attention. I forced my best 'I-just-kicked-ass' neck-jut and strode down the stairs hoping to look glamorous. I think I heard her snort.

The following week I got the fantastic news that I'd won a main role. My dad was overjoyed. And, most importantly, I had won the role over guess who . . . Greetccheen! My feeling of exhilaration lasted well into the night, when I calmed down and decided to read the play to see what I had actually got myself into.

It was called *Terrorism*, and was written by the classic Russian playwrights the Presnyakov Brothers. It was a series of vignettes that eventually tied themselves together, and, thankfully, it was damn good. When I got towards the end of the play, I stopped reading mid-sentence. My character does what? She likes to be tied up? Okay, I can live with that. But . . . what? She actually *gets* tied up? Then she gets *raped* on stage. My exhilaration took a sharp downward turn as my predicament became apparent. Not only was I to do a play with a mouse-hater, but I would have to be raped on stage every night of the run. Damnnn yooou, Greetccheen!

Then I found out that Igor, the director of *Terrorism*, wanted us to *vocally* do all the sound effects in the play – the noise of an aeroplane, of the birds and wind. He was a lunatic. The production was either going to be exceptional and talked about for years, or the biggest, most laughable pile of shit ever put on in New York. The bets were in.

ılıllılılı

When I took my father to the airport, he told me that it was all up to me. He said if *Terrorism* was going downhill, it just meant I had to work harder and longer to make the production better. 'Easy!' he said with a joyful smile.

As I watched him enter customs I felt a pang. I'd always basked in the immense capacity for joy he had and missed it when it wasn't there. But as I waved him goodbye I felt the surprising warm jolt of my own happiness and silently thanked his genes as I made my way home.

That night, I went out to meet Dieter and Alex at the Marquee Club. Outside there were swelling queues of sequinned, hair-straightened, bright-white smiling partygoers. I hated waiting in line, so I stood near the roped-off private entrance and tried to look like I was equal parts important, glamorous, and waiting for somebody. Sure enough, a few seconds later, Puff Daddy and his entourage of giant bodyguards came along. I smiled familiarly at him then hooked on to the back of his train and entered the club. Weaving our way through, I was shoved into position just behind Puff Daddy. It was fascinating to watch the buzz that was generated at our passing, okay, okay, his passing. Girls' faces lit up, people started up a chant, men stiffened and grinned nervously. At the back of the club we climbed the stairs to the exclusive 'top room'. I pretended to swagger and pout my way up the post-modern staircase, looking down at all the non-famous people, clenching my butt cheeks for maximum effect. Inside, my pal P Daddy and I got separated but his bodyguard gave me a slip of paper with an invitation to their secret after-party. I gave it to a guy in a lemon-coloured sweatsuit for ten bucks and a packet of cigarettes.

'You could've gotten a thousand!' exclaimed Alex.

Damn.

Although getting rich by hawking P Diddy tickets wasn't on the horizon, my acting career was picking up. The director of a film Gian-Luca was doing called to offer me a role. I would be playing a madam of a brothel that the main characters frequented.

Relishing the chance to play a madam, I accepted on the proviso of a no-nudity clause.

'Of course there's no nudity,' the director replied, shocked. 'I'm a Christian!'

I didn't quite know how being a Christian meant no nudity in the film, but I went along with it.

The scene was a lot of fun to do and the director was happy, so two weeks later he called me in again, saying they wanted to extend my character and shoot again in a week.

The shoot went well, except for an airhead assistant who couldn't quite understand that I was *acting* a madam and that I couldn't in reality 'hook him up'.

Next, I heard on the grapevine that Igor was going to include dancing and (cringe) singing in *Terrorism*. I still had time to shoot myself.

ııılıllılılıı

Finally, rehearsals for *Terrorism* began, and the other actors involved were talented and the director was as weird and fabulous as I'd hoped he'd be. He asked me to play two additional characters as well as the vixen who gets raped: I was also to play a simpleton alcoholic and, lastly but certainly not least, my most cherished character – I was to play a dog. Move over, Ophelia, new heights had been reached.

The cast had bonding exercises for an hour a day. They were supposed to help us work together, coordinate our collective senses and work out our bodies, concentration, memory and instinct. I failed to see how spelling out a word with our chairs did that, but was still hopeful.

Another of Igor's training methods was to make us try to develop our mental telepathy. We each had to sit across from a partner and telepathically send them a message to stand up or nod their head or something. It was supposed to develop non-verbal communication between the actors on stage. I sat there with my partner, fiercely looking into her eyes and sending a telepathic message that she should pick her nose. It didn't work.

My biggest scene in *Terrorism* was the one that climaxes in an awful rape scene where my character ends up screaming for her life. Once I finished that scene and wiped off my tear-streaked face, I would do a twenty-second costume change and make my way back on stage as Bernice, the drunk suburban office worker. Two scenes after that, I went on as The Dog.

Walking home one day after rehearsal, head down, deep in thought about my roles, I was startled back to reality as a taxi cab hurtled past an inch away from me. I looked around as if for the first time. New York rose out of me, the city of light and energy. It was stupendous and alive and sordid and powerful and gentle and sweet and it was my everything. I loved the city as if it were a person.

Axel and I were sleeping in the same room by now, so we'd been meeting strange and interesting New Yorkers to interview for my old room. One guy, six foot six, cried sweet happy tears when he spoke about leaving Alabama for New York; a gay guy said he was the happiest he'd ever been coming out (literally) to the city. All these people, converging on this city of light to make their lives better, to forget their pasts, to follow their passions. Each of them spoke about New York as if it were a sanctuary, or a dear friend, or a fine piece of ass. The old adage was so true: You're a New Yorker before you even arrive in New York.

When I arrived home that day, a Harvard graduate who worked as a voice-over artist came to see the room. He was charming and pleasant and very keen to move in. During the interview, I excused myself to go to the bathroom, and when I came out he had changed completely. He seemed nervous and somewhat disgusted. He made a feeble excuse about the rent being too high then left abruptly. I settled down on the sofa then spied the reason lying on the coffee table. I had made a reminder note to myself for Costya, the talented actor in *Terrorism* that had to faux-rape me. It read:

Babes — the last rape was great, but remember not to punch me in the face when gagging me (arm is okay) and to be careful of not

throwing plate at me when having sex (got cut on lip last time).
Towel is okay to throw.

   Love Bella

Hmmm.

ııılıılılılı

I relished the chance to play the vixen/raped woman as it was a
fantastic challenge, but secretly enjoyed playing The Dog twice
as much. I loved physical comedy and this was a sure-fire opportunity to have a blast. I created three dogs. One was a dumb/
stoned dog with a floppy tongue and an idiotically happy expression; the second was a tiny terrier with a manic smile and a tight,
twittering body; and the last was a bulldog with crooked legs
and protruding teeth. I showed all three versions to the director
and he ummed and ahhed, then finally settled on the dumb/
stoned one.

   The first time Igor asked me to show my Dog to the other
actors, I got good feedback and most of the cast enjoyed it. But
one actor didn't.

   'Totally absurd,' he said. 'I think we need to cut that whole
character out.'

   'Why?' asked Igor.

   'Because *I'm* in that scene and I don't want to be upstaged by
a goddamned dog!' he retorted.

   The rest of us hid our smiles.

   Although it was funny, there was a lesson for me to learn
there, and it was about ego. Actors in general don't want to
play characters who look bad, seem unkind, bitchy, rude, arrogant or unlikeable (or to be upstaged by a dog). I guess nobody
wants to look bad, but an actor's job is to portray the whole
of the human experience, so I wanted to explore that idea by

working on a play called *Rosemary with Ginger* by Edward Allan Baker in class.

Rosemary, my character, was belligerent, obnoxious, awful-looking, slovenly, paranoid and half-crazed. Perfect. I chose tight-fitting, snow-washed jeans (five dollars from a put-out-looking rocker chick at an op shop) with a bra-less singlet that exposed my flabby pot belly, and put gel in my hair to make it look greasy and gross. I looked like shit. Next I perfected the walk, a kind of animalistic slouch, pelvis leading, low to the ground, powerful, with quick-moving arms like weapons that threatened. Pretty disgusting and very Rosemary. Then I developed a hellishly annoying whine to her voice and then allowed myself to be as obnoxious and slovenly as possible. I had more fun than I could remember. The performance itself was especially enjoyable as, by being so base, I had somehow freed myself on stage and was full of an energy and joy that infected the audience so that people were snorting and belly laughing. Even the ever-critical Robert Castle clapped. I liked being slovenly, lesson learned.

ıılıılıılı

For *Terrorism*, we rehearsed every evening for four hours, seven days a week, for two months. With my already overflowing schedule, it was a whopping challenge. Especially the horrendous heights I had to reach as the rape victim, the easy tomfoolery of the drunk girl and the physical comedy of The Dog in such rapid succession. The rape rehearsals in particular began to affect me on a day-to-day level. I felt the tension in my bones as each night I mounted the stage and relived the tears and fears.

Maybe because of that, my insomnia came back with a vengeance. Or perhaps it was because I partied too much into the wee hours and my body clock was oiled with vodka. For the last few weeks in particular, I'd been sliding in and out of these clouds of insomnia. Sometimes I almost fell asleep in class, other times I'd lie in bed with adrenaline pumping through my body until it grew light outside. Often, during the day I'd be walking around like a ghost, my sleeplessness like a fuzzy cloud following me everywhere, separating me from the real world and putting weights behind my eyeballs. As soon as my head hit the pillow, I would come alive with random thoughts. About life, the future, films, acting, family, friends, why feijoas taste so damn good. All kinds of thoughts were whirring and clamouring for attention, half-finished ones always replaced by fresh panicky new ones. The physical pain of getting up after four hours' sleep in forty-eight hours was enormous. I began to feel half dead.

But I forced myself to do the work that needed to be done outside of class. Regularly, Axel would come home and see me either down on my hands and knees barking at the furniture, pleading to an imaginary person to stop raping me, or over-dosing on energy drinks to keep me going.

Igor was wonderful but also a bit crazy. As we approached opening night, he would suddenly rip out dialogue and reorder the scenes, changing the intention of the scene as often as he yelled at us. We plotted putting a fake mouse in his shoes, but we – okay, I – chickened out at the last minute.

But truthfully I loved it like I loved onion cheese dip. Mmmm, cheesy. The long hours, the character analysis, the stage, the challenges, even Igor's outbursts filled me with delight. (I was on a stage in *New York* with a crazy famous *Russian* director who was *yelling* at me. Yes!) I loved it, loved it with all my heart. I'd learned so much at Strasberg that year and *Terrorism* was the icing on the cake.

Then, when the much-anticipated opening night loomed, my joy rapidly turned to terror at the thought of screwing up or falling off the stage. But performing on a New York stage was a hit of adrenaline like nothing else, and once I was up on stage my terror dissolved rapidly in the pure pleasure of being absorbed in my characters. Happily the audience enjoyed it too and gave us a standing ovation. So thankfully all the weirdo stuff Igor had put us through had paid off in spades.

Afterwards, people came up to us to shake our hands and tell us nice things. The principal of Strasberg, Caroline, hugged me and joked that I could now teach at Strasberg. A playwright with yellow hair said he wanted to turn my Dog character into a solo performance. 'Thank you, but no' (on the grounds I would be typecast). One guy said my Dog looked like a bad version of Cheech Marin, 'And not in a good way,' he added. I told him his tie looked like a limp fish. But Axel was there, and came every single night after, proud as punch and beaming like a maniac.

I was alarmed, though, that Ana Strasberg, the wife of the late Lee Strasberg, abruptly left straight after she'd watched my rape scene.

'Oh shit. But why?'

'She said it was too disturbing to look at.'

And so were her earrings. But huh, who was I to judge?

But my main source of pride was the snippets of conversation we all eavesdropped on outside once the play was over.

I heard one man, a large fat guy, say, 'My favourite was that sex scene, it was kind of horrendous and sexy. I had goose-flesh.'

His wife rolled her eyes and gave him a shrewd look.

His daughter piped up. 'I liked the drunk woman in the second scene, she was the stand out.'

'You're both wrong. The actress who did the doggie was the best, he was just so cute! He reminded me of my little Trevor.'

I stepped out of the shadows and puffed my chest out. 'It was all me!' I said, grinning maniacally.

They turned to look at me, so I stopped in my tracks. Wife pulled Daughter closer to her and Fat Guy lowered his stance.

'Leave us alone,' said the Wife, not for a second recognising her little Trevor incarnate.

I went to the laundromat with Axel a few days later and a woman approached us to ask if I was that actress from *Terrorism*. I put on my best 'Who me?' face and hid my grin.

'I couldn't take my eyes off you, you were really powerful,' she said, smiling kind of maniacally. 'Very sexy, too,' she added.

I swallowed. Was she hitting on me and about to ask me to squish her fake boob? I looked down at her shoes and they weren't sensible, so I figured I was safe. I thanked her and chatted a little. When she left, Axel and I continued folding our washing in silence for a while, then looked up to meet the other's eyes and laid a languid high-five on each other.

'Your first New York celebrity sighting,' he said as he folded some trousers.

'And the fact that she was slightly mad and wanted to sleep with me didn't detract from that at all.'

'You betcha,' he agreed, grinning.

ıılıllılılı

When the play's run finished, I needed a bit of rest after the constant juggling of *Terrorism*, Strasberg and classwork. I wanted time to walk around the house naked and take bites out of blocks of cheese and put the rest back in the fridge. I'd been feeling a bit like a circus clown, juggling balls. So the next day, I dropped all of my balls and relished the chance to read, write, sing and slide across the floorboards in my socks. Unadulterated freedom with a block of cheese and Aretha Franklin blaring from the speakers. Couldn't get much better than that, I reckoned, as I shook my booty for no one in particular.

19

Prostituting myself on the altar of acting, Tropicana violence and how I found religion

A N OLD FRIEND, RUPERT-THE-CHEF, arrived to visit me for a few days. He was a New Zealander who was working on a tiny speck of an island nestled in the Caribbean. Arriving in New York, initially he was overwhelmed by the pace, the lights, the people. But after only a few hours he was bitten by the New York bug – hard. He loved it: I could see in his eyes the same fervour, the same excitement I still felt for it.

Jacinta was a beautiful but annoying Polish girl I knew vaguely from Strasberg. She was the kind of girl who could turn on her sexuality like a tap, control the amount and pour it over whoever she wished, always with results. One night, she had come over to visit, spied Axel, liked what she saw and turned on her tap full bore. The fact that I was there and trying like hell to give her my version of the evil eye (a kind of a squint with a fast left–right motion) did nothing to quell her desires. I tried to keep images of my grandmother's sparkly rings out of my head as I looked at her sideways. Yet somehow it wasn't all about jealousy because she did it in an almost blinded, brutal way, as if it wasn't about anybody else. Like a machine gun, she fired off questions to Axel about age, career and rank but didn't really wait for the answers. I was fascinated watching this predator-type girl, strong, seductive, working her thing. Her eyelashes and pouts worked overtime, alive and animated, her top falling off her shoulders. Gesturing hands swept her breasts as she talked. It was kind of like watching an out-of-control fire, transfixing and also kinda scary. It wasn't a natural flirt with a man, it was premeditated, an act, a game.

If somebody began talking, she'd grow tense and interrupt in a louder voice. Rupert and Axel and I became open-mouthed, getting more and more uncomfortable as she bombastically savaged the conversation to her side. Even though she was adept at manipulation, subtleties slipped through her web like stones. I suggested we should get ready to go to dinner, which Axel took as a chance to escape.

Rupert and I both looked up pleadingly at him but he just smiled abruptly and whispered: 'Can't think, blood rushing to penis,' then gave a hefty roll of his eyes and got the hell out of there.

Jacinta attached herself and we went to get tapas. We sat down at our table in uncomfortable silence. I looked at the menu.

'There are so many kinds of shrimp here,' I said, for lack of anything else to say as I watched her nonchalantly slip her strap off her shoulder so that it dangled alluringly on her arm.

She looked at me as if I were a demented child. 'Well, dah, of course, Bella, this is a tapas restaurant.' She turned to Rupert, rolled her eyes and gave a loud snigger.

Why you little . . .

Rupert looked like he had a bad taste in his mouth. I went outside for a cigarette.

When I returned, I was startled at the change in Rupert. She had been alone with him for maybe five minutes, but in that time she had spun her silky sexy web around him and he was hanging off her every word like a puppy dog. It was like she had drugged him: his faculties gone, his humour gone and his perspective. She was the sex dealer and he was her john.

When a woman turns on her sexuality full bore, it's a spectacular thing. With the suggestion of sex and a fluffy tail swished in their faces, man becomes less stable than jelly. But this was on a whole new level. It was determined and precise, as though the outcome was linked to her very existence.

Now, to be honest, if there had been any suggestion of Rupert getting laid then I would have been in there. But I knew it was only about power and that she had no intention of coming through with the goods. Initially I stood by watching her game being played out, with horrified fascination, but then it really started to bug me. She was getting Rupert's hopes up and was treating me like crap as she viewed me as competition.

I thought of my own friends and had a mad desire to see them and de-foul myself from the charms of Jacinta.

I stood up and made my excuses to leave. Jacinta looked up at me and suddenly all traces of the vixen disappeared, and in her place was a small girl swallowed by apprehension.

'Can I come too?' she asked in a small voice. 'I don't have any other friends.'

I studied her face and it hit me: she hated herself, she couldn't help herself. The only way she thought she could relate to people, or be liked by them, was through her sexuality. She had become a master at it. Her sexual-ness gave her momentary hits of acceptance; droopy-eyed proclamations of adoration; sex-addled brains working overtime to soothe her, affirm her. And it was all lapped up, every last compliment. Perhaps if she received enough it would stop her trembling? Her forced words, her desire for attention, all came from this overriding desire to be accepted, and yet she was aware of it, and hated herself for it. I saw the artifice slip away to reveal her. So often we judge too quickly, before we know the secrets and tremors that lurk inside somebody.

Later, when Rupert and I debriefed and I'd told him about the hurt I had seen on her face, he gave me a look.

'She can't help her hurt, Bella, I saw it too. But it doesn't mean she needs to be a tyrant. Everybody has pain, but it's a choice as to how you deal with it.'

'You're just shitty 'cause you didn't get laid,' I retorted.

But he was right. It reminded me of something my mum used to tell me. She'd said the thing that differentiates us as people, is how we deal with difficult things. It was about the rational and thoughtful choices we make that help to keep the demons at bay.

It was such a simple idea, that we needn't be slaves to our pain and did in fact have a choice. I wondered if Jacinta knew that. But perhaps hurt goes too deep in some people and they can't change. But was it because she couldn't or wouldn't? Or a combination of the two? The question thrashed around in my head until I was so thoroughly sick of the dilemma that there was only one option left to me: I just had to go on holiday. Connecting random events in life so I could justify taking a holiday has always stood me in good stead.

ıılıılıılıılıı

That weekend, Axel and I took a greyhound bus trip to Atlantic City for our de-Jacintanising/romantic getaway. *True Romance*, eat your heart out. The only other passengers on the fifty-seater bus were an old, leather-faced couple who played blackjack with the seriousness of junkies trying to score, and a young black man with 'Lies and Life. Death Equals Truth' on a button on the front of his baseball cap. I wore short shorts, a singlet, boots and aviator sunglasses, which gave me the kitsch American B-grade road-trip movie look I was after. Axel didn't look enough like Christian Slater in his elegant olive-green pants and white T-shirt, so I ruffled his hair.

'Yo mama doesn't love you,' I told him.

He scowled.

'Perfect.'

We arrived at the Tropicana resort and casino that stood on the boardwalk near the ocean, jostling for attention with the larger Trump and Caesars casinos along the strip. As we joined the long queue to get our room keys, I glanced around and saw that almost everybody there was madly chewing gum, making the place look like a surreal stable. In line we stood next to an aged woman with burnt freckly skin and shoulder-blade tattoos. Next to her was a bunch of Low Rent frat boys who kept high-fiving each other and checking out the young chicks with ankle tattoos of love hearts or a generic boy's name stencilled on top of 'Forever'. I fitted right in with my aviators and Patricia Arquette slouch.

Waiting our turn in the queue, I scanned to my right and my heart stopped. I spied a wiry-armed man setting up two tatty pint-sized deck chairs for his two scraggly kids, who lurked under his shadow. A layer of cold sweat broke out on my skin and I breathed in sharply. He was completely saturated with violence; it emanated from him like a chemical.

He pointed his fiercely tattooed hand at the two frightened kids, warning them to sit down and not move. I couldn't take my eyes off him. He seemed to actually leak violence. The way he stood with his hands shoved in his pockets as he glared at his scrawny kids. The little girl looked exactly like a scared mouse with her sticking-out ears. She began searching her brother's face for reassurance and the boy, with tough shoulders and scared eyes, patted her arm kindly, as their father looked on with a sneer. I had a sudden mad desire to pick up the little girl in my arms, take her brother by the hand and lead them away from the man forever.

Axel looked at me, read my thoughts, and shook his head.

The hotel was pretty garish and wall-to-wall with poker machines with their blinging sounds and bright flashes of light. Fake gold fountains spurted multi-coloured water into the air as punters wandered about in various stages of greed. We took the elevator up to our well-appointed room with Gaultier blue-and-white striped panelling and a view of what looked like Springfield from *The Simpsons*. We spent our first three hours ordering room service in between bouts of testing out the springs of the king-sized bed. When we finally emerged from our marathon, we made our way down to the beach with tousled hair and a kind of stunned-mullet look on our slack-jawed faces, walking bow-legged. Sigh, hotel sex is what holidays are all about.

We strolled on to the smooth, wet sand and plucked seashells from between the boulders until we found a bright sunny spot near the water's edge. Australia rolled around in my mind as the sand stuck to my body and the heat made my shoulders melt with a sigh into the towel. Ah, the warmth and comfort of the beach. We lay there all day, dreaming, talking and cuddling, then occasionally upping our lumbering bodies and splashing into the cool surf as people bandied balls over our heads and whacked at each other with soft rubber bats. As the sun began to sink and the cool shadows of the nearby mountain darkened us, we went back to the hotel to shower and change, the jets of cool water stinging our lobster-red bodies.

After dinner and a play at the casinos, we left the bling behind and made our way back to the peace of the darkened beach to dance in the glowing froth of the ocean. Then we twirled around in the sand as the bells and whistles of the nearby casinos stung the air. I loved the ocean, like a life-long friend or a fierce cuddle. I opened my arms to it and breathed in the fishy, salty smells.

I turned to Axel, who was digging his toes into the sand, deep in thought.

'That little girl today in the lobby,' he said, looking up at me.

'The one with the fucked-up father?'

'Yeah. I can't stop thinking about her either.'

The little girl's beautiful big ears loomed in my mind. I turned to look at Axel; his face was filled with sadness. 'Is there something else wrong?' I asked him.

He thought for a while then answered. 'I don't know what to do. In life, I mean. Career-wise. It feels so stupid when that little girl . . .'

I knew that chestnut pretty well.

'Music,' he continued, 'it's just not realistic. It doesn't pay. How could I even afford a family on it?'

'You could turn to prostitution.' I answered helpfully.

He looked at me with a sullen expression.

'Oh, bullshit,' I said.

He looked surprised.

'Did Chris Cornell say it was too hard?' I continued, knowing full well the singer from Audioslave was a hero of his. 'Did he say, "Well, there's no money in it, so I'll get a job at Burger King"? No, he didn't. He loved music, wanted it to be his life, so he persevered.'

'Bella, I'm not Chris Cornell. Only, like, two per cent of people make it. Be realistic.'

I hated it when he talked like that. It was at these moments that missing James became physical. 'Yeah, but the bottom line is you gotta have talent, and you have that, yeah? The other thing you need is the desire to do it. Plus those two per cent of people fight for what they want, they don't give up. Life is so bloody short, you know. Bloody short. So there is no reason you can't be one of those people. You can do it, Axel. I believe in you with all my heart, and I'm not just saying that to get laid. Well . . .'

'Yeah, but how?'

I thought back to my Sydney days. 'The first step is admitting what it is you *really* want. Second step is devising a plan. There are heaps of things you can do to get ahead. Motivate your current band into playing more, join another one, get an agent. Practise more –'

'Yeah, but what's the point of practising when I'm not performing?' he moaned.

It was like trying to motivate a sea slug.

'It matters when the day comes that you're playing in front of a big-time record producer. Every extra second you put into rehearsing will get you that inch closer to getting signed. Plus, I like to think of you at the studio drumming, it makes me horny.'

He threw sand at me.

I told him a story my father used to tell me. When he was a young buck he entered the esteemed Theatre Corporate of New Zealand's director-in-training program. There were forty other people in the class, equally or more talented than my father, all vying for a permanent director's position in the theatre. Danny told me that at the start of the course he'd made a vow to himself that he'd work harder and longer than anybody else in the room. At the end of the run, Danny got the coveted director-in-residence position. The head director said it wasn't only because of Danny's talent, it was because he didn't take it for granted and he had worked harder than anybody else.

The next day, Axel and I lined up with the blue-rinse set to catch our bus back to Manhattan. I got wedged in-between an icy-cold vent shaft and a huge fat woman with four nostrils. Trip from hell. The woman spluttered and roared in her sleep like a demented monster as I stuffed tissues down my ear canals. Every now and then she would let out a hearty chuckle and then doze off again, the machine inside her clanking to life with roars and squeaks. I kept expecting to see steam coming out of her ears. When we finally pulled in to Manhattan I was half-crazed, and as I was clambering over her to exit my seat, she slipped me a crumpled five-dollar note.

'Sorry about the noise, honey, you know how it gets at this age.'

So unexpected and so very sweet.

As we walked to the subway station, Axel spoke up.

'Like Joss Stone,' he said pensively.

'Huh?'

'The singer. She wanted Lauryn Hill, the woman from the Fugees, on her album, so she called Lauryn's mother five times a week for two months to get in contact with her.'

'Huh?'

'Perseverance,' he mumbled, then got lost in thought again.

In the next two weeks, with his newfound motivation, Axel doubled his hours practising at a rented studio, joined another rock band, a sexy trio from Israel called Branch of Life, and encouraged his own band, TimeCode, to get more gigs. Things began to look up, and all because he let go of his fear and had the courage to listen to his desires. You just can't beat that feeling of dreams materialising in front of you. My thoughts turned to my own dreams, and I realised with surprise that I was beginning to feel hazy about my own future, but, like the emotionally healthy gal I was, I pushed it to the back of my mind and let it fester silently until I was ready to deal with it.

Back in Robert Castle's class, Gian-Luca and I were doing a scene from the film *Kramer vs Kramer*. We played an unhappily married couple that breaks up. As was the norm, Robert drilled us about our characters' relationship.

'In this scene, you're breaking up, but I imagine they had been having difficulties for a while before that.'

'Yes,' responded Gian-Luca.

'What sort of problems?' asked Robert, turning to me.

'They probably didn't communicate, fell out of love ...' I replied.

'What about their sex life? Were you still physically attracted to each other? Or had that gone too?'

'Gone,' replied Gian-Luca. 'They probably hadn't slept together for a long while.'

'How long?' asked Robert.

Gian-Luca's beautiful face rumpled up in thought. 'A very long time, I think.'

'Yes. But how long, Gian-Luca?'

'Oh, probably as much as three days.'

The class erupted into belly-rocking laughter. Ah, my beautiful Italian stallion!

I got a text from Axel during the class: 'Call me when you can.' I forgot about it, but when I got home he told me in a very serious voice that he'd had an argument with his Jewish mama.

He had wanted to open a recording studio for musicians, so he'd called up his parents in Tel Aviv to see about getting a loan from an Israeli bank. His mother suggested he go to LA to stay with a rich relative there and work for him in the diamond trade to earn the money he needed. Axel replied that he didn't want to leave his life in New York.

'Or Bella,' he said.

'But you know it's not going to last with her,' his mother responded.

'Why?' he asked, taken aback.

'You might as well let it end now.'

'But you know how I feel about her.'

'Yes,' she said sympathetically. 'But there's no future with her, is there?' Then the words were spoken. 'I mean, she's not Jewish.'

She told him that if we were together he would be hurting their family, destroying all of their Jewish tradition. He would be the traitor who destroyed the family name.

Axel didn't agree with her.

'It's my fault. I just haven't raised you right,' she responded sadly.

He said he told her that he didn't think that an old Jewish rabbi should determine who he could or couldn't love. But by the shake of his voice, I thought that perhaps she had more influence on him than he was letting on.

Coming from the family I did, it was difficult for me to see her point of view. She'd said that her worst nightmare was if her grandchildren weren't Jewish. In Jewish culture, it is the mother that hands down the religion to her children, so she had a lot of pressure on her to fulfil that. She had probably spent her whole life upholding her Jewish convictions, handed down from her mother, and didn't want to see them disappear. I could understand that.

'She'll come around,' I told him. 'She wants you to be happy.' Then I gulped.

ılıltılılı

Over the next few days my thoughts would constantly return to the Atlantic City conversation about career that I'd had with Axel.

Something was really beginning to bug me, but my thoughts felt obscured and unformed. Perhaps it was just from feeling a little low after the excitement of *Terrorism* and the bright lights of Atlantic City. Before I could really be honest with myself, I was distracted by another visitor from Aussie land.

My cousin and friend, Kylie DuFresne, a talented and sexy film producer from Sydney, came to visit for two weeks. On her first day we went to Central Park and rowed in the pond. It was a beautiful day with a slight nip to the air, but the balmy sunshine seeped through our layers and warmed us. The pond was bright green with algae and ringed with small gazebos, where people were signing their nuptials, dressed in wedding dresses or tuxedos. A group of flummoxed-looking Asian tourists were taking it in turns rowing with one oar each and going round and round in circles with delighted squeals. An old man with a nylon fishing line connected to an old stick sat on a rock and waited for his supper.

The park was alive with buskers and artists and musicians. People wandered hand in hand, the deep green foliage like a background in a painting. Joggers ploughed up and down the paved roads and lovers twisted along the winding paths. We stumbled across a roller disco derby near the fountain from the *Friends* sitcom. There were all sorts of people skating in the fenced-off area: young couples, burnt-out hippies, muscle men and drag queens. A tiny older woman who looked to be in her late sixties dressed in a black Lycra jumpsuit was spinning and jumping into the air, doing splits and cartwheels, her skates blasting sparks as she landed. A giant black man who looked like Forrest Whitaker was gently leading a shaking, lily-white gay guy around by his hand. There was a Cheech Marin look-alike who rolled willy-nilly with a gentle stoned pace. It was New York in a nutshell: these diverse types all getting together for their Sunday skating in the park, all encouraged, accepted and enjoyed by each other. The crowd, like me, was watching their enjoyment and feeling it mingle with our own. The old woman in Lycra parted her red-painted lips to sing as she rolled past us, 'We're all Friends and Freaks'.

That week, I got the news that Axel's parents were coming to visit us from Israel. I hid all pagan memorabilia and artworks with expletives and stocked up the fridge with matzo balls. Knowing how much they thoroughly disapproved of me, I was ready and willing to disapprove of them. When they arrived, even though they could both speak English they spoke only Hebrew when I was in the room, evidently trying to convince Axel to be with a nice Jewish girl. In the beginning I made excuses for them, but as the days wore on I became more and more miffed at their rudeness. It got to the point where I considered lacing their matzo balls with ham.

I'd see Axel and his mother arguing often, and one day, after I'd heard my name being spat out once again, I decided to say something. If she wanted to talk about me, she could do it to my face. I skolled the rest of my orange juice for courage then went into the sitting room where they were arguing and put on my best air-hostess smile.

'Hi. Sorry to interrupt here, but I heard my name being mentioned. If you guys want to discuss me and my lack of Jewishness, then I'd prefer you did it out in the open.'

They both blinked at me.

I felt my courage draining into the floorboards.

'Um, Bella, we were just talking about whether you wanted to come with us to the Statue of Liberty,' said Axel.

I coughed. 'I'll be serving in-flight snacks very soon.'

When Axel's parents and Kylie had gone, I was left twiddling my thumbs. *Terrorism* was over, I was up-to-date with all the Strasberg performances, and my love life, for once, was working well, despite my offer of eggs and ham to Axel's parents. All was strangely good and easy. It wouldn't last anyway, I figured, so I decided to complicate my life a bit and audition for some more New York films.

I auditioned for and won the role in a short film by an up-and-coming director named Richard. It was a great script about a blind woman who hires a PI to see if her husband has been cheating.

I realised a lot of my acting had to do with reading the expressions of the other actor in the scene, so playing a blind woman presented a challenge. I'd seen actors overplay blindness and wanted to avoid that, so I researched thoroughly and watched videos on blind people and learned about the different types of blindness. One of the crew members, who came in on the fifth day of shooting, kept staring at my breasts as if he were trying to bore holes through my blouse. Later I was told he'd thought I was actually blind and thus wouldn't notice his perversion. Gotta love perverts!

Fresh from the success of the blind film, I figured it wouldn't be too hard to get another acting job, but many weeks later, after emailing like crazy, speaking to everybody in the know and generally prostituting myself on the altar of acting, there was not even a whiff of an audition I could go to. That's the heart-wrenching thing about acting. Acting, as one of my favourite actors Maximilian Schell once said, 'is madly and completely about luck'. Blind, castrating, mother-fucking luck. I thought back to my Sydney days and figured I could always sulk.

It felt scary, having a career based entirely on luck. If I wanted to be a lawyer, I could study, pass my bar exam, then get a job in law. Sure, luck would come into it to a certain degree, but it wouldn't be so horribly dependent on it as acting was. I didn't want to just sit around passively waiting for Lady Luck to honour me, so I laboured on, even applying for crappy girlfriend/ alien roles. But still *nada*. There was nothing for it – I had to call my mum.

'I, I, I don't wannna be an allieeennn.'

'Bella, what are you talking about?'

'Waaaaa. Luck' – hiccup – 'Waaaa. Acting. Don't wanna . . .'

'Your luck has dried up and you have to make an alien film, right?'

'Yeeeeeessssss,' I wailed. 'I mean, nooooooo. I, I –'

'Bella, you've chosen a difficult career and you have to prepare yourself for these down times. There will be more. But the good times outweigh the bad, yeah?'

(Sniff) 'Yeah.'

'And if that ever changes, you can always do something other than acting. Like professional fly fishing.'

Hearing those words, I felt both a flood of relief and a new-found resolve to try to act my age. Then I apologised to my mum for being a pissant. When I didn't have the pressure of *having* to be an actor, I knew how much I loved being an actor. Fuck fly fishing. I would stick it out, through the hard times and the good. I understood that I had to accept the precarious nature of luck – but really making it work for me was another thing entirely. I had to think outside the box.

I called up Daiana, a good friend from Strasberg, and asked her to bring over a lot of champagne and to spread the word. Soon enough, a bunch of Strasbergians arrived and we bejewelled ourselves in flapper clothes left over from a costume party and began to twirl around the room as we incanted our guardian spirits (Oscar Wilde, Shakespeare and Heiner Muller) to give us a break and get the Gods of Acting Jobs to smile upon us. None of us actually believed in guardian angels, or Heiner Muller for that matter, but it was fun – and, oddly enough, it seemed to work.

The next week I received three phone calls: one from a TV channel that I'd auditioned with three months before, asking me to host a segment on their new travel show, one from a film-school grad who wanted me to play a role in his new film, and one from a concerned East Village citizen who offered me one dollar for every dog poo I could clean off the streets.

Spooky.

Sure, it could have been coincidence. *Or* it could have been a super-duper flapper-god-Shakespearean-evoked near-life experience.

'Or maybe not,' came Axel's dry response after I'd confessed.

But I knew that whenever I released my tight grip on what it was I wanted (and had a bit of fun doing it), then it magically materialised. Not always in the form that I'd envisaged, but nonetheless there, just like our new-found guardian angels.

ılılıllılı

I got a phone call the next day from Zoë.

'Zo, I never heard back from Mary the casting director. I mustn't have got the role in the film, huh?'

'Oh, shit, sorry, babe. I thought they would have got back to you by now. They went with Rosario Dawson for the part. They probably needed a name actor. I'm really sorry.'

'No, that's cool.'

'Bella, what's that noise in the background?'

'A chainsaw and my neck bone.'

'Don't top yourself just yet. I called because I want you to get your ass over to California to visit me on the set of *Grindhouse* and have a beer with QT and me.'

'No dice. I'm busy sulking,' I answered. 'Anyway, I like my beer straight up, without any QTs.'

'No, dickhead, Quentin Tarantino.'

'I knew that.'

'Anyway, get your ass on a plane.'

'But I'm as broke as a two-dollar ho's back.'

'Huh?'

'On sailor night,' I added for further clarification.

'Don't worry, I'll pay,' she said. 'But you have to fly me over for your next blockbuster movie. Deal?'

'Would an alien movie count?'

'Even if you're its butt-double, honey.'

'Cool!'

I was off to Santa Barbara to see Zoë Banoe and hob-nob with Quentin Tarantino. My suicidal thoughts would have to be put on hold for the time being.

20

Bitch-slapping *Il Direttore*

THE PLANE TRIP WAS a bit of a nightmare. An old-smelling woman kept falling asleep and drooling on me. Her head wobbled precariously on her frail neck and her snores kept making her head tilt forward sharply. I found myself continually catching her head mid-plunge before it could snap off and roll down the aisle. I wondered if she'd slip me a fiver at the end of it.

I finally arrived at the Marriott hotel in Santa Barbara late at night, where I met up with Zoë. She looked just the same, perhaps a bit more buff. She was cheery and in great spirits. It was lovely seeing her; I always felt the sensation of slipping into a warm bath of childhood memories when I was near her. Which would then remind me of our childhood you-have-to-fart-underwater and sink-the-plastic-boat games that we somehow never tired of.

We were late for dailies, where the crew and cast watched the footage they'd shot that day, so went downstairs into a small dark room and watched the film of Zoë on the bonnet of a super-charger going a million kilometres per hour. In the scene, Kurt Russell's character was speeding alongside Zoë's car and bashing into it, making her slip and slide precariously from one side of the bonnet to the other. It was enthralling! Whenever Kurt's car plunged into hers I felt a plunge in my stomach and gripped tighter onto Zoë's arm.

When friends or family see me in a film and something nasty is happening to me – if I'm getting beaten, or crying, or being hurt – they get affected. I look at them strangely and can't work out why it would affect them. I mean, it's not really happening, it's acting, yeah? But seeing Zoë on that bonnet, I finally understood. It looked so damn real. At one point, Zoë, still on the bonnet, was screaming out her friend's name for help. 'Kim,' she yelled. 'Kiiiimmm.' It sounded so New Zealandish – so sweet and funny – that I laughed so hard I snorted my complimentary Sprite through my nose and sprayed it on the person in front of me. Zoë and I changed seats. As I continued to wail with laughter I heard a wild, fabulous laugh coming from the front of the room, rising and crescendoing with mine. I peered into the darkness and saw the outline of Quentin Tarantino. Holy hell! I was in the same room as Tarantino! And we were laughing at the same thing. We've bonded, I thought, then gave myself a mental high-five.

Afterwards Zoë and I went upstairs to her luxurious hotel room where we jumped on the bed and caught up on each other's lives. Knowing how difficult it is to do your first acting role, I was anxious to see if she was okay, if she was stressed out or not. But by her ready wit and undaunted enthusiasm I could see she was taking to it like a duck to water. We talked about Axel and Strasberg and filming and careers like cocked-up galahs until we were all up-to-date with our dramas.

Later that night, we went to Quentin's room a few doors down to join the posse. I was introduced to the Wu-Tang Clan, a bunch of incredibly smart, funny and witty guys who were visiting their mate Quentin on set. I hadn't heard their music before, but by the end of my holiday I was to be a devoted fan. When I sat down on the sofa with my drink, I looked up and saw the tall figure of Quentin Tarantino staring down at me. He had a slight awkwardness that came from being so tall, a very dynamic presence and humour-filled eyes flashing with smarts. He held out his hand.

'Hi, I'm Quentin, you must be Bella,' he said. 'Your reputation precedes you. It's really good to finally meet you.'

Quentin Tarantino knew my name! Wait – *reputation . . .* ?

'Yeah, I know,' I said, before I knew what I was saying. 'I mean, I don't mean I have a, er, a reputation. Well, okay, I do, but not the, um. Um, I meant, I know you, ah . . . well I don't know *you*, I , er . . .' I stopped mid-sentence. 'I'll just stop talking now.'

He looked at me while I bored a hole into the floor with my stare. When I looked up, his mouth was twitching with a smile. I shook his hand and we grinned at each other.

The next morning, Zoë and I kept the blinds closed and watched DVDs and ordered room service. I liked knowing superstars.

At around midday we made our way to a small Danish-themed bar to sit in a beer garden, chug down some steins of beers and munch on hamburgers, Danish style. Whatever that is. Quentin and his friend, a lovely roller derby girl, joined us and we spent a great afternoon together, eating, guzzling beer and belly laughing.

My impression of Quentin that day was that he was a really good egg. Effervescent, immensely funny, passionate, sharp as a whipper snipper with new blades, open-handed and good-hearted. I liked him a lot, despite the fact that he made constant fun of my accent, though he did quite a brilliant mimic of an Aussie accent himself.

There was a steady stream of locals and tourists dropping by our table and asking for a photo or autograph. When we were about four steins to the wind, yet another group of Midwesterners approached our table.

'Excuse us, we're big fans, can we take your picture with us?'

Quentin gave me a wink.

I scraped back my chair and stood up. 'Sure,' I answered.

I wobbled myself over to their waiting camera and stood there expectantly.

'It's okay, really,' I said, eyeing off their hesitation. 'I won't charge you for it or anything.'

'Oh . . . good,' said the perplexed young man slowly.

Click.

I could see Quentin, Roller Derby Girl and Zoë giggling in the background, until the ever-gracious QT got up and posed for them himself.

At one stage, Quentin leaned over to me and put his hand on mine.

'Bella, I wanted to thank you for all the acting talks you had with Zoë before we began shooting. It was really excellent advice,' he said.

'No worries, Quentin, you're welcome,' I replied, blushing like a Heinz bottle.

I badly wanted to ask him if he had even seen my audition tape for Abernathy and what he'd thought of it. But he would have mentioned it by now, so I was pretty sure he'd never had the chance to watch it. And if that was the case, it would have been uncomfortable for both of us for me to bring it up. I clinked glasses with him instead.

We moved from the Danish Hamlet and drove to a pub with a

giant faux windmill, which felt like entering the back of beyond: it was a large old-style pub with flickering neon beer signs and a few sloshed locals cheerily chatting with the owner, Vince. We hitched ourselves to the bar and ordered more beers, shot pool and put coins in the jukebox.

'Bella! You have crappy taste in music!' said Quentin, laughing.

'Yeah. So . . . You have crappy taste in fashion!' I retorted as I shimmied away.

Finally, Quentin and Roller Derby Girl left to get ready for the evening's festivities so Zoë and I slammed back more vodka Red Bulls in the hope that it would sober us up.

Quentin has a huge collection of original 35 mm prints of films, and his lovely assistant Pilar got *Pretty Maids All in a Row* couriered over from his collection back in LA to watch at a local cinema they'd hired for the screening.

Zoë, Daniella (the friend of Zoë's who had taken me to the Venice Beach festival in LA) and I arrived late and pretty tipsy to the screening. I sat next to my mate Roller Derby Girl who was next to Quentin. All I can remember of the 1970s drama was the sausage-like imprints of the male actors' appendages in their tight seventies synthetic pants. In the theatre, many of the crew were asleep in various states of drunkenness. I felt my own eyelids grow heavier than my will to perve on the actors' pants, then fell promptly asleep. But apparently not only did I fall asleep, I began to snore. Loudly. Apparently Quentin leaned over and shook me to wake me, or at least stop the hideous noise; but I swished him away like a fly and fell asleep again, resuming the blood-curdling snore of the unconscious. When the gentle whirr of the projector stopped and people were leaving the cinema, I woke up. Timing was everything. I wiped the drool from my face and peered across at Zoë.

'What happened?'

'You fell asleep and were snoring.'

'Loudly,' added Daniella unhelpfully.

'What?'

'Quentin tried to shake you to wake you up but you just pushed him away then fell asleep again. And snored.'

'You were like a machine,' marvelled Daniella. 'The whole cinema were plugging their ears.'

'You're kidding, right?' I asked, every bone in my body willing it to be a joke.

'No,' said Zoë, breaking into a peal of laughter. 'You should see your face!'

'Oh shit, I'm so sorry, I'm so embarrassed . . . I . . . I need to . . .'

'Get a nose plug, yes, I know.' She took in my stunned-mullet face. 'And another drink, come on.'

Embarrassment took on a whole new meaning, even for me, that night.

ılıllıllılıl

Rosario Dawson from *Sin City* and *Clerks II* had been given the role I'd auditioned for, so I had prepared myself to hate her thoroughly, but after one minute in her company she had me enthralled. She was quite fantastic. Very beautiful, very strong, fiery, extremely intelligent and she had an excellent debauched sense of humour. Zoë, Rosario and I spent a lot of time in our hotel rooms talking about politics, sex and life. I love it when women get together and everything is laid on the table. Nothing is sacred as you talk intimately about penis size, fears and dreams, and penis size.

The next day, Zoë and I woke up while it was still dark and, wiping our red-wine-stained mouths, made our way to the car that would drive us to the set. The lonesome country road wound around grassed corners, bypassed Michael Jackson's Neverland ranch and a small primary school (I'll leave *that* one alone), then tapered out into farmland. Base camp was set up a few kilometres down the road from where the next car chase would be shot. Occasionally a farmer would lumber past on his tractor, gaping at the bustling city of vans and trailers and equipment that had sprung up overnight.

On set I met Kurt Russell, who played the villain. He had a warm energy and a deep plentiful laugh. I liked him immensely. I had the privilege of watching Kurt, Zoë, Rosario and Tracie, the actress playing 'Kim', do their magic in the final scene, the dramatic and amazing car chase that has since become so famous. Cameras were hooked up to various parts of the stunt-cars and inside a specially equipped truck that followed at a break-neck speed. Quentin invited me into the camera truck with him to see the chase up close and personal, which was a blast.

It all made me froth at the mouth. The speeding cars, the equipment, the bustling crew members, the actors pacing and preparing; the camaraderie. There was a ribald sense of camaraderie there, like on other film sets. That ease of instant family. All the faces I saw were filled with seriousness and joy; that satisfied look of somebody who is doing a job they love. *Il Direttore* in particular. His face was radiant as he went from heightened concentration to spontaneous laughter.

Later that night, when we got back to the hotel, Quentin spied Zoë and me, ran up to us and squished my cheeks.

'You are sooooo cute!' he joked.

'Ooow oww!' I replied. Then managed to get out an apology about snoring during his movie.

He pulled my hood down, hooked it under my chin and squished my cheeks with his big hands.

'Don't worry about it,' he said as he squished my cheeks harder.

'Oow, oww, let meeee go!'

'But you are so adorable,' he mocked. Then planted a big fat kiss on both my cheeks as I tried to squirm out of his grasp.

I didn't know whether I should kiss him back or knee him in the balls.

'Stop squirming and let me kiss those cheeks of yours,' yelled Quentin.

'Noooo,' I yelled.

'Why not?' he said as he twisted them harder.

'Confused . . . grandmother . . . oww . . . Italian . . . owwww . . . pain,' I managed.

Saved by the bell, Rizza from Wu-Tang phoned so they gas-bagged for a minute or two then Quentin gave Zoë and me a big wet kiss each and frolicked off to meet his mates.

I adored that about Quentin. His ability to be a highly articulate man one moment then switch into an enthusiastic, tender cad in the blink of an eye. I'd found him to be generous in spirit as well as intellect. He was quite becoming, as my grandmother would say. Or, as I would say: A very fine piece of ass.

Later, in our pyjamas, Zoë and I went to Quentin's room to hang out.

'I know you can't hide anything, Bella,' said Quentin.

'Huh?'

'I want to show you the trailer for *Death Proof.* You watch it, and I'll watch your face while you're watching it, deal?'

But what if he could really read my face, *à la* Ron NaVarre, and discovered that I thought he was 'becoming', or that I was thinking about him in a compromising position? I'd have to give an Oscar-worthy performance. I folded my legs up underneath me and plonked my head on my knuckles. 'Okay, bring it on.'

I watched the crash scene from the first part of the movie and it was so hideously cool I forgot all about his imaginary arms wrapped around me. I high-fived him and told him it was great.

'Good shit,' came his response, along with a sexy smile.

My mum on the bog. My mum on the bog.

Quentin had an encyclopaedic knowledge of film, and when we turned to the subject of Australian cinema, I was left feeling like the idiot I was.

'I did see *Mad Max*,' I said hopefully.

He looked at me doubtfully.

'Let's talk about acting,' I said. 'Safer ground.'

He told me about doing a reading at the Actors Centre, early in his career. He was as nervous as hell because he hadn't finished reading the play he and the rest of the cast were to read in front of all manner of luminaries. Halfway through, when they reached the part he didn't know, he froze. Then, just in time, he reminded himself to let go, and to just be in the moment. From there his reading actually improved and he was on fire.

'With acting, always be in the moment,' he told me.

He also said the best acting advice he got when doing a reading was to do it as though you were doing a radio play: no pauses. Excellent advice. His final piece of advice reminded me of the conversation Axel and I had had in Atlantic City. When he was younger and working in a video store, the thing that differentiated him from other aspiring filmmakers was that he wanted success more than anybody else. He said always to watch and learn and never presume you know anything. I told him about Strasberg and how I had tried to become a sponge and soak up all the information I could. Then –

'They never saw you coming!' he interrupted.

'Yeah,' I answered, returning his grin.

'So, tell me, what did you work on last?' he asked.

I told him a bit about my characters in *Terrorism*.

'I would've liked to have seen that dog,' he said.

'Your wish is my command.'

I got down on my haunches and showed the various dog characters I'd come up with. Zoë and Quentin clapped in unison. There I was, in Quentin Tarantino's room, with my childhood friend, on my hands and knees pretending to be a dog as *my mum on the bog* echoed around the cavern of my head.

I knew in retrospect I'd be kicking myself for embarrassing myself like that, but at that moment I was having more fun than I could remember.

21

Indulging in cheese, cheerleaders, Cheeks and Christmas (and bad poetry)

S UMMER GAVE WAY TO autumn and Halloween arrived, trans-
forming New York into a colourful carnival of outrageous
costumes and munted party-goers. Union Square was the place
to be. It was a furnace of sex-charged teenagers parading and
flirting, snapping tourists, drunks and feather boas. Packs of
dancers and buskers ploughed the pavement for all they were
worth, earning their rent money for the month. I stepped out
of the way of a Father Christmas being chased by a group of
squealing Japanese tourists. There were men wearing large card-
board cartons painted to look like dice; there were all manner of
monsters, with giant platform shoes and waving tentacles. I saw
a group of teenage girls in Heidi outfits flirting with a pack of
wolf men. There were Roman gladiators, pimps in giant mink
coats, harlots, surgeons with bloody aprons, vampires, sumo
wrestlers, even a bright orange road cone that was being herded
by a roadworker in a hard hat. My favourite costume took a

while to register: a tall guy in a Tropicana shirt with a stocking over his face, clutching a bag of Huggies. He was Nicolas Cage's character out of *Raising Arizona.*

Axel and I headed uptown and wended our way through a surreal mix of Obi-Wan Kenobis and gorillas and monks and ghosts hurrying about. On the way back downtown on the packed subway, a young, pretty Puerto Rican woman dressed in a cheerleader costume began jostling for space with a rather elegant woman in a tree costume. Being New York, they began to have words.

'Stop sticking those fucking branches in my face,' muttered the Cheerleader.

'Then get your ugly face outta my branches,' retorted the Tree.

The Cheerleader turned to the Tree. 'You got a fucking attitude, bitch.'

'Give it a rest, go-go girl,' answered the Tree as she ruffled her branches.

'It's Halloween and I ain't taking no shit from a goddamn tree! So how about you just shut the fuck up.' The Cheerleader had an inch-thick scowl plastered on her brightly made-up face.

'Get over it, bitch,' came the Tree's reply.

'Oh yeah!' shouted the enraged Cheerleader.

And with that, she lunged at the Tree and smacked her in the face. The Tree's glasses went flying. Momentarily stunned, the Tree retaliated by twisting her torso and slapping the Cheerleader with her branches. That enraged the Cheerleader more, and she lunged at the Tree again, scratching at her eyes and throat. They began to have a full-scale punch-up, branches snapping and pompoms flying – the other commuters, like me, watching in absolute horror. They were brutal. When they both took a break to regain their balance I took the opportunity to gently lay my hand on the Cheerleader's arm. She turned around as if I had stung her. After a few beats of evaluating my intentions, she pulled her arm away violently but she didn't lunge at the Tree again. The violence and threat from the two pissed-off chicks was actually quite scary – it wasn't until afterwards in the retelling that I saw the funny side.

ılıllıllılı

That week, I got a call from James. He'd just moved into a new apartment in Midtown and was inviting me over for dinner. In his voice I heard the man I knew: civilised and funny and kind. I realised I wanted to see him. I mentioned it to Axel and his face turned down into a sneer and he said: 'I *prohibit* you to go. A proper girlfriend wouldn't see her ex-boyfriend!'

'You're kidding, right?'

He looked at me and glared. I could sense an argument coming.

'Well, thanks for helping me make up my mind, Axel,' I said, as I took my keys and coat and left him to his medieval proclamations.

James had prepared plates of hors d'oeuvres and cooked a delicious roast chicken salad. He could still detect the sound of a champagne cork popping through a metre of concrete, but he didn't drink one drop that night. He spent time showing me how to create a web page for my acting. Then we talked about politics for a lively hour, then moved on to art. As I sat listening to his energetic ideas, I couldn't help comparing him to Axel. James had always had the ability to keep me startled and engaged intellectually.

I asked him about his career and he said he wasn't really putting his heart into it. I could see he wasn't very happy. I asked him, above all, what it was he wanted for his life.

'Love,' he said, his tanned face creasing. The way that word slipped out of his mouth, I knew he'd been savouring it for a long time. He was being vulnerable and honest. 'I miss love, Bella.'

I felt an incredible sadness emanating from him. His drinking problems, his self-esteem issues, his work stresses, nobody to be excited about. It made me angry. He was a fun, smart person underneath all the alcohol, but he continued to throw it all away on the bottle. But it wasn't my place to fight his battles for him anymore.

'You still have lots going for you,' I soothed him.

'Yeah, like what?'

'You're not grey yet.'

He managed a smile.

'It's a choice,' I said, after we'd sat in silence for a bit. 'I know it seems crazy to think that the solution to all of your problems lies in such a seemingly simple thing as a choice. But that's the truth of it.'

When I was ready to leave he took me in his arms and held me tight. 'I love you, Bella, I'll always love you. I fucked a lot of things up,' he said, conviction in his low voice. 'I regret most of those things, but never us.'

ıılılılılıılı

A book I once read categorised how we love. I think there were four categories: the gift-giver, the toucher, the verbal, the server. You have to ask yourself, if you're walking down the street and a big bubble of joy rises up from thinking of a loved one, what is your next response? Do you want to touch or kiss them (the toucher), buy them something nice (the gift-giver), call them and tell them your thoughts (the verbal), or think of something nice to do for them (the server). I am a GG, or Gift-Giver. I skip into a shop and buy a little present. That's how I show love and, unfortunately for my family and friends, also how I feel loved. My poor parents go into paroxysms every birthday and Christmas. My mother says it's like buying a gift for Idi Amin. I've tried to become a toucher or even a server, but nothing doing. I equate love with gifts, and it gets more complicated. The time spent buying the gift, the thoughtfulness, the number of gifts and the price – all get analysed into my internal Am-I-Loved computer, and either I'm lacking or loved. Horribly black and white and horribly embarrassing. It doesn't even make sense, because I'm not expansively materialistic. My ten-year-old jeans and penchant for plastic cheese slices prove that. That Christmas, as usual, I went overboard. The presents I bought Axel were crammed up underneath the branches of the tree and spilling out onto the living-room floor.

I love Christmas. I love it. I look forward to it like a kid. I like the festivities. But this year was different. I was experiencing my first Christmas away from my family with a man who didn't even believe in Christmas. I tried to explain to Axel about the pagan fertility tree and a nice old man named Saint Nicholas but he wasn't buying it.

Christmas in New York, though, was something else. The TV was inundated with diamond-lathered women hugging their handsome and generous spouses and kids playing and smiling happily, urging us to buy Disney. There was the lovely big Christmas tree at the Rockefeller Center, the lights upon lights stacked as tall as buildings, Macy's window displays, and hurried shoppers darting about, just like in the movies I saw as a kid.

One day, Axel arrived home with a big smile.

'Baby,' he said, 'I have an early Christmas present for you!' He looked a little frightened.

I eyed him suspiciously.

'Shut your eyes,' he commanded.

Then I heard it – a soft little squeaking noise. He'd got me a rat? I listened closer.

There it was again! It was a meow.

I opened my eyes and stared at him blankly.

'You got me a kitten?' I asked, every commitment-phobic bone in my body rattling.

'Well, not exactly a kitten.'

He opened a cage and out walked a large poo-brown tabby with a broken ear and a snarl.

'And he's sick,' added Axel.

'Sick,' I repeated.

'He just needs a little medication is all. An injection twice a day for a month,' he added quickly.

I reached out to pat the cat and he took a chunk out of my finger with his claws.

'Nice. Er, thanks, Axel,' I said, rubbing the blood off with my shirt. 'Shouldn't we be getting him back to his owner now?' I asked hopefully.

'No! He's yours, baby! Merry Christmas!' He grinned. 'I wanted to buy a cat from the pound, to save a life, and Cheeks here was the friendliest one. He gave me a cuddle right away, he's really very affectionate.'

'Sure, I can see that,' I mumbled, as Cheeks and I eyed each other off.

I lived with Axel, we were a couple and now we had a cat. That sounded suspiciously like commitment to me. What next? A baby? Marriage and a golden carriage? Shudder. It was entirely possible I still had a bit of an issue with commitment. And a cat – a cat was a bloody big commitment. A large scary one at that. No, siree, that wouldn't gel. But Axel's beaming face loomed into my view and I didn't have the heart to kill his joy. Perhaps I could kill the cat? Hmm, too messy. Cheeks and I would just have to sort out our differences. I spent the next few days alternating between ignoring him, bribing him with food, jamming a syringe down his throat and wiping blood off my fingers.

Global warming had definitely arrived. There was absolutely no snow and the weather was only cold enough for a light sweater. In Central Park, tulips were sprouting out of season, and upstate, bears were coming out of hibernation too early. On Christmas Eve, Axel and I went out to buy our last-minute Christmas stuff. I was determined to experience a white Christmas, even if there was no snow. I put on a big coat and a fluffy white snow hat; Axel sympathetically joined my protest and wore a leather jacket and snow goggles. Happily sweating under our winter attire, we got some cheers from a few locals and a little girl even offered to throw her ice-cream at me.

James called that day too, to wish me a merry Christmas. He was zooming off to Bloomingdales to meet his personal shopper to get gifts. He sounded cheerful and it was nice to hear him in good form.

On Christmas Day, we woke to an overcast sky. We shoved shallots, eggs, cheese and dill into a pan and whipped up an omelette, then sank into the sofa, eating greedily and eyeing off the gifts. Even Cheeks was excited as he chewed off the bows on the gifts then pawed around the furniture. It was highly possible that Axel and I had overcompensated for his Jewishness and my absent family. We had thirty-eight Christmas presents under the tree. We played 'I'll show you mine if you show me yours.' Amongst other gifts, I got a new mobile phone, a hair straightener, a diamond ring, earrings, a leather-bound notebook, a red polka-dot dress, fluffy handcuffs, a

Sony Cyber-shot camera and a digital video recorder. Score. I was loved.

Axel was so cute. After he'd unwrapped all his other presents, he got to the small, tatty-looking, second-hand speakers I'd bought him and I could see a momentary flash of disappointment on his face, then he showered my face in kisses and made a great show of liking them.

'Sorry, babe,' I said. 'I did tell you I couldn't afford the ones you wanted. I just didn't think you were worth it.'

He managed a laugh.

Then I went into the closet and withdrew from its hiding place a huge box smothered in bows and ribbons. His eyes grew wide and he started breathing heavily.

'Don't come yet, honey,' I grinned.

He unwrapped it almost reverentially.

'What have you done, baby? What have you done?'

When he saw the state-of-the-art, floor-standing speakers, I knew I would come a distant second in his life from then on. Even the fluffy handcuffs he'd bought me didn't get a trial run until well into the afternoon. Ah, credit cards can be a wonderful thing.

Once we had finally found the handcuff key ('Damn, this always happens,' said Axel) and my wrists were back to a normal size, our friends started to arrive. We ate roast chicken and fourteen kinds of cheese and drank an obnoxious Christmas punch I had concocted from vodka and white wine. Everybody brought little gifts and the starving artists brought poems they'd written. I hurried into the bathroom and scrawled one on some toilet paper for Axel.

Baby,
My defences slip away and reveal me.

Your eyes close and I watch.
You're timeless.
Alive.
Inside of me.

He read it, got a bit misty-eyed, then passed me over his crumpled piece of paper:

Roses are Red
Violets are Blue
Sugar is Sweet
And so are you.

Well, I wasn't with him for his originality.

That day I got an email from my mum. I'd written one to her about how I was missing her and my dad.

Dearest Belle, I'm sad you're sad but because we're going through the same thing it's a comfort in a weird way. It's a real grief, having you so far away. Christmas certainly triggers that off, the memory of all our lovely Christmases, the feeling of our family coming together so cosily, a rounding off of the year, a grounding thing which is based on a lifetime of family ritual. But as I've said many a time and oft – it is so worth it for your happiness and success and wonderful life in NY.

My mascara trails didn't dry for an hour. Hell, I missed her.

22

Fear and fitting in

ONCE THE FLASH AND fervour of Christmas died down, the weeks began to plod along in an uneasy way. I felt disconnected from life, like I wasn't a part of it. Somehow I felt it was linked to my mother's email, but I couldn't fathom how. Even Axel and I had come to a strange place.

It seemed almost an overnight thing. We'd eat together and it was like eating alone. At night, we didn't hold each other. When he went to work, I didn't notice him leaving. 'I love you,' I said; 'I love you,' he said – but it was rare that I could settle into those moments. I missed the tang of love on my tongue. Sex was regular, but when I lay underneath him we'd move our bodies in unison with passionless pleasure. I wandered around the house, watering plants and feeling empty. From experience, I thought this phase would pass. I think from experience, I knew that however much I tried, I couldn't kick-start the passion, it had to return when it was damn well ready.

I loved the occasional moments when we'd look at each other and it was as if a murky barrier had lifted and we'd see each other as if for the first time. He'd come home from work and we'd hold each other, soothingly, gently. Then our fingers would press into each other's skin with passion newly unfolding. We'd kiss, and it felt like years since we last did. We'd look at each other with studying, lustful eyes and I'd breathe again.

Those moments used to be strung together like a necklace, continuous jewels of happiness. But the necklace had become unstrung lately and those moments had become single expectant jewels that sometimes dropped into my day to remind me that the love was still there, or that it was growing weaker, I didn't know which.

I think a lot of people believe they'll find their answers in love. I know I did. In those first stages of love, you feel so good and confident that your world becomes saturated in gleaming, irrepressible colours. But when the pheromones die off and reality comes crashing through, that all-consuming, all-protective bubble of early love pops and leaves you feeling deserted, meaningless, even resentful. You have to say goodbye to the fierce lovemaking, the sideways glances and the flowers, and accept the next phase. The phase of the individual. You open your love-sick eyes, stretch and look about you. Things have changed, the soothing feeling of togetherness has dissipated and you are left alone.

Immersed in my alienation, I was forced to look at myself and my life without any filters. The truth was, I had become depressed again.

I couldn't muster any enthusiasm for day-to-day life. I bought bread and went to school like a robot, sort of numb and deadened. When I was alone, I'd weep all the time, then cringe at my tears. Sometimes my body would startle awake and Axel's body would enter mine and I was alive for a spark of a moment, but then the dull cloud obscured and I moved to the mechanical thrust of my depressed momentum.

I was thoroughly sick of myself, for my obvious penchant for depression, for my inability to cope with it. I was sick of the stupid pattern constantly reasserting itself. After everything I had been through, it was if I were back at Cancer Town, scoffing down coconut cream cakes.

I tried to talk to Axel about it, but he was a drummer and he gave me a drummer's advice: 'Just cheer up.' That wasn't *quite* what I needed to hear.

I sat in Central Park near the duck pond, turned my back to the throngs of tourists and let the tears slide down my cheeks. I felt like such an idiot. Here I was in New York City, an actor in training, living my dreams, and all I could do was cry fat useless tears. If I were to try to beat this damned depression, there was only one way I could start. I had to be honest with myself.

There was a life force in me that was blunted, curbed and caged. And it was dissolving under my constant scrutiny and that of others. I had a mad desire to let it out and trash my room and be an angry young woman with no inner voice dictating my movements.

Okay, so I was angry, that was a start.

I was confused by the many treacherous paths ahead of me. It was as if the world had broken open and I could see the guts and entrails, the mechanics of life. I saw the giant blossoming tree of life, its branches crossing the sky like a network of highways. I saw my distant future caught in a rain drop at the end of each branch. So many possibilities, so many threats.

Okay, I was confused as hell, and well on my way to the funny farm. But?

I only had a few more months left of the safety of Strasberg and then I had a working visa for only one year. One year of stiff competition, one year to 'make it'. One year to prove myself as an actor or I'd be kicked out of the country. I felt the pressure sink into my bones. What if all the energy and money my parents and friends had put into me was wasted? What if I let them down? What if I wasn't good enough? I would return home a big-assed failure.

Bingo. I felt fear flooding me and spreading its tendrils through every part of me.

I puffed out my chest with indignation and began to rationalise as the fear swelled at my heart and made me righteous. I didn't really want to be an actor anyway. I didn't want to be broke and struggling, shimmying up to shiny-suited people to book a job.

My newfound moral indignation began to warm at my cheeks and I felt the honourable glow of the fearful and the deluded. But as I looked out at the ducks splashing between the reeds, thoughts rose thickly through my head and became distant and somehow unimportant. The one thought that kept niggling at me was the blissful welling excitement of finally knowing that I'd hit the nail on the head: I was full of shit.

I was supposed to be a strong, independent woman, but here I was being an utter pussy, letting my worm-tongued friend – fear – get at me. Again.

The thing about fear, I realised, is that it is a hell of a lot smarter than me, it never sleeps, is always vigilant and always has silvery words at the ready: 'Don't be an actor. It is too hard. Give up now. You know you want to.'

But where would that lead me? By listening to my fears and condemning acting to the 'too difficult' basket, I'd just become bitter and roll my eyes at fresh young talent while I whiled away my life in regrets.

Is that what I wanted?

Nope. Not by the hairs on my chinny, chin chin.

I knew I wanted to be a working actor. Something in me clicked. It was too late to turn back. I couldn't rationalise anything away. I had to come head to head with my fear and conquer the bitch.

I remembered a documentary that Natalie and I had watched, called *March of the Penguins*. There was a telling scene towards the end, when an albatross was intent on choosing one of the fluffy chicks for his lunch. The chicks huddled together in fright, sensing their perilous situation. The albatross made a lunge for one of the unfortunate fellows, but, stumbling, only managed a bit of a peck. The irate and very brave chick fluffed his indignant feathers and chirped angrily at the huge beast twenty times his size. This miniature show of defiance obviously ruffled the albatross, and with a confused look, he backed away and tried his luck with a less frightening fellow. Another chick, scared out of his wits, made a break for it. The albatross reacted immediately to this display of fear and scampered after the little guy, who with a peck and a snap became his lunch. Lesson learned: fear will get you dead.

When I arrived home from the park, I sat down on the sofa to think. I was tired of fear controlling me. Fear as a puppet master. It would have me crawl into a hole somewhere and make me feast off the bullshit it told me. It was folly to follow fear, to listen to its soothing words. So what would Ron do? I guessed he'd tell me to voice my fear and breathe it out, then to stop eating my sandwich in the middle of class.

'Okay, I'm mind-bogglingly, pathetically, unbelievably, earth-shatteringly afraid of failure,' I said to the empty room.

I breathed into the emotion and allowed it to be there. Somewhere close by I heard the pitiful wailing of a baby in a full force of tears and realised with a fright that it was coming from me. They weren't the silent wet tears from a stubbed toe, it was the noisy *waaa* hiccup *waaa* of a bloody big baby. I think I actually said 'I want my mummy' too, not that I'd ever tell anyone that.

It felt so good to cry like that. I was burping up all my fears and accepting they existed. I couldn't have fought my fears through rationalisation or intellect, I had to embrace them, accept them and only then could I conquer them. It was fear at the root of my depression, it was the nucleus that everything bad had spiralled from. It was my inner Hitler and denial had given it strength.

For a few days afterwards, I figured that my I-want-my-mummy/crying purge had weeded out all my issues because I felt lighter and freer. I contemplated going to the zoo to see if I could stare down a snake or wrestle with a crocodile. But soon enough I realised that I'd won the battle but not the war. I knew with a sinking heart that I hadn't weeded out all of my issues. Perhaps I could blame Axel?

I watched him cooking dinner in our tiny kitchen. He really was the most awful cook. He thought he was an Israeli Fernand Point, but, suffice to say, he managed to kill toast. However, he'd dish up his disasters so proudly and would sulk so profoundly if I didn't like them, that I always ended up lying and saying it was great, cooing at him like a mother pigeon.

Making pigeon noises at your lover as you boldly lied to his face probably meant that something wasn't quite working in the relationship. But I'd have to deal with that later. Right now, I had to work out what was happening to me.

I began to realise that in the past few months, as I'd slid towards depression, another kind of fear had been at work in my life, too – the fear of not fitting in, not being good enough.

When I dressed in the morning, I'd think of the universal 'they' and try to work out what clothes would make me acceptable to 'them'. So that I'd be accepted.

At Strasberg, instead of giving performances with the intention to learn more or to improve, I'd do them so that the teacher would say how good I was, or so students would congratulate me afterwards. So that I'd be liked.

I would find myself anxiously mulling over zillion-dollar anti-wrinkle creams and make-up products to cover my wrinkles and my disappointing self. I'd buy brand-name products because the commercials said I would be fun and adored if I did. I remembered something I'd read in a book: if you are trying to show off to people at the top, they will look down on you anyway. If you are trying to show off to people at the bottom, they will only envy you. I was aware that my new idiocy would get me nowhere, but I just couldn't seem to stop myself.

I felt my fragmented self slowly slipping further and further away from my understanding as the days wore on. Perhaps my little tango with FF, or fear of failure, had spilled over into a belief that I wasn't good enough to succeed. That I wasn't good enough as I was.

One day I found myself standing in front of the mirror, fresh from the shower, looking at my reflection with such aversion, such distaste, that it shocked me. I'd always believed that beauty was deeper than skin; that positive energy sears through someone's skin and lands all around them in warm, affecting waves, and *that* is beauty. I mean, I liked to dress up and look good, just like anybody, but it usually wasn't so life and death as it seemed to have become. But there I was, staring at myself in the mirror, wishing I was someone else, disgusted at my own face, blaming, angry. It forced me into a wake-up call. Why was I being such a dickhead? Why was I trying so desperately to fit in, when a few months ago I was planning to buy a cape and take over the world?

There seemed to me to be a biological imperative to fit in. Like in the animal kingdom, there's an impetus to work together, fit in, not stray, so as to ensure the survival of the species. It was just like us humans, it wasn't a desire, it was a need.

Attempting to fit in wasn't some esoteric or flighty thing that only teenagers did. It was real. It is our biology telling us, urging us on towards straighter hair and a whiter smile. Perhaps thousands of years ago when the impulse to fit in was developed for survival of the group, we needed it to, well, survive. But now, in modern day, an individual can physically survive on their own. Then again, what about the other deeper needs, like contact, affection, acceptance? Perhaps we still have that primal impetus to fit in not only physically but *emotionally* with a group. The need for acceptance is a primitive instinct played out through biology, fuelled by our fears.

But the issue went deeper. It wasn't only about our desire to fit in, it was also about the group's desire to make us fit in. I felt like one of those giant balls of rubber bands bunched around a pencil that you see in offices. Each input I received subconsciously or consciously from family, friends, TV and magazines added one more rubber band to my ball, and what happened? I got covered in these layers until my pencil was completely lost from sight. I had to get back to the pencil. I had to get back to myself.

I figured I would make my life easier by giving up smoking, so I hid my remaining cigarettes under the sofa in the bedroom. Every so often I'd run in there and with Herculean strength push the sofa aside to get at them. Then with every iota of my willpower, I'd back away (let out a scream) and run out of the room, slamming the door behind me. Cheeks would watch me with distaste and lick his balls.

Axel texted me every half hour.

'Have you broken? Are you smoke free?'

'I hate it and I hate you.'

'Good, you haven't. Talk to you in another half hour.'

I found myself walking past the neighbour's door and trying to catch a whiff of smoke from between the cracks. I was confused as all hell about who I was, or even wanted to be, had turned into a fat-ass blob of rubber and was homicidal from cigarette withdrawals. I was in good shape. Then I checked my bank balance. Seven dollars and fifteen cents. Phew, just enough for cigarettes.

That afternoon, I got a text from James.

'I bought this really expensive smoked chicken but it tastes so bad and is too expensive to toss. Can I make you dinner?'

Ha ha. Sounds ridiculously inviting, but I'd have to take a rain check.

Just then, Daiana and Natasa, my two Strasberg friends, knocked on my door. They careered into the room with spirit and energy, spied my downcast face, plonked onto the sofa next to me and kindly listened to all my bullshit.

'So what do you want?' Daiana asked.

'I want to feel that lustful desire for life again. And to stop being so ridiculously dependent on what others think of me. Or being so dangerously susceptible to advertising. I want to scrape away all the bullshit, have an annual car wash of the senses and de-layer myself. In a nutshell.'

'No, I mean wine or juice.'

Daiana and Natasa and I talked at each other until five in the morning. As we talked it began to dawn on me that I'd been living without love. Love for the funny things people did, for the flannel hat of an old guy, for friends, for the view outside a window, for life in all its strangeness. When you look at life through love, things become less threatening. Ah, love. I wanted to feel its lustful beauty again.

I had a thought. I pushed open the window and leaned out. 'I loooove you, New York!'

'We love you too, you fucking nutcase,' came the cheerful reply from the streets below.

ıılıllılılı

Over the next few weeks, I began to make choices. Small ones at first, then bolder ones. I began stripping away the artifice that surrounded me (as well as the hideous clothes I'd bought). I threw away my wrinkle creams and let my ripeness shine on through. I wore clothes that I liked and began to get out from behind the beast of ingratiation and politeness and began to get to know myself again. And I wasn't as bad as I'd feared. Granted, I still told bad jokes, but I accepted them, and accepted me. It seemed a little too easy. Didn't I have to suffer more to get happy? Evidently not. This choice thing was the bomb.

Sometimes the world cracked open and I could feel my dull haze lift. I could feel the freshness of the world on my face as though I had been sleep-walking. It was good to feel that, the birth of an idea, the rediscovery of the world.

I was getting more positive every day. It felt good to be in control of my destiny and not at the whim of fear. I really liked the whole choice thing, and would go to ice-cream shops to test out my new choice prowess. Chocolate, please.

The one thing that wasn't as simple as choosing an ice-cream flavour was my relationship with Axel.

Watching him from across the dinner table one night, I got a bizarre image of us in my head. We were hanging in midair. Then a soft wind would blow and we'd occasionally bump into each other and occasionally his parts slipped into mine. But otherwise, we just hung there, slowly turning in the air. By all appearances we were hanging side by side. But we didn't choose to. We were hanging next to each other because our limbs were tied. We presented ourselves to the world: 'We're by each other's side and all is good in our world.' But it wasn't true.

I was beginning to feel like the unfair stereotype of a wife. Striving for some notion of perfection that I knew didn't exist, yet still resentful that it didn't.

23

Starry nights, a mini-break to Texas for the premiere and how I got my leg eaten by a zombie

SPRING AND SUMMER came and went as I continued to go to Strasberg, see friends, make short films and do theatre shows. Life had a gentle hum to it after the highs and lows of the past few months, and I relished the easy pace. Axel and I were pottering along well enough. The sex was always really good so I was content to let our relationship continue. Horniness was the great healer, I reckoned.

But despite our commonality through rumpy pumpy, I was having some difficulty talking to him. One night, after trolling through the MoMA, I came home excited and inspired.

'Hell, there was Picasso and Klimt and I saw van Gogh's *Starry Night!* I actually saw it! Fuck –'

'*Starry* what?'

'*Starry* – it's a painting.'

I'd always known Axel wasn't very interested in anything other than drumming and my being naked, but I'd made allowances because of his hotness. I mean, hell, I still had to use my fingers to count. But I'd get those looks from people when he'd insist that Nelson Mandela was a type of soda. Those, what-the-hell-are-you-doing-with-him kind of looks, which seemed to be increasing in frequency. But my friends weren't dating him, I was. And he was good in bed, damn it.

But one night, after a particularly painful explanation of why we needed gravity, I asked him point blank, 'Axel, are you interested in more education in the future, perhaps?'

'I didn't finish high school.'

'So? A lot of people didn't finish high school, such as Thomas Edison, Bill Gates, Richard Branson, it doesn't mean you can't strive for betterment –'

'Who are they?'

'Edison was – eh, forget it.'

Suddenly a light bulb lit up his brown eyes. 'I read in *Maxim* that Paris Hilton didn't finish high school. And just look at her now . . . she's really hot!'

'Yes, Axel, yes she is,' I replied as I slowly backed out of the room.

'Anyway, learning is stupid,' he called after me.

Anyway, learning is stupid! A sudden image of James swam out through my frustration. A sharp physical pang startled me awake; I missed the Good James. We used to stay up for hours and talk, that kind of exuberance was so rare to find; he'd opened worlds for me that I hungered for. James had his faults too, I was the first to point that wee little fact out. But when he was in good form, and sober, he had been so interested in the world, he embraced new things, new ideas. I missed being inspired by my partner and taken on wild journeys of heart and mind. But whenever I felt my heart fluttering over memories of the Good James, the knee-jerk sadness would immediately well up and I'd remember that he'd always be my half-finished statue, hewn from pain. Axel, on the other hand, was real, maybe a little *too* real, but real.

That afternoon I got a call from Zoë, telling me to get my ass down to Texas to go to the *Grindhouse* premiere with her and Quentin Tarantino.

'Couldn't possibly.'

'Excellent! I'll get a driver to pick you up at the airport.'

ılıllıllıl

When the day broke, I slept through my alarm, got dressed and ready in thirty seconds, but still managed to miss my Supershuttle bus to the airport. Jumped into a cab. Driver took me three blocks then confessed he didn't have a toll pass to get into JFK. Got out of the cab. Found another one. Fell asleep. Woke up on the wrong side of Manhattan.

'Yo, where are we going?'

'To the airport, miss,' came the slimy response.

'Um, so why are we in bloody Africa?'

It clicked. He thought I was a tourist and wanted to scam me for more money. As the good New Yorker I had become, I yelled at him, and like the good New York cab driver he was, he yelled back. I jumped out of the cab as we both threw the middle finger at each other and grinned.

I got into another cab and the driver told me he wouldn't take me to the airport.

'Why not?'

'I don't like airports.'

'O-kaay.'

I got into another cab and bribed the driver to go as fast as hell, promising extra money if he got me there with time to spare. He was a Mexican version of Morgan Freeman in *Driving Miss Daisy*. I saw an old lady on a cane wobble past my window.

An excruciatingly long while later we arrived. I had two minutes before my flight left.

'Give me my extra ten dollars!' he demanded.

'You didn't get me here on time!'

'Fuck you, give me my extra ten!'

He looked mean.

'Okay, wait here and I'll go to an ATM.'

I hightailed it across the terminal in my wobbling heels as the final boarding call blasted from the speakers. Found an ATM, which swallowed my card. Took another card out, got cash. Gave to cabbie. He demanded more.

'Five extra for waiting!'

I didn't care how mean he looked. 'Um, how about fuck you?'

He took in my bloodshot eyes and furious expression.

'Okay,' he said abruptly, then, smiling, wished me a good flight.

I ran to the check-in and yep, I had missed the final call. I popped out some tears but it was to no avail.

The clerk finally took pity on me and booked me onto another flight in half an hour.

'But it's at LaGuardia Airport, across town.'

'How long is the bus ride?'

'Twenty-five minutes,' she said. 'You'd better run.'

I sprinted to the bus and clambered aboard. When we finally arrived at LaGuardia, I hurtled up to the check-in and was told I'd only just made it.

My chest heaving, I grinned gratefully at the gay attendant. 'I' – huff – 'want to' – puff – 'have your babies.'

'I don't like fish.'

'Huh?'

'Nothing.' He grinned. 'Can I have your ID please, ma'am?'

I looked everywhere but couldn't find it. I realised I had left my purse on the bus. *Shit!*

I raced back to the bus stop. No bus. I sprinted with all my luggage smashing against my thighs and shins to the company's rep, who walkie-talkied to someone. After listening to the response, he shook his head. Just then, like a lovely mirage, around the corner came the bus driver waving my purse with one hand and navigating the rickety old bus with the other. I thanked him profusely and sprinted back up the three flights of stairs, across the terminal to the boarding gate. Red-faced and breathing like a serial killer, I gave the attendant my ticket and ID.

She looked at me sourly.

'Flight's closed.'

I felt hot tears blob out of my eyes.

Just then, Nice Gay Guy Who Didn't Like Fish gallantly shouldered Nasty Woman out of the way.

'Let the lady through,' he said, like a hero in a film.

I gave him a hug and sprinted through security, got all my perfumes and make-up confiscated and finally got on the plane – off to Austin, Texas.

ıılıılılılı

I arrived in Austin, seven hours later, and was picked up and taken to the InterContinental where Zoë and the rest of the cast were staying.

Zoë and I tackled each other onto the plush sofas of her hotel room and said our traditional hellos by knuckling each other and grinning maniacally. We popped open some pinot grigio and chatted excitedly until a stylist arrived and applied make-up on Zoë. We ummed and ahhed about her choices of dresses and settled on a sexy Jessica Rabbit leopard-print with Stella McCartney shoes. She looked unbelievably stunning, like a fifties movie star with smouldering eyes and red, red lips. I wore a white Marilyn Monroe-style dress with gold beading, teamed with red shoes and lips. So, this was the big-time.

We left the hotel with Kurt Russell – who always looked infinitely younger in the flesh and damn sexy – and some other cast members of *Grindhouse*, and went to a local Mexican restaurant that served soggy nachos and excellent margaritas.

Quentin spied me from across the room and, elbowing people out of the way, let out an almighty roar, 'Belllllaaa!' He gave me a big, enveloping hug. I forgot he was such a huge superstar as his affection was so embracing he seemed like a cherished friend. I really liked Quentin, I liked his warmth, his humour and quirks. *My mum on the bog.*

After dinner we headed to the premiere. When we arrived in our Hummer there was a heaving crowd of fans and press outside the cinema, as if it were a rock concert. People were jostling and elbowing one another to get closer to the stars. When we got out of the vehicle, almost immediately the fans started to swamp Zoë and she was dragged off to the red carpet to do interviews, while I stood around and tried to look inconspicuous.

Inside, the atmosphere was electric. Quentin and Robert Rodriguez got up and roused the crowd with expletives and enthusiasm. Industry people I spoke to said American premieres were usually filled with agents and managers who stood around with plastered smiles and clapped politely on cue. Quentin shouted to the crowd: 'This is Aussstin, Texas! This is not a room full of Hollywood slimeball agents and managers. This is the reeeall deal' – a huge cheer from the crowd – 'so let me hear you scream! I want to see you yell and shout and have fun with this movie, interaction is what it's all about, Ausstiin!' – huge roar – 'and if you see a Hollywood slimeball agent, you have my full permission to knock 'im out!'

The reels and gags rolled onto the silver screen to roaring cheers and rabble-rousing shout-outs. *Death Proof*, Quentin's film, was as fun as all hell. He'd created a clever, exuberant homage to the C-grade films that he was raised on and the pace never let up for a second. Zoë was ridiculously good. Her spirit and incredible physical dexterity splashed onto the silver screen with gusto. It was great seeing her up there, my childhood friend who I always saw in my mind's eye with face paint and pigtails, kicking ass and being an action hero. Hell, yeah. The role I had been up for, Abernathy, was played beautifully by Rosario Dawson, but as I slurped back my free beers I couldn't help but think of how I would have played it.

At the after-party I took the role of unofficial bodyguard for Zoë. It took almost an hour to get to the VIP room as after every few steps excited fans and impressed crew members would stop Zoë to congratulate her stellar kick-assedness. Zoë was so elegant and charming and real that people stared at her with a slightly glazed look in their eyes, as if they had just fallen in love. I gently moved her on from group to group and we finally made it to the backroom, where we played, for some strange reason, a paper–scissors–rock championship with much enthusiasm and spilled drinks. I was introduced to the very handsome Robert Rodriguez and his waif-like girlfriend Rose McGowan, who scowled at me in a really cool way.

At the after-after party, Zoë grew tired so went back to the hotel, while Quentin and I and Danny Trejo – that cool pock-mark-faced Mexican from *Once Upon a Time in Mexico*, *SherryBaby*, *Desperado* and 137 (!) other films – danced like demons. We 'hardcorers', as we named ourselves, stayed up talking about the film and Hollywood as the bar owner chortled along with us and made strong drinks. It was a great night, climaxing in me eating a tequila worm from the mouth of Roller Derby Girl and Danny showing me how, if he were a zombie, he would eat my leg. (A kind of quick munch-munch action with an upward rolling of the eyes.) Quentin and I danced, our limbs flailing like crazy people's, and when I was as trashed as a pussycat could be, he drove me in his limo to my hotel where I squeezed into the bed next to Zoë. I liked the big-time.

When I got up the next day, Zoë had already left for her early morning plane back to Los Angeles, so I spent the day exploring Austin with its hundreds of musicians eagerly performing in the cafés and bright tree-lined streets. It was a perfect break to refresh myself before the last throes of Strasberg and my nearing graduation. Little did I know, it wouldn't be quite as simple as that. My period was late.

24

Doing the baby blues and wearing banana fronds

M Y PERIOD WAS LATE. Like, two weeks late. Axel kept kneading my boobs to gauge when it was coming. I started feeling hormonal. I cried a lot and fell asleep a lot. But I hoped it was just African Sleeping Sickness. Then, overnight, I transformed into Anna Nicole Smith. My boobs grew and grew like strange monsters from *Alice in Wonderland*. Axel continued to unhelpfully knead them. I really started to get scared when I ate four hamburgers, half a roast chicken, a wheel of brie and two tubs of ice-cream, all without faltering, in one hour. I brushed the worry from my mind and reckoned it was just my fat genes finally coming out.

'Maybe you're pregnant?' said Axel one night over dinner.

'What!' Our unspoken etiquette of denial was in danger of being violated.

'If we don't talk about it, it can't happen,' I reminded him.

He looked at me.

'But I can't possibly be pregnant. I'm just eating a lot because . . . I have tapeworms, and my boobs are bigger because I'm just going through, ah . . . late puberty.'

'That doesn't make sense. You need to stop being in denial, so that when you get tested it won't be such a big shock.'

'I'm not in denial. I could have a baby! We could row to the Amazon and have a baby there. And wear banana fronds. It'd be nice.'

'That's how you see it, isn't it?'

'What?'

'Like it's not possible.'

'Well, it's not possible! I'm not pregnant. I don't want to be pregnant.'

I had already become strangely hormonal. Very Earth Motherish. As if a part of me was becoming the tiger mother that would protect her cub at all costs. As hormones flooded my system, I could sense the change in me. I felt protective, strong, as though I'd found this well of secret and immensely powerful femaleness that I hadn't tapped into before. I'd seen glances of it in the eyes of my own mother and it always made me feel safe, but now I was feeling the same thing, and it scared the living hell out of me.

'Okay, truth is, I'm afraid. Like, very afraid.' I told Axel about feeling Earth Motherish and we both tried to imagine me draped in banana leaves. I told him I knew the timing was wrong, really wrong. I told him I didn't know what was happening to me and that when I saw kids on the street, for the first time in my life I felt clucky. I told him that with my fifteen-hour days, I didn't know what I would do with a baby. I told him I still felt like a kid myself. I told him that I was ready, that I wasn't, that I just didn't know.

Axel took the day off work to come to the pharmacy with me

to buy a pregnancy test. We got it home and unwrapped it as if it were a time bomb.

I peed on it.

I waited the allotted time.

Two blue lines appeared.

'What does that mean?' asked Axel.

'It means you're a total bastard.'

I was pregnant. Our eyes met. In that fraction of a second everything was said. The immense fear and anticipation made us both shake like wet kittens and we drew together and held each other. Very tightly.

I was a total mess. I couldn't think straight because the kamikaze hormones would make me alternate between feeling violent and feeling like singing old show tunes, often at the same time. Plus, I was falling asleep at odd times. And, my unearthly long days at Strasberg were making my head hurt.

I was at a crossroads. Sure, the idea of being pregnant at the *worst* possible time of my life could be construed as a negative, but I didn't need to *feel* negatively about it. It was my decision as to how I reacted to this new 'adventure', right?

So there I was, only a few months away from graduating from Strasberg. I had fought so many of my demons and even managed to scrape by the obstacles they'd placed in my way (with only a small amount of permanent damage). Would I have to give it all up to have a baby, to wear palm fronds?

I could be an earth mum and buy cool little outfits. I could finally say I was a real grown-up. I could take long baths and see my swelling belly float in a bevy of bubbles. I would be a good mum. Cheeks and I had grown to love each other – that counted for something, didn't it?

But I didn't want to throw away everything I had fought so hard for, to wipe sick off my blouse. I didn't even have an income. Neither did Axel, for that matter – he'd been fired from BB Kings for being chronically late. Plus he still thought 'reciprocity' was a 1990s rock band. But was I any better? I still liked to suck lollipops and twirl my pigtails, for godsake. Were either of us ready?

I thought about my career, Strasberg, my OPT year, about financial woes and my already overloaded schedule, now to include a baby? Why was I even considering keeping the baby? Immense battles had been fought and people had died so that I had the choice to have it or not.

I thought of Axel. I could clearly see his big, gentle hands holding our baby. I loved Axel. Together, in love, we could overcome any obstacles, right? Then I thought of our recent troubles.

One night a few weeks ago we had sat up in bed talking.

'The problem with you, Bella, is that you think life is easy. You think you can do anything you want to,' he said out of the blue.

'What are you talking about now?'

'I'm just sick of your head being in the clouds. Life isn't like that.'

'Did you have a crap day?'

'No.'

'So why are you saying this all of a sudden?'

'It's not all of a sudden, you just don't want to see it. I don't see life like you do. Life is shit and that's the way it is.'

'That's not true at all, that's just your own crap.'

'Yes, Bella, it is true,' he said, conviction in his eyes. 'I don't believe that life is easy, it never has been and it never will be. You go around saying how anything is possible when it's not. It pisses me off.'

'But it is true,' I insisted. 'Anything is possible, I mean, within reason. You know it's true, don't you?'

'There's no use talking to you.'

'Axel, I don't understand where this is coming from, really. I mean, life is *not* meant to be hard – it's all a lie. Life is meant to be easy and that's the truth. You can do whatever you want. The only thing stopping you is yourself, your own attitude.'

'Bullshit,' he replied. 'I have no schooling, no money, no stability. These things stop me, it's not in my control. It's not up to me.'

'Bullshit to you. That's denying your responsibility. If you *wanted* to, you could start arrangements to go to school, begin saving money. It's all up to you. Life doesn't hold you back unless you let it, it's a choice and that's the fucking truth.'

I looked at him, and with a sinking heart I knew he didn't believe a word of it.

'What about what you said about your music, about trying and perseverance?' I continued.

'Yeah, well, that was then.'

I felt the bottom sink out of me. If he really did think all that, what hope did he have for a good life? What hope did we have for a good life together? Out of nowhere, I got a sudden vivid – and now, I understood, prophetic – image. I saw my daughter in years to come, standing near a wooden kitchen table with Axel standing over her saying, 'You can't do it, life is hard, get used to it.' I shuddered.

Once I was pregnant, I brought the subject up again. He recanted and said he had never said anything of the sort. Bloody lying men.

One night, as we lay in bed together, he kissed me gently.

'Everything will be all right, my softness,' Axel said as he stroked my face.

Most men seem to want the soft part of a woman, but some don't, some like the fire in our eyes and the strut in our walk. I wanted a man who would love me for both.

'What are you thinking about?' he asked.

'Too much, babe. So, tomorrow we need to make an appointment with the doctor and see what our options are, okay?'

'Yes . . . hey,' he said, a bright idea furrowing at his temples. 'Now that you're pregnant, we can have sex without a condom!'

I sank into his arms and kissed him.

ıılıılıılıılıı

The next morning, we slept late and just managed to get to our doctor's appointment on time.

'You're not pregnant,' said the doctor.

'Er. Ah. What?' I stammered.

'Nope, I've tested your blood and you're not pregnant.'

It was the same crazy doctor I'd gone to before. I punched myself for ever having gone to her again. But she was free. I looked down at her mismatched socks and glared.

'Look, I'm really sorry, but is there another doctor who could confirm that?' I felt bad for her, but this was my future we were talking about.

'Sure,' she said brightly, as though I'd asked her if she liked coloured pencils.

Dr Reynolds, a fifty-something, severely dressed woman examined me.

'Yes, your hCG levels have dropped. It seems you had a chemical pregnancy.'

'A chemical what?'

'It's very common, fifty per cent of pregnancies are chemical. Most women don't even get the symptoms of pregnancy before the foetus miscarries. It seems you were sensitive and picked them up.'

'So I miscarried?'

'No, it was a chemical pregnancy.'

I couldn't work out exactly what she was talking about, but I gleaned just enough to know I was out of hot water.

'Thank you very, very much, doctor.'

As I walked out onto the street I experienced a blinding flash of clarity. I could finish Strasberg and I could plan when I wanted children. I could now also decide what to do about Axel. A great rush of air came from my lungs.

Axel came up behind me and put his arm around me. 'You okay, baby?' he asked, sadness swallowing his words.

'Yes, baby, I'm okay. I'm okay.'

On the way home we listed all the positives of our non-pregnancy.

'I don't have to read a billion books on burping and nipple drippage – that's a big plus.'

Axel looked at me startled. 'You would have read a book on how to be a mother?'

'Not *how* to be a mother, Axel, but yes, all that cool technical stuff that I would have had no idea about.'

'It should have come naturally!' he insisted. 'My mother didn't have to read any books,' he added rather indignantly.

'Axel, you tool – I mean, darling little block-head. I wouldn't have *had* to read books on babies, but I'd –'

'That's crazy. What kind of a woman would read a book on how to be a mother?'

'Sometimes people like to learn new things. Get knowledge from people who have been there before, who have wisdom to impart.'

He looked at me and blinked, then his eyes grew unfocused. 'I'm hungry,' he said.

That afternoon Rene called to see how the doctor's appointment had gone. I told her about the chemical pregnancy.

'Thank god, Bella. I'm so relieved. I couldn't have imagined you two doing the baby thing just yet. How's it going with Axel anyway?'

'He keeps saying the most astonishing things. The other day he told me that life was crap and to get used to it. I mean, who says that other than a character from a Mike Leigh film? And he said it was stupid to read books on motherhood, that it should just come naturally.' I lowered my voice. 'He doesn't know who Edison is.'

'But?' she prompted.

'I love him. And on the flip side, he's also lovely and kind. And hot. I could open up his world. I could help him grow and learn and change. He's worth it,' I added uncertainly.

That afternoon, I caught the subway uptown to do some shopping and think about things.

I loved Axel, and that was all that mattered, right? I'd read the storybooks, I'd listened to the John Lennon songs; love is all you need.

But I needed more than love to be in love. I needed us to be right for one another. I needed us to have things in common, like morality and life view. I wanted to stop explaining what the government did and why we needed gravity.

If he *wanted* to grow, if he *wanted* to learn, then I would have been at his side. But he didn't. He was who he was and he was content being who he was.

I looked up and saw an advertisement on the train's scarred walls. It was a public-service announcement on illegal guns. 'Get Your Priorities Straight' it threatened.

What were *my* priorities? They were acting and Strasberg. Short and sweet. There and then I decided I would do all the things I dreamed of before I left Strasberg. I would play Blanche, and Martha. I would try to get some kick-ass references and leave Strassy with a bang. The challenge was set.

25

The grand finale with kisses and splits, Blanche and Martha, as well as getting blessed by wet agents and Father New York (or off on a new adventure)

I N MY LAST TERM at Strasberg I eagerly enrolled in a class taught by George Loros, an actor famous around New York for being on *The Sopranos* and pretty much every other TV show that ever existed. Initially he terrified the hell out of me, with his burly body and deep commanding voice which rose in fury when students disobeyed. But his class was my last chance to play Blanche in *A Streetcar Named Desire* before graduation, and even the fear of swimming with the fishes didn't dissuade me. Plus, I still had weird hormones floating around me, so if he tried to mess with me he'd find an Earth-Mother-Tigress waiting.

Blanche was a Southern belle who had landed on tough times. Her young lover, who she found out was gay, shot himself after she discovered his leanings. Then her family house was sold out from under her and she had to live in a decrepit hotel where she sought love in all the wrong places. She journeyed to her sister's house, never admitting the depths to which she had sunk. There she was raped by her sister's husband and gradually turned to madness to escape her wretched life.

I set about on my routine with gusto, learning lines, plotting peaks and troughs, developing Blanche's walk and mannerisms and working on the Southern accent. I was to play the scene, with one other actor, in which Blanche confesses her past sins and finally lets the cloud of madness obscure her. Blanche tries her hardest to keep herself together but she quickly falls apart as her past eclipses her present. The scene seemed to me to be about that delicate balance between the past and the present. She veers towards one, then to the other, then finally the battle is resolved when the unwholesome weight of the past wins.

Playing her was a great honour and a dream come true, with her complexity, her Southern values, her dream-saturated life, her horrific past, her madness and vulnerability. Up there on stage, under the lights, Blanche came alive inside me and I felt the overwhelming pathos of her life. Being Blanche reminded me of how fragile we all are. Blanche's fragility was worn on her sleeve, barely concealed under her Southern charms, but it was still there, glimmering and tender, like all of us. She also reminded me how necessary it was, in my own life, to learn the lessons the past had taught me.

Afterwards, when George congratulated me and said it was good enough to take to Broadway, his comments didn't affect me the way I thought they would. Don't get me wrong, I was damned appreciative (in fact, I said 'thank you' six times), but I had turned a corner and I wasn't performing for his or anyone else's accolades. I was doing it for myself.

My friends and I went out that night to paint the town red. When I got home, still pretty drunk, Axel was getting ready to catch a bus to Atlantic City for a weekend with his mates. He was in a foul mood.

'What the fuck is this?' he demanded as soon as I walked in the door. He had my journal in his hands.

I looked at him. 'You read my journal? You asshole!'

'Don't call me an asshole.'

'Then' – hic – 'don't read my journal' – hic – 'asshole.' The room was beginning to spin. I opened my journal to see the last thing I'd written.

I love Axel, I really do. Sometimes I wish I didn't. I don't think I can do it with him any more. He inevitably says 'life is shit' but he's given up before he's even started. I try to make him see but he just won't. Then I see him suffering and I try again, but he just won't listen – the stupid circle keeps reinventing. What the hell do I do? Crap, I'm not any better. I'm a fuck-up; we're all fuck-ups. But you have to try and not be a fuck-up, that's what counts, isn't it? Trying.

I really didn't want to be dealing with this half-sloshed. I looked up at him and he was glaring with all his might. 'So, you think I'm a fuck-up?'

'I think that you don't try. I want you to be happy, Axel, I want us to be happy together. I wish' – hic – 'you would just try is all.'

'Fuck you,' came the eloquent response.

'No, Axel, fuck you,' I said, trying to keep my head still. 'I've been through the whole happy/unhappy thing and I know what I'm talking about. Mostly.'

'What are you talking about?'

I braced myself. 'I spent a lot of time trying to get happy, then more time making sure I stayed happy, do you know what I mean? It's hard, I won't say it isn't, but it's what you gotta do – try, grow, expand. And then the rewards are there.'

'What rewards? You're full of shit.'

'Being happy. Being happy with yourself and your life. Feeling it inside of you, all the time, like a . . . like a nice thing. Like an ice-cream inside you.'

'A nice ice-cream?'

'Look, let's just save this for when I'm sober, okay?'

'You're talking about getting famous or getting a million dollars, aren't you? Do you think that means you'll get happy?' he snorted.

'For fuck's sake, it's not about money, it's about *being happy*. Before I came here, I thought happiness was a right, and when I wasn't happy I'd get pissed off that the joy of life seemed to always be passing me by, you know? Like a damned carnival I wasn't invited to. But you know what? Happiness isn't a right at all, no, no, no, not at bloody all. You can't just sit back and wait for it. You have to seek it, earn it. Yes! Work hard for it, do things you're not comfortable with, get out of your comfort zone, take risks. Learn, grow!'

He looked at me blankly.

I tried a new tack. 'Like that guy, Will Smith, in *The Fun of Chasing Things*. He never gave up.'

'You mean *The Pursuit of Happyness*?'

'Yup, if –'

'Then if you just try, you magically get happy, right?' he said sarcastically. 'You just don't understand at all, do you?'

'No, Axel, no. You don't understand.'

He didn't want to open his eyes and take on the world, even his own world. I loved Axel, I mean, he'd even managed to part me from some of my hard-held commitment-phobic issues, but . . . I knew my heart wasn't strong enough to pour more time and energy into a man who wasn't ready to fight his own battles, or at least try. We are all fucked up in some way, but as my mother told me long ago, it's *how* each person deals with their own fucked-up-ness that counts.

'Axel,' I said, swallowing slowly. 'We're pretty different and perhaps we need to admit that and move on from one another.'

'You don't love me anymore?'

'Yes. I do,' I said honestly. 'That's a problem. I mean, we could go on like this forever, but what about the future? Life. We don't want the same things –'

Axel glared at me. He picked up his bags and left, slamming the door behind him.

Once he was back from Atlantic City, he would push his palm out and say, 'I don't want to talk about it.' I thought *I* was good at the whole denial thing but he had a black belt in it. We continued to live together for the next couple of weeks, sorting out our things and arranging everything. He wanted to punish me for breaking up with him so he'd ignore me completely, or make sure that I'd see him flirting with other girls. Technically we were broken up but it still ripped me in two to see it.

Sometimes I saw Axel as a malevolent figure who had control over me in ways I hated. Other times I saw him as a confused little boy who was in up to his neck and acting out. One night he sent me twelve roses and a note reading, 'No matter what, I love you more than anything else in the world. Meet me at Bua Bar at 8,' so I went to meet him. I figured he had begun the process of accepting what we needed to do and I was intent on helping and supporting him through it. At least a really good friendship could come out of it.

When I arrived, he was drinking a beer with Jamie, the waitress. He saw me come in and a smile spread over his face. Keeping eye contact with me, he raised his arm and brought it up to Jamie's cheek. Softly, like he was touching precious silk, he stroked her. Then he turned his head towards her, leaned in and kissed her passionately on the mouth.

I was so filled with hurt and disgust, it felt like a fire was spinning up my spine and I was liable to do anything. My body wanted to rage against him, my knees wanted to give way, my mind wanted to shut down. We locked eyes and both our masks fell away. He discovered that I did still love him; and I discovered him for the person he really was.

It had taken a year to fully understand Axel. They say people show their true colours in a predicament; and his were splashed across that bar for all to see. I knew his limited world view affected his quality of life and future, but it also gave him a single course to take when faced with a problem, which was vindictiveness and cruelty.

I moved into my friend Natasa's house, and in the weeks after the separation I still felt hurt and anger but I also felt a lot of relief. I'd seen him for who he was, and no matter how subversive love was, it couldn't convince me that I missed him.

When I was with Axel, I felt I had to protect my *joie de vivre* as if it were a delicate child, shielding it behind my skirts, safe from the criticism of his world view. So, after the break-up I began to feel lighter than I had in a long time, as if the physical weight of his negativity had lifted off my shoulders and I could embrace life again.

In a sense, the suffocating weight of Axel and his surprise cruelty had been worse than the alcohol-induced anger of James, because it was more nefarious, more insidious. With James, I knew he was aware of his anger and was always contrite. I didn't want an Axel who only fulfilled the physical in me and left my other needs gaping wide open. Or a James, who fulfilled all my needs, but who had so many problems with alcohol that he really could fulfil none of them. To hell with men! I had to get back to what my heart really hungered for.

ıılıılılılı

I was finally ready to play Martha, the kingpin in *Who's Afraid of Virginia Woolf?* It was a tough role because the character is drunk, complex, wild, in pain, fierce, intelligent, witty, lonely and powerful. Elizabeth Taylor played her in one of the best performances in living memory and I was as daunted as hell by her exceptional performance. How could I make Martha my own? Should I allow myself to be influenced by Taylor's amazing performance in the movie? How could I not?

In my last weeks of school, I worked hard to try to develop and perfect her character, tormented by Taylor's performance and generally having a hard time of it. I spent hours developing her physicality. She was tough yet vulnerable, grounded yet manipulative. I had to incorporate all of those traits into her walk, the way she held her shoulders, her head, her heart. For example, her toughness, raunchiness and powerfulness of character would have encouraged a low-to-the-ground centre of gravity and a kind of staunch sensuality to her body. Yet her manipulative nature and cerebral leanings would make her lighter on her toes and result in more lucid, angular movements. I worked on her drunkenness too, and finally discovered the only believable way to act drunk was to act as if you were trying *not* to be drunk. She had a lot of sexual anger, and thinking about Axel and Jamie's kiss came in preeetty handy. Bless. I worked on her vulnerability a lot, and explored the reasons for it. Then I covered up the vulnerability with toughness and let it glimpse through only when she least expected it. But even so, it was extremely difficult and I felt like I'd only really scraped the surface of her character.

When I finally did play Martha, in Robert's class, it felt like a mountain had been climbed. The huge emotional burdens Martha carried were so draining that afterwards I was drenched in sweat, and when I left the stage my knees buckled and I fell onto the ground.

Up there on stage, I glimpsed the momentous willpower of Martha. She kept up an extraordinary level of energy, constantly tormented by the battle between her mind and her heart. She couldn't choose, wouldn't choose between the two and she never let up. She was an absolute dynamo of a character. I felt over the moon to have got inside her for even that brief a time.

I felt proud of myself for having tackled her and that I'd overcome my fear of taking on such a daunting character. I'd taken my own rocket ship to the moon and had dangled up there in space. Those few moments were bliss enough in my book. And I didn't even mind the bruises on my knees that made me look like a two-dollar hooker. One day, when I was Martha's age, I would play her for the whole two hours. Now, that would be a rocket ship to the monkey fondle.

A couple of days after that performance, Robert handed me an envelope.

'What's this?'

'For you,' he said mysteriously. Then he opened his arms and drew me into a hug.

When I got home I opened it.

I consider Ms. Vendramini to be one of the most outstanding actors I've worked with in several years. Her character work is creative and imaginative, never clichéd. She exhibits a depth of emotional expression, conveying inner strength and vulnerability simultaneously, one of the primary marks of a talented actor. She has a rich gift for comedy and a deep, striking talent for serious work . . . Ms. Vendramini can make a significant artistic contribution to the theatre and the cinema. She has my highest recommendation.

I couldn't read the reference any further or else I would have stripped off naked and done my Travolta dance. I felt like there was a pure silky ribbon that tied me to the memories of all the good things that had happened to me in New York; they became one big, joyous, chaotic, heavenly mass of kaleidoscopic images. It was one of those moments when the joy in your chest becomes physical. I felt proud of myself.

Inspired, the next week I contacted an actor's studio and went to listen to seven casting directors speak about the trade and afterwards had the opportunity to audition for them. I chose a comedic scene about a humorous Jewish woman trying to sell a house. When I finished they handed me their feedback forms, which I grabbed up and took to the next room to devour. 'Very funny,' wrote one. 'Bad choice of clothes,' wrote another. But I got a casting for a Robert De Niro film out of it, so all was good. Not that I won the role, damn it. Although the casting director, Kate, did say she liked my top.

ıılıılılıılılı

After the rigours of doing Blanche and Martha, I wanted to do some more comedy, so for my last performance at Strasberg, Alex and I played the title roles in the farcical comedy *King Ubu* by Alfred Jarry. The play evolved out of the Dada movement, and revolved around a slovenly and hideous couple, Ma and Pa Ubu. We padded our bodies in layers and layers of material to gain extra pounds and I roped two rolls of toilet paper in my pants to create an unlikely ass. I drew on thick black eyebrows three inches above my eyes and we grimaced and beat each other up on cue. Physical comedy was glorious but exhausting. At the end of each performance, my make-up was ruined with rivers of sweat and Alex and I would slump into a heap and use my posterior toilet paper to mop our brows.

Like all the roles I'd performed at Strassy, we would do them multiple times to work on them, and sometimes other students

and outsiders would come in to watch. During one of the performances for *King Ubu*, an acting agent was in the audience,
a young woman named Sally, who had just set up a brand-
spanking-new agency and was looking for actors.

'Can you play characters other than fat obnoxious ones?' she
asked me afterwards.

'Maybe,' I answered as I sucked in my belly.

'Good. Come in next week with a prepared monologue and
we can go from there.'

That was a gift from the gods. As Strasberg drew to a close,
I'd been sending my headshot and résumé off to lots of agents
and had only received one reply. To get the good roles, you need
to have a good agent, and you can't get a good agent without
having had a good role. For actors beginning in their careers, it
is a tough cycle to break.

The one agent who had got back to me was from an established
New York firm. He was a great old geezer who used to manage
Jim Morrison and Janis Joplin back in the day. We chatted amicably about my career for a while then he offered to sign me on
as a freelance actor, which meant that it was a non-exclusive
contract and I could still work with other agents. I thanked him
and told him I'd let him know as soon as possible.

I went to see Sally at her offices and did a monologue for her.
She liked it and said she would sign me up too, but that if she was
going to work for me, she wanted to do it on an exclusive basis.

I had been pretty terrified about even attempting to get an
American agent. I'd heard so many horror stories about actors
trying unsuccessfully for years to get one. But there it was, two
of them were interested in signing me up – admittedly, one was
wet behind the ears and the other had wet stuff coming out of
his ears, but hey, who was I to be picky?

I mulled over the options and decided to go with Sally as she seemed the hungrier of the two and she also had offices in LA. Plus, she had a good departure clause where I could leave her agency if it wasn't going well.

When I sat down with Sally to sign the contract she asked me whether I planned to go to Los Angeles.

'What do you mean?'

'Well, you have an OPT visa for only one year, yes?'

I nodded.

'New York has five television shows, LA has five hundred. There are no films being made here, Los Angeles has more studios than I can count. Get the picture?'

'You think I should go to Hollywood?'

She raised her eyebrow and smiled.

I called up Gian-Luca to get his advice.

'Bella, are you kidding? LA is full of dickheads, you wouldn't last a minute over there. New York is the place to be, it's the largest theatre hub in the world.'

The day before, in class, my teacher George Loros and I had gone through *The New York Times* and counted the Broadway theatre productions that were playing. Shockingly, there were only five dramas, four of them with limited releases of four-week runs, and yet a massive forty-seven musicals on Broadway.

'Trust me,' George had said, 'if I could do theatre for the rest of my life I would, but there's no work – there are only musicals for the tourists – plus theatre pays shit.'

I told Gian-Luca what George had said.

'So what?' he replied. 'Theatre is what I want to do, and it doesn't matter how hard it is, I'll do it in New York.'

'I thought you were going back to Rome to buy a house?'

'Yeah, I know, but . . .' he trailed off.

'Do you want to do theatre or film?' he asked me, changing the subject.

'Both.'

'Okay, but if you *had* to choose.'

'Film.'

'Then get your ass to Hollywood, my baby.'

I sat on a park bench and watched the New York crazies holler past me. Sun melted down on my shoulders and made the petals of the flowers ooze their beautiful smells into the air. A homeless guy lost in layers of rags ambled past and a young black man with his beautiful Spanish wife cooed over their small child rolling in the grass. I loved New York, no question, but I also knew the crazy city would keep being crazy, with or without me.

I thought of Los Angeles and the people I'd met there, the actors and filmmakers jostling for a part of the treasure. I thought of Zoë and Bianca, Sally and the Like People. Of the sunshine and the miles of pristine beaches. The deals and schemes and parties and premieres. It was just as crazy as New York, but the difference was it was packed full of acting jobs. I knew those jobs attracted squillions of actors and the competition would be fierce, but I reckoned, with a bit of Aussie luck on my side, I could be up for the challenge.

I was smiling. Hollywood, huh?

Just then a truck rumbled past me on the cobblestone road. 'Hollywood Dry Cleaning' it announced in large swirly black letters. It was fate. I turned to a homeless guy splayed out on the bench beside me and grinned.

'I'm going to Hollywood.'

He opened his eyes to incisions then clamped them shut again. A small smile formed on his face. 'I met James Caan once,' he said. 'Maybe you'll see him there.'

'Maybe,' I answered, smiling. 'Maybe.'

ılıllıllılı

Two weeks later, on my way home from seeing friends, I spied James sitting in a café on Eighth Street. He was reading a magazine with Charlize Theron in a sexy gold dress on the cover. His movements were soft and less panicked than I remembered them. Usually I would have hopped into the café, cuffed him and plonked myself down for a catch-up. But I felt awkward somehow. I stood for a bit, then I left before he noticed me. A few weeks before, I'd heard that he'd established another charity. I should have at least gone up to him to applaud him for it.

That afternoon I decided to stop being a chicken and I called him up to congratulate him.

'Oh, on Belletheron? Thanks, yeah, another of my brilliant schemes to rid the world of evil.'

'You called the charity Belletheron?'

'Yeah.'

'You named it after Charlize Theron? I'm both frightened and intrigued.'

'You said yourself that it would be either her or Angelina Jolie you'd jump the fence for.'

'Yeah, but –'

'So every time I go to work I'll be reminded of you and Charlize. Together. In bed.'

'Sick, sick, sick. You've outdone yourself.'

'Well, it was either that or naming it "Aussie Girl with Freckles and an Embarrassing Celebrity Crush on Charlize Charities Incorporated".'

He paused and his voice became a bit halting.

'Listen, Bella, I wanted to talk to you about something else. I was going to wait, but now that . . .' He trailed off.

His voice sounded different. It was calmer and deeper than I'd ever heard it.

'What?' I asked, sensing the seriousness. 'Is Charlize pregnant with your love child?'

'I've been sober for three months.'

'What?'

'I wanted to tell you face to face but, well, now you know.'

'I –, I –,' I began.

'I still have a long way to go,' he said, 'this is just the beginning of a long road ahead. But with you and Charlize by my side –' he joked.

'James, this is the greatest news. I –, why –, what made you finally do it?' I asked. 'Did the planets align?'

I heard his voice smiling. 'What do you want to hear? That your lectures finally sank in? That my love for you broke my stony heart and I saw the light.'

'That would work.'

'Okay, then. My love for you broke my stony heart and I saw the light.'

'So – I mean – Wow. I'm really lost for words.'

'So the planets have indeed aligned?' he asked.

We laughed, then we both fell silent.

'James, I'm proud of you.'

'Thank you. That really means a lot to me. Listen, Bella, I have to go, but perhaps we can get together soon, go for an exciting vegetable drink together?'

'Sure. As long as it doesn't have any vegetables in it,' I mumbled back.

ıllıllılılıı

My very last day of Strasberg came around and I hugged the admin staff and my extraordinary teachers and friends goodbye. Two of my teachers, Tim Crouse and Bill Hopkins, who were directors, each asked me if I'd like to take a role in their respective films. In my time in New York, I'd built up lots of acting contacts, casting agents knew who I was, I'd scored an agent and I'd worked with some good directors. And there I was throwing it all away to start at the beginning again in Los Angeles. Was I stupid?

'Yes, but despite that, I think you should still go,' said my mum. 'You've learned a lot, so now is the time to put it all into use. You'll be fighting fit and ready to hit the ground running in LA.'

As I got off the phone, Gian-Luca busted through the front door of Natasa's apartment.

'I'm coming with you!'

He was talking so fast his words were running into each other like dodgem cars as he swirled around the room and picked things up and put them down at random.

'I was gonna go to Rome and buy a house. Buy a house! Give in, that was what I was going to do. I was going to give in! Not me,' he said, pounding his chest. 'I'm coming to Hollywood with you, baby. I'm coming with you!'

⑅

In the next few weeks, amidst the excitement of travel plans and graduation parties, my thoughts continually returned to James. We planned to meet one morning in a coffee shop near Natasa's apartment. I hadn't told him that I was leaving New York.

Even from across the room, I could see the change in him. His skin was glowing and he seemed so much more self-possessed. Not in a showy, arrogant way, but in a quiet and more determined way. He still made me laugh hard enough to rupture something but he also had a quality of stillness about him that I'd never seen before. Even his conversation seemed more lucid. He told me about how he had quit drinking.

'It was the hardest thing I've ever done,' he said, the truth of it hitting at his words. 'I've been going to AA and I do private counselling sessions once a week. I've got medication to help with the anxiety. I feel like an old man,' he laughed.

'You look wonderful, James.'

'Thank you. I feel pretty good.' He paused for a bit, gathering his thoughts.

'Here, I have something for you,' he said, as he took a small blue flower out of his jacket pocket. 'I've been trying to decide what to get you to show my appreciation. I thought emerald earrings would look beautiful on you – but I didn't want to receive a black eye.'

'Emerald earrings would have been fine in the circumstances, considering what an asshole you were. Plus it wouldn't have been trying to "buy me", like giving me fifty bucks for a massage with a happy ending would be.'

'Yeah, I'm still a little blurry on the distinction, and I didn't want to take the risk.'

I chuckled. We'd often argued about where the line in gift-giving was drawn and he was at least trying to understand.

'So, here,' he said, placing the small, perfectly blue flower in my hand. 'To steal from Renee Zellweger: thank you for making me a better person.'

'You're welcome, James,' I answered. 'But Renee didn't say that, she said "You complete me".'

'No, she didn't, "You complete me" was Jack Nicholson's character in that obsessive compulsive film.'

'No way. Who's the film buff here? Say it.'

'Okay, I submit to your higher authority, Bella, you are.'

'Uncross your fingers when you say that.'

'No.'

'Damn, the drunk you was so much easier to scare.'

'You better believe it, I drink whole eggs now without flinching.'

'But still just as sick, I see.'

As I was getting ready to leave I kissed him and told him that I wished him every luck with his new life.

'That will have to extend to LA,' he said.

'Huh?'

'We're expanding the company to Los Angeles. I'll be spending a lot of time over there in the next eight months, so I'll need the luck there. But I'll come back to New York often. I plan on being in your face once in a while so you won't forget me entirely.'

'No need, I'll be in yours. I'm moving to Los Angeles, too,' I told him.

'What?' he said, looking somewhat shaken. 'Really?'

'Really.' We looked at each other from across the table and I saw a smile full of surprise and tenderness spread across his face. Then he seemed to check himself and he cleared his throat and said rather haltingly, 'In LA, I doubt you'd want to take up your time with an old alcoholic like me, but perhaps you'd let me take you to dinner on the odd night?'

'Ash long as thoshe eyes come with yoo . . . cowboy,' I faux-slurred.

We smiled and a mountain of memories seemed to pass between us. Then, as if we'd unlocked a box we weren't ready for, we grew quiet.

'We'll see,' I said to him.

Just then, Jackie, James' assistant, came into the café in a flurry of papers and cell phones.

'Bella, sorry, I have to go,' said James as he motioned for Jackie to wait. 'But here, take this.' He passed me a small package. 'Don't open it until you get home, okay?' he said. Then he held me at arm's length and surveyed me as if I were the only water for ten miles. 'Ah, it was really good to see you again, Belle.' Then he turned and left, disappearing into the thronging sidewalks of New York.

When I got home, I opened the package. Inside was a pair of emerald earrings and a note.

'Churchy, this is not me buying you, this is me thinking you'd look exceptional in these. With all my heart and all my gratitude, James.'

I smiled to myself and looked out the window and saw the bright street carpeted in the mottled shadows of a giant tree. It made the pavement look like it was a river, alive and shimmering.

I went to the bureau and took out my aeroplane ticket and the letters of reference from my teachers. I started to feel the strong, excited buzzing in my stomach that I'd come to know so well. It gave me goose-bumps and made my heart thump like a rabbit's foot on firm grass.

I wanted to go to Hollywood and test myself. I wanted to stand on my own two feet and be completely me, the soft and the hard, the bright and the dark. I wanted to go there, as me, with all my foibles, all my bliss. I wanted to test my acting, as well as the person I had fought to become.

I looked out the window again and saw the river of New York below me. Shopkeepers with sacks of oranges wobbled past and beautifully dressed women wove their little dogs' leashes between the feet of passers-by. Then I saw a sign, literally. A fundamentalist Christian was holding up a placard that read 'Tomorrow' in bright friendly letters, as in tomorrow Christ would come. It felt prophetic somehow. That word: Tomorrow. When I was disillusioned, or unsure, tomorrow seemed so vast and coldly threatening. But as I watched the religious man twirl his fingers at his sign, I knew that for me, right at that moment, tomorrow was so saturated in hope and sunlight that I wanted to leap out the window and fly down to meet it and bask in its promises. Somewhere subterranean and pure inside of me, I knew that life's strong branches were supporting me, holding me up to the sun so I could feel the warmth on my face.

I walked out onto the street and I felt the blast of New York assault my senses. I saw a homeless guy go past on his knees as he stalked a pigeon. Then I saw a businessman on his mobile phone do one of those Sinatra skips as he enthused about a deal he'd just done. I was going to miss New York. I thought about all the things that I'd been through here. I'd lived and breathed the city of my dreams, fallen in love, twice, got halfway pregnant, performed on a New York stage, travelled, made friends, got into adventures, shot films, met weird and wonderful characters, conquered (some) of my demons and become a confident actor.

New York was like my father, protective and strong; like my mother, smart and loving; like Axel, passionate and cruel; like James, fractured and brave; like Cheeks, cute and furry – without the furry part. I pursed my lips and blew a kiss out into the New York air to mingle with the cab fumes.

'So long, and thanks for all the fish, beautiful, beautiful New York.'

The homeless guy stopped chasing his pigeon and looked up at me. 'You're talking to yourself,' he commented sagely.

'I know.' I smiled. 'I fear I have finally become a true New Yorker.'

'Without fear there cannot be courage,' he said, then suddenly smiled.

I knew that smile. I recognised him!

He was the old Union Square philosopher guy, 'You're that guy!'

He let loose that same broken-door tooth grin that broke through his chops and lapped all around the features of his face.

'Got some spare change?' he asked me, his eyes twinkling.

I handed him what I had left in my pocket.

'And remember,' he cautioned, 'love as hard as you possibly can. Then watch out for the killer bees.'

And with that he ambled off into the streets of New York, irrepressible, familiar, alive. Just like I hoped to be.

500 per
1000 max per 7
working days.